The Voice of the Analyst

The Voice of the Analyst contains personal narratives by 12 psychoanalysts, each taking the reader through his or her unique path toward developing a voice and identity as an analyst. All come from different backgrounds, theoretical orientations and stages of their careers. The narratives are courageous and uncommonly revealing in a profession that demands so much reserve and anonymity from its practitioners. This book demonstrates that the analyst's work is a product of their characters as well as training and theory.

The narrative form in this book offers a refreshing and necessary companion to the theoretical and clinical writing that dominates the field. The editors show the importance of developing a unique voice and identity if one is to function well as an analyst. This endeavor cannot be accomplished solely through technical training, especially with the isolation that characterizes clinical practice. There are pressures that analysts experience alone in their practice, from patients and themselves as well as other professionals, forces that render technical training and theory alone inadequate in facilitating the development of one's analytic voice and identity. Enter the form of the personal narrative presented in this book.

This fascinating compilation of narratives shows how the contributors bear striking similarities and differences to one another. Despite their different backgrounds, they display commonality in their sensitivity towards mental and emotional states and their wish to heal suffering. However, they also exemplify wide differences in motivations, interests, and what makes them tick as psychoanalysts. *The Voice of the Analyst* will be a great companion book for established psychoanalysts and psychoanalytic psychotherapists and those in training, as well as mental health professionals keen to understand what it takes to become a psychoanalyst and to enhance their personal and professional development.

Linda Hillman, PhD, practices as a psychologist and psychoanalyst in New York City and Westchester County. She treats adults, adolescents, children, and couples. She is a Clinical Supervisor for the City University of New York, and a member of the New York University Postdoctoral Program in Psychoanalysis and Psychotherapy. She has published on the psychological implications of teaching writing as well as co-authored several papers on group relations. She is also a published poet and has played leadership roles in a number of volunteer community organizations focused on youth, mental health, and education.

Therese Rosenblatt, PhD, is a psychologist and psychoanalyst in private practice in New York City and Westchester County, New York. She treats adults, children, adolescents, couples, and families. She leads parenting groups privately and at the Early Childhood Development Center in New York City. She is on the faculty of the Metropolitan Institute for Training in Psychoanalytic Psychotherapy. She is Adjunct Clinical Supervisor at Yeshiva University and Pace University in New York and an active member of the New York University Postdoctoral Program in Psychoanalysis and Psychotherapy.

Psychoanalysis in a New Key book series
Donnel Stern
Series editor

When music is played in a new key, the melody does not change, but the notes that make up the composition do: change in the context of continuity, continuity that perseveres through change. Psychoanalysis in a New Key publishes books that share the aims psychoanalysts have always had, but that approach them differently. The books in the series are not expected to advance any particular theoretical agenda, although to this date most have been written by analysts from the Interpersonal and Relational orientations.

The most important contribution of a psychoanalytic book is the communication of something that nudges the reader's grasp of clinical theory and practice in an unexpected direction. Psychoanalysis in a New Key creates a deliberate focus on innovative and unsettling clinical thinking. Because that kind of thinking is encouraged by exploration of the sometimes surprising contributions to psychoanalysis of ideas and findings from other fields, Psychoanalysis in a New Key particularly encourages interdisciplinary studies. Books in the series have married psychoanalysis with dissociation, trauma theory, sociology, and criminology. The series is open to the consideration of studies examining the relationship between psychoanalysis and any other field—for instance, biology, literary and art criticism, philosophy, systems theory, anthropology, and political theory.

But innovation also takes place within the boundaries of psychoanalysis, and Psychoanalysis in a New Key therefore also presents work that reformulates thought and practice without leaving the precincts of the field. Books in the series focus, for example, on the significance of personal values in psychoanalytic practice, on the complex interrelationship between the analyst's clinical work and personal life, on the consequences for the clinical situation when patient and analyst are from different cultures, and on the need for psychoanalysts to accept the degree to which they knowingly satisfy their own wishes during treatment hours, often to the patient's detriment. A full list of all titles in this series is available at: www.routledge.com/series/LEAPNKBS.

RECENT TITLES IN THIS SERIES:

Vol. 41 *Understanding the Sexual Betrayal of Boys and Men: The Trauma of Sexual Abuse* Edited by Richard B. Gartner

Vol. 40 *Healing Sexually Betrayed Men and Boys: Treatment for Sexual Abuse, Assault, and Trauma* Edited by Richard B. Gartner

Vol. 39 *The Voice of the Analyst: Narratives on Developing a Psychoanalytic Identity* Edited by Linda Hillman and Therese Rosenblatt

Vol. 38 *Interpersonal Psychoanalysis and the Enigma of Consciousness* Edgar A. Levenson and Edited by Alan Slomowitz

Vol. 37 *The Organizational Life of Psychoanalysis: Conflicts, Dilemmas, and the Future of the Profession* Kenneth Eisold

The Voice of the Analyst

Narratives on Developing a
Psychoanalytic Identity

Edited by Linda Hillman and
Therese Rosenblatt

LONDON AND NEW YORK

First published 2018
by Routledge
2 Park Square, Milton Park, Abingdon, Oxon OX14 4RN

and by Routledge
711 Third Avenue, New York, NY 10017

Routledge is an imprint of the Taylor & Francis Group, an informa business

© 2018 selection and editorial matter, Linda Hillman and Therese Rosenblatt; individual chapters, the contributors

The right of the editors to be identified as the authors of the editorial material, and of the authors for their individual chapters, has been asserted in accordance with sections 77 and 78 of the Copyright, Designs and Patents Act 1988.

All rights reserved. No part of this book may be reprinted or reproduced or utilised in any form or by any electronic, mechanical, or other means, now known or hereafter invented, including photocopying and recording, or in any information storage or retrieval system, without permission in writing from the publishers.

Trademark notice: Product or corporate names may be trademarks or registered trademarks, and are used only for identification and explanation without intent to infringe.

British Library Cataloguing in Publication Data
A catalogue record for this book is available from the British Library

Library of Congress Cataloging in Publication Data
Names: Hillman, Linda Harbaugh, editor. | Rosenblatt, Therese, editor.
Title: The voice of the analyst : narratives on developing a psychoanalytic identity / edited by Linda Hillman and Therese Rosenblatt.
Description: New York : Routledge, 2018. |
Series: Psychoanalysis in a new key book series ; 39 |
Includes bibliographical references and index.
Identifiers: LCCN 2017009056 (print) | LCCN 2017034313 (ebook) |
ISBN 9781315681375 (Master) | ISBN 9781317399971 (Web PDF) |
ISBN 9781317399964 (ePub) | ISBN 9781317399957 (Mobipocket/Kindle) |
ISBN 9781138929135 (hardback : alk. paper) | ISBN 9781138929142 (pbk. : alk. paper)
Subjects: LCSH: Psychoanalysts–Biography. | Psychoanalysis–History.
Classification: LCC BF109.A1 (ebook) | LCC BF109.A1 V65 2017 (print) |
DDC 150.19/50922–dc23
LC record available at https://lccn.loc.gov/2017009056

ISBN: 978-1-138-92913-5 (hbk)
ISBN: 978-1-138-92914-2 (pbk)
ISBN: 978-1-315-68137-5 (ebk)

Typeset in Times
by Out of House Publishing

For my husband Marshall and sons Zachary, Sam, and Jacob
from Therese with love and gratitude

For my husband Michael and children Jessica and Daniel
from Linda with appreciation and love

Contents

Acknowledgments xi
List of contributors xiv

1 Prelude 1
LINDA HILLMAN AND THERESE ROSENBLATT

PART I
Narratives 11

2 All origins are suspect: becoming a psychoanalyst 13
FRANCISCO J. GONZÁLEZ

3 From Ebbets Field to 82nd Street: finding my way 26
TED JACOBS

4 Psychoanalysis and me 37
LISSA WEINSTEIN

5 The voice endures 50
MITCHELL WILSON

6 Becoming myself: resuming a derailed adolescence 62
THERESE ROSENBLATT

7 Becoming a psychoanalyst 77
JACK DRESCHER

8 Hiding in plain sight 94
LINDA HILLMAN

9 Curiosity didn't kill the cat: (or how I became a psychoanalyst) 109
CAROLYN ELLMAN

10	Developmental struggles in psychoanalytic training: developing a psychoanalytic identity JONATHAN EGER	123
11	The dice popper: how we describe what we remember RACHEL ALTSTEIN	141
12	My psychoanalytic self: discovery, embrace, and ongoing formation DOROTHY EVANS HOLMES	156
13	Untranslatables SPYROS D. ORFANOS	167

PART II
Reflections　　　　　　　　　　　　　　　　　　　　185

14	Themes and variations LINDA HILLMAN AND THERESE ROSENBLATT	187
15	Rethinking psychoanalytic training and beyond LINDA HILLMAN AND THERESE ROSENBLATT	201
16	Coda LINDA HILLMAN AND THERESE ROSENBLATT	208

Index　　　　　　　　　　　　　　　　　　　　　　　　210

Acknowledgments

The authors are very grateful to Donnel Stern for including us in his authors' series and for his generous and enthusiastic help in moving this project forward. We would like to thank the Psychoanalytic Society of NYU Postdoc for their belief in our project and for supporting us with the award of a Scholars Grant. Mina Samuels has been a brilliant, thoughtful editor who has helped us navigate any obstacles we have encountered in the process and helped us more fully articulate our voices. Danielle Knafo was invaluable in helping us develop our proposal for Routledge.

We feel deep gratitude and admiration for our contributing authors for making their inspirational and courageous stories a part of this book. Their essays helped shape our conclusions, and we share a belief in the power of narrative to encourage other analysts in the development of their identities and voices. They made our writing better by sharing theirs.

Linda: Many thanks to my close friend and colleague, Lissa Weinstein, whose exceptionally keen mind and discerning eye for language was invaluable in helping me to shape my narrative. Thanks also to Marilyn Hillman, a wonderful editor, who helped me tell my story. I am so grateful for her support and thankful for all the shared life experiences that have informed the development of my own voice.

Thanks to my very close colleagues and friends, Kathe Hift, Ellie Esposito, and Steve Solow for their support and encouragement. I feel lucky to have them by my side in this ongoing journey of becoming a psychoanalyst. Thanks to Harriet Arnold and Stephen Hillman, my mother and brother, and my friends who have been nothing but encouraging and patient along the way. Profound thanks to Delia Battin who has helped me find and share my voice and made this enterprise and so much else possible.

My thanks to my patients, whom I respect and admire for the risks they take. I feel honored that they allow me to sit together with them, engage with them about their most personal wounds, losses, loves, and reparations. Their bravery and their struggles move me and challenge me to grow as a therapist and person.

I am so grateful to have worked closely with Therese Rosenblatt on this book. She has been a wonderful partner, and the challenge of integrating our voices has been enriching and exciting.

My deepest gratitude goes to my family. My husband Michael Chayes' boundless intelligence, sense-of-humor, and creativity have enriched my life beyond measure. His love and support for my growth in all things and in particular, in the writing of this book, have never waivered. With his generous and thoughtful input, he always makes my writing better. My children Daniel Chayes and Jessica Beckley-Chayes and my son-in-law Ben Beckley-Chayes are a constant source of inspiration and joy. Their encouragement and belief in me make all things possible.

Therese: I am eternally grateful to my patients without whom I would not be an analyst and would not have written and edited this book. They give me purpose, joy, and enthusiasm about getting up in the morning. I am honored that they trust me with their intimate confidences and allow me to be the person that helps them find their way in life. I continually learn from them. They teach me how to be a better analyst and a better person with humility. I thank my supervisees as well.

I am indebted to Tom Lopez for hearing my voice, believing that I had something valuable to say, and encouraging me to develop and express my thoughts in writing.

I thank Carolyn Ellman, Ted Jacobs, and Rich Lasky for giving me astute feedback on my own narrative as well as much needed support for telling my story.

Steve Solow and Carolyn Ellman have been instrumental in helping me cultivate my analytic thinking. Words cannot do justice to how that has facilitated my development as an analyst. Nancy Dallek has shown extraordinary and unwavering confidence in my abilities as an analyst, and I never stop appreciating that. The members of the Education-Colloquium Committee of the Contemporary Freudian Track at Postdoc with whom I have been happily meeting for 15 years, Jo Lang, Rich Lasky, Ken Feiner, Linda Jaffe Caplan, Linda Eidelberg, Desnee Hall, Paul Hymowitz, Annette Berman, Elle Esposito, and Steve Axelrod have provided a warm and welcoming environment where we can discuss analytic issues with like minded colleagues. I thank Jonathan Eger and Ricardo Rieppi for planting the seeds of this book in my mind by inviting me onto their panel and Marsha Levy Warren for nourishing these seeds. I remain eternally grateful to the late Martin Bergmann, who influenced and animated my thinking profoundly, taught me so much of about psychoanalysis that has become a part of me and offered an environment that encouraged my thinking.

My deep gratitude goes to Nicole Klemens who has kept me sane and organized in general and throughout the writing of this book. I am greatly appreciative to my family and friends who have cheered me on in the writing of this book and who have tolerated and understood the months of lunches, coffees, and conversations that have been deferred until the conclusion of this book.

I am especially appreciative to Linda Hillman my co-editor on this book. Through our collaboration, which has been enriching and fruitful, I have learned precious lessons in blending our voices and creating a good professional marriage.

Finally, my greatest debt of gratitude goes to my husband Marshall Sonenshine and sons Zachary, Sam, and Jacob Sonenshine. I could not do what I do without their love, support, respect, and unending belief in me. It amazes and sustains me every day.

Contributors

Rachel Altstein is a psychoanalyst in New York City. Before entering the psychoanalytic field, she worked as an attorney specializing in prisoners' rights, criminal defense, and anti-death penalty litigation. She is an associate editor at *Psychoanalytic Perspectives* and a member of Beatrice Beebe's Infant Research Board. Altstein writes about the psychoanalytic writing process.

Jack Drescher, MD, is a psychiatrist and psychoanalyst in private practice in New York City. He is Clinical Professor of Psychiatry, New York Medical College and Adjunct Professor at New York University's Postdoctoral Program in Psychotherapy and Psychoanalysis. He served on APA's DSM-5 Workgroup on Sexual and Gender Identity Disorders and the World Health Organization's ICD-11 Working Group on the Classification of Sexual Disorders and Sexual Health. He is author of *Psychoanalytic Therapy and the Gay Man* (Routledge, 2014) and emeritus editor of the *Journal of Gay and Lesbian Mental Health*. He is also an expert media spokesperson on issues related to gender and sexuality.

Jonathan Eger, PhD, is an advanced candidate in psychoanalysis at the New York University Postdoctoral Program in Psychotherapy and Psychoanalysis, where he is an active member of the Contemporary Freudian Track. He serves as member-at-large on the board of directors of the Division of Psychoanalysis (39) of the APA. He is an Adjunct Clinical Supervisor of psychology graduate students at Yeshiva and Pace Universities, and is in private practice on the Upper East Side of Manhattan.

Caroline Ellman, PhD, is Adjunct Clinical Professor and Supervisor for the NYU Postdoctoral Program in Psychotherapy and Psychoanalysis; Fellow (Training and Supervising Analyst) and Faculty at the Institute for Psychoanalytic Training and Research (IPTAR); Training and Supervising Analyst at the Contemporary Freudian Society; member of IPA and CIPS; senior editor of *The Modern Freudians: Contemporary Psychoanalytic Technique Self* (Jason Aronson, 1998) and *Omnipotent*

Fantasies and the Vulnerable (Jason Arsonson, 1997); and co-editor of *A New Freudian Synthesis: Clinical Process in a New Generation* (with Andrew Druck, Norbert Freedman, and Aaron Thaler; Karnac Books, 2011). She teaches and writes on the topic of envy including "The Empty Mother: Women's Fear of their Destructive Envy" (2000, *Psychoanalytic Quarterly*, *69*, 633–665) and "Desire Beneath the Elms: An Evolutionary and Developmental Model of Envy" (2012, *Canadian Journal of Psychoanalysis*, *20*, 229–245), and is in private practice in New York.

Francisco J. González, MD, is a Personal and Supervising Analyst and on Faculty at the Psychoanalytic Institute of Northern California. Since 1997 he has also worked as a staff psychiatrist and supervisor at Instituto Familiar de la Raza, a community mental health clinic serving the Latino community. His published work often investigates the imbrication of sociocultural process and individual subjectivity, and has included work on film, immigration, queer sexualities, perversion, relationality, and archaic mental states. His psychoanalytic writing has received the Symonds Prize and the Ralph E. Roughton Award. He serves on the editorial boards of *Psychoanalytic Dialogues* and *Studies in Gender and Sexuality* and practices in San Francisco and Oakland.

Dorothy Evans Holmes, PhD, is a Teaching, Training, and Supervising Analyst in the Psychoanalytic Education Center of the Carolinas. She is Professor Emeritus at the George Washington University where she was Program Director and Director of Clinical Training of the Professional PsyD Program. She is also a Teaching, Training, and Supervising Analyst Emeritus at the Baltimore Washington Institute for Psychoanalysis. Dr. Holmes has written extensively on intrapsychic influences of race, gender, and their impact on psychoanalytic treatment process. Currently, she serves on the Board of Directors, National Register of Health Service Psychologists, the Program Committee of the American Psychoanalytic Association (APsaA), and its Task Force on Diversity. Dr. Holmes has received numerous honors for her scholarly work on cultural factors and cultural trauma, including having been the plenary speaker for the National Meeting of the APsaA, January, 2016. She is in private practice in Bluffton, SC.

Ted Jacobs, MD, is a Clinical Professor of Psychiatry (Emeritus), Albert Einstein College of Medicine and a Training and Supervising Analyst, New York and IPE Psychoanalytic Institutes. He is the author of *The Use of the Self: Countertransference and Communication in the Analytic Situation* (International Universities Press, 1991); *The Possible Profession: The Analytic Process of Change* (Routledge, 2013); and co-editor of *On Beginning an Analysis* (International Universities Press, 1990). He is the author of over 65 articles and book reviews on a variety of analytic subjects.

Spyros D. Orfanos, PhD, is ABPP Clinic Director at the New York University Postdoctoral Program in Psychotherapy and Psychoanalysis; Senior Research Fellow at the Center for Byzantine and Modern Greek Studies, Queens College, City University of New York; and on the editorial boards of *Psychoanalytic Dialogues* and *PsycCRITIQUES-Contemporary Psychology: APA Review of Books*. He is past president of the International Association of Relational Psychoanalysis and Psychotherapy, the Division of Psychoanalysis (39) of the American Psychological Association, and the Academy of Psychoanalysis of the American Board of Professional Psychology; founding board member of the Stephen Mitchell Relational Studies Center; national and international lecturer and author on the arts, clinical process, creativity, culture, immigration, and social justice; producer of six music albums: *Greek Songs for Romantics and Realists*, *Enchanted Night* (Greek), *Ay Amor* (Spanish), *Mauthausen* (Hebrew), *Essentially Ella* (English), and *On the Shores of the Moon* (Greek); co-editor (with Eliot Jurist), of "Psychoanalysis and the Humanities," special online issue of *Psychoanalytic Psychology* (2016, *33*, Suppl. 1); and is in independent practice in NYC.

Lissa Weinstein, PhD, is a Professor on the Doctoral Program in Clinical Psychology at the City College of New York and the Graduate Center, a Faculty Member of the New York Psychoanalytic Institute, and a fiction writer. Her interests include the interrelationship of neurobiology and psychoanalysis, the function of repetition, as well as film and literature studies. She won the Heinz Hartmann Jr. Award with Dr. Arnold Wilson for their papers on the work of Lev Vygotsky and psychoanalysis and was given the Margaret Marek Award from the International Dyslexia Association for *Reading David: A Mother and Son's Journey through the Labyrinth of Dyslexia* (Penguin, 2003). Recent publications include "The Neurobiology of Personality Disorders: Implications for Psychoanalysis" (*American Psychoanalytic Association, 57,* 361–398) and "Personality Disorders, Attachment and Psychodynamic Psychotherapy" (*Psychopathology, 47,* 425–436), both with Larry Siever; "It's Only a Dream: Physiological and Developmental Contributions to the Feeling of Reality" (Chapter 8 in *The significance of dreams: Bridging clinical and extraclinical research in psychoanalysis*, Karnac Books, 2012), and "Why Bion? Why Now? Novel Forms and the Mystical Quest" (*Psicoanalisis, 61,* 91–93).

Mitchell Wilson, MD, is a Training and Supervising Analyst at the San Francisco Center for Psychoanalysis, and a Supervising Analyst at the Psychoanalytic Institute of Northern California. He has been awarded the Heinz Hartmann Memorial Lectureship at the New York Psychoanalytic Institute in 2002, the *Journal of the American Psychoanalytic Association* Journal Prize in 2003, and the Karl A. Menninger Memorial Award in

2005. He is an associate editor of *JAPA*, and on the editorial board of the *Psychoanalytic Quarterly*. Dr. Wilson has published widely on a variety of topics that cohere around a theory of ethics, desire, and the psychoanalytic process. He is currently working on a book project, "The Analyst's Desire and the Ethical in Psychoanalysis." He is in private practice in Berkeley, CA.

Chapter 1

Prelude

Linda Hillman and Therese Rosenblatt

We were having lunch at the Parkway Diner, immersed in one of our wide-ranging conversations when we came up with the idea for this book. We had dived into a discussion of our psychoanalytic practices, as well as our lives—our children becoming adults, our marriages, our own new phase of life, and more specifically, the relationship between our lives and our work. In particular, we discussed how we were changing in our beliefs and the ways we think about ourselves as psychoanalysts. We had recently formed our own two-person writing group in which we shared our separate writing projects and ideas for future papers, so talk about our writing threaded through our conversation.

There was a moment when we recognized that we were both deeply engaged in exploring the on-going developmental journey of becoming a psychoanalyst, and within minutes, we made the decision to develop this book. The conditions were right. We were both poised (and free enough of some family responsibilities) to take on a large project and begin expressing our own voice and thinking in our professional field. We knew that we were naturally effective collaborators. Already our combined thoughts and ideas had led to more expansive and original conclusions than the sum of our individual input. Our mutual respect, admiration, and sometimes disagreement was in itself an example of how the process of identification with one another modified our individual attitudes to create one collaborative voice, an aspect of the very topic we wanted to explore.

We share a strong belief that becoming a psychoanalyst is very much about the character and development of the person of the analyst and that this process is a life-long journey. Starting well before formal training and continuing through decades of practice, analysts continue to change and develop both their understanding of theory and technique as well as the depth, subtlety and sophistication with which they learn to use themselves in the treatment situation. While we know a good deal about the development of technical skills and the structure of training that analysts receive, we know much less about how individuals develop their own analytic style, thinking, voice, and the integration of their personal development with their training. We are taught to help our patients find their way through their internal and external conflicts, fears, and longings to find their voice, and yet the psychoanalytic establishment as a whole has not focused on the analyst's development of his or her own voice either through training or in professional writings. A central goal of our book is to open up the discussion about the process of becoming a psychoanalyst and specifically, about the development of a psychoanalytic identity and voice.

We present personal essays from twelve psychoanalysts who have distinguished themselves in the field through a variety of developmental journeys. This is a group diverse in age, seniority, background, gender, race, theoretical orientation, as well as interests. Each developmental journey is unique. The purpose of presenting these narratives is to provide an opportunity for learning, personal inspiration, and support, as well as to loosen some of the constrictions that may inhibit creative, productive, and responsible training. Our aim is to inspire you to consider your own experiences and analytic identity in fresh ways. We would like to bring this discussion into the community as a whole and explore the idea of the analyst's developmental journey as a lifelong process.

Even the period of formal training in institutes, with it's primary focus on theory and technique barely addresses these developmental issues despite the requirement for a personal analysis. A huge part of the development of an analyst is ignored in the very environment in which it might be best addressed. There is little or no discussion about how we have found our way into psychoanalytic training. What are the roots of this interest and what are the known and unknown motivations for doing this work? Formal training often leaves the young analyst with the impression that theory and formally taught guidelines and technique are all we need for this work. Without a more balanced developmentally oriented training, the young analyst can be inadvertently encouraged to hide behind theory, making it more difficult to authentically respond to the patient. She often emerges from training with a sense of inadequacy and shame for not living up to the idealized image of the restrained, silent and anonymous psychoanalyst, always with a parsimoniously worded and perfectly timed, eloquent interpretation.

Traditional American models of the technique of psychoanalysis were largely derived from the 1950's practice in America. These models claimed that anything other than interpretation was considered a violation of technique. They portrayed the analyst as a blank screen and as neutral except for an occasional countertransference experience. Even countertransference was considered to be purely elicited by the patient, and a hindrance to the work of the analysis. This method of taking the person out of the analyst led for years to a method of teaching that dehumanized the process and left trainees out in the cold. Freud's real classical technique was distorted by his followers. He himself was personable and friendly and had a real relationship with his patients (Lipton, 1977).

We believe that the isolation of the analyst's working conditions can foster a sense of shame for not living up to some imagined ideal and at times inhibit the analyst's creativity. While supervision can relieve some of that isolation for the analyst-in-training, it can often create a pressure for the candidate to conform to the style of the supervisor. Our hope is that sharing our narratives can relieve some of this isolation, offer support for the individual creative process, and encourage a freer development of voice and identity for the analyst.

Here we address what we mean by "voice" and "identity" and why we believe the narrative is the most effective and eloquent way of conveying aspects of the development of analytic identity.

Voice

Finding one's voice has become a popular phrase in today's culture. Often we hear it from those who have been culturally, politically, or psychologically disenfranchised or those who feel they suppress or defer their voice to others with more authority or privilege. Women, for example, continue to find their voices within a male-dominated society (Gilligan, 1982). This version of voice has to do with the right to express an opinion, have a say, be heard, counted, and in essence, to be empowered.

In these pages, we hear from analysts about the development of their analytic voice, a concept that has to do with the expression of the analyst's particular individual, professional identity including a sense of empowerment. Until the relational movement and the introduction of the concept of inter-subjectivity, the analyst's voice was not even acknowledged as present in the treatment. Analysts were supposed to be silent, unobtrusive, and blank screens on which patients could transfer their innermost feelings and thoughts. Historical notions of abstinence, anonymity, and neutrality bred into us a dread and embarrassment about self-exposure.

Yet, even before the arrival of two person psychologies, our clinical experience has always shown us that our patients hear our voices loud and clear. They react and change in response to our interventions and they often refer to something we have said to them. There is now considerable literature (Davies, 1998) citing instances of patients who know more about us as their analyst than we explicitly tell them. We have always struggled to find the right balance between leaving room for the patient's voice to unfold and introducing our own voice in the room when necessary and useful

The definitions of voice cluster around one of two distinct poles, the metaphoric and the literal. In the metaphorical realm, voice is linked with such words as identity, persona, self, and style. Just as we can identify a writer's unique voice, we can speak about the voice of the analyst. We mean that each analyst has a style that makes them identifiable as them. It embodies the analyst's physiology, personality, education, experience, thought, and feeling. We are bound by that. It is human to strive for cohesion and consistency. It is this consistency that is an achievement and that is related to identity. Even the flexibility to adapt one's voice in response to each patient, is part of one's uniform voice. Our voice inevitably changes over time with our development and the evolution of our mood, mindset, etc. We adapt our responses to each particular patient as well as to a single patient within his or her analysis. Yet even with the evolutions and variations in our style, there is a certain stability to our voices as analysts. The adaptations we make are all components of one integrated voice.

"Creating a voice … might be thought of as a way, perhaps the principal way, in which individuals bring themselves into being, come to life, through their use of language" (Ogden, 1998, p. 426). Ogden adds "individuality of voice is not a given, it is an achievement" (p. 444). Fred Pine (2006) writes that psychoanalytic knowledge is a matter of "hard-won experience" (p. 3) and alludes to "the time it takes to develop one's own voice as a clinician" (p. 3). He goes on to write that the finding of our voices reflects a synthesis of what we take from our own analyses, supervisors, patients, and our personality. The authors in the following chapters describe their own unique journeys, the influences, the environments, the struggles and passions, and the identifications.

The more literal definition of voice as sound emitted through the mouth as speech also resonates for us as analysts. After all, psychoanalysis is the talking cure that is heavily based on the spoken word. The words we choose, why and how we choose them and what they sound like as well as the tone, affect, cadence, mood, direction, and inflection are central in our work. As in poetry and literature, pauses and silence are an aspect of voice. What is not said may matter as much as what is said. Based on more current developmental and psychoanalytic theories, we now understand that pre-verbal utterances can take the form of somatic or bodily communications. Voice can manifest itself in other modalities in the treatments, such as movement and drawing. Such non-verbal expression is likely true for analysts as well.

Writing itself is a form of literal voice though it is to be distinguished from the verbal. For several authors, writing is an especially meaningful aspect of their voice and for most, writing serves as a foundation in the further development of voice and self differentiation—a step towards the creation of self and analytic self.

In the following section we discuss our idea of the meaning of identity and how we use it in this book. The development of voice is a major building block towards the achievement of a mature identity. Voice is the vehicle of expression for the thoughts, feelings, and sensations that comprise identity whereas identity itself is an abstract idea of what it means to know who we are as a person.

Identity

Identity has several meanings depending upon the context and the particular discipline. For our purposes, we are referring to a sense of self, providing sameness and continuity in personality over time. It is a representation to ourselves and others of who we think we are, feel ourselves to be, and who we want or strive to be. It is both conscious and unconscious. Even as identity is consistent, it is ever changing, evolving, as we continue to discover ourselves anew, accrue more experiences and identify with others in our lives. Our analytic identity as we discuss it in this book is all about who we strive to be and who we feel ourselves to be as analysts.

Although the term identity is not primarily a psychoanalytic term, the term identification has a robust history in psychoanalysis beginning with Freud's (1917) discussion of the identification with the lost object in melancholia, "the shadow of the object fell upon the ego" (p. 249). In psychoanalysis, we have come to understand identity as being derived from our identifications. According to Freud, identifications are primarily object related. During childhood and infancy there are unconscious, primitive identifications with caregivers and family members that serve as the very first steps towards separation. If I am like Mommy, I can feel close to her and don't actually have to be in her arms all the time. Freud's idea in *Mourning and Melancholia* is that by identifying with the attachment object, we can relinquish it.

There is a developmental pattern to the consciousness with which identifications form. Early identifications take place before boundaries between self and object are set (Sander and Perlow, 1987 in Smith, 2001). Then there are the increasingly conscious and deliberate idealizations and identifications that children, teenagers, and young adults form. Later still, adult identifications can again become less deliberate and conscious. However, Smith (2001) suggests such easy distinctions between early and later or primary and secondary identifications may not be so clear-cut in the everyday realities of life.

This developmental pattern seems to recur for young psychoanalysts during training and after. During training candidates can be more deliberately imitative of teachers and supervisors, as Jonathan Eger points out in his chapter. While he uses the example of the candidate who is the child of two analyst parents, the same may be true for other candidates as well. Later still and continuing indefinitely after training, when learning is less formal, analysts' identifications can again become less deliberate and conscious.

For the analyst in training, identifications may take on special significance as a way to reduce the terror of feeling alone—or the "splendid isolation" (Freud, 1925, p. 22) of what Ken Eisold (1994) calls "the analyst's lonely work" (p. 794)—and of not knowing what to do. Identifying with one's supervisors and analyst may also reduce the pressure inherent in being the target of patients' varied and sometimes coercive projections, all while being expected to heal or at least to be of value to the patient. Henry Smith (2001) describes these early identifications with teachers and supervisors when he says that "alliances (meaning identifications) can form prematurely to abort the painful process of finding one's own voice" (p. 799).

As analysts, we are expected by others and expect ourselves to develop our own voice and at the same time to adhere to one or several theories that are derived from someone else's voice. The question is how best to assist each candidate in the development of his or her own clinical voice. Fogel and Glick (1991), who write about analysts' transferences to theory, state that "an essential aspect of a mature, independent psychoanalytic identity can only be fully acquired and consolidated some time after the completion of formal analytic training. We call this the acquisition the analyst's autonomous theoretical identity" (p. 397).

Identity, unlike identification, is not entirely object related. It is in part at least, derived from our temperaments. We may feel ourselves to be outgoing, introverted, creative, analytic, spontaneous, outspoken, slow to warm up, and so on. This aspect of ourselves, our in-born temperaments (something that we observe in infants and toddlers), may be the most challenging part to integrate into our identity as it is the part most often protected and defended against. As a result, having an awareness of one's own temperament leads to more effective functioning in life and work.

Our identities, inclusive of our identifications as analysts and our in-born temperaments, are composed of different aspects and sources, many unconscious. The more obvious sources are relatives, friends, lovers, teachers, patients, institutions, readings, and theories. Others are from more surprising sources like place, politics and neurology. As you will see in the following narratives there are striking variations and similarities in the consciously recognized categories of influences emphasized by the analysts in this book. While some express strong identifications with readings and theories, most discuss people and institutions. Family of origin is mentioned as influential for some and less for others. For several authors, race and sexual orientation are formative and intrinsic to their identities.

Susan Levine (2007) talks about our "analytic persona" (p. 81). Analytic persona relates to who we are as a total person in the context of our work as analysts. The melding of our personal and professional selves reveals itself to be true in the narratives that follow. This blending is eloquently articulated by Jane Kite (2016). She writes that as analysts, our character and personality is at the center of our work. She argues that in training as psychoanalysts, we overemphasize theory at the expense of taking responsibility for the centrality of character, most of which is unconscious. Kite's idea relates directly to the thesis of this book which is that the development of analytic identity and voice is central to our work as analysts.

Ricardo Bernardi (1992) observes that differences (in identity) among analysts reflect each analyst's psychic reality, however, these differences threaten analysts' narcissistic equilibriums. Bernardi references Sandler's idea (1983) that analysts have "implicit theories" (1992, p. 520) that are personal to them, are products of that analyst's unconscious thinking, and are very much partial theories though they may be more useful than established theories. Pluralism in psychoanalysis, or the ability to consider the validity of different perspectives, is an achievement of the conscious ego according to Bernardi. In fact, many analysts are greatly influenced by the personas and viewpoints of other analysts and incorporate aspects of those others into their self-concept. These changes may cause destabilizations that complicate development and cause conflict in the analyst as she attempts to find her own voice while making herself available to shifting identifications. This struggle for smooth integration and acceptance has to be part of the analyst's psychic work. Yet as John Klauber (1983) writes, it is "surrounded by a peculiar silence" (p. 45). This book aims to pierce some of that silence.

If, as Roy Schafer (1979) asserts, we are always becoming an analyst, what does that say about the process of becoming a fully formed analyst? It means that there is no moment when we have completed our identity formation. It is ongoing. Does the rate of change slow down with experience, seniority, and maturity or increase as one becomes more comfortable with complexity and change? In the narratives of the more senior authors in this book, identities appear to have solidified with a protracted process of thought and experience over the years. Yet, in Smith's (2001) view we humans are promiscuous in our identifications throughout the lifespan, sometimes even absorbing an imprint from a casual contact. Martin Bergmann was fond of reminding students that he was always learning from his patients. The narratives of the senior analysts in this book demonstrate clearly that they remain open to change and absorbing new ideas.

Since we have been working on this book, we both feel that the process of formulating our thoughts and representing them in writing has transformed how we think about ourselves and our work. The very act of writing, as Mitchell Wilson so aptly points out in his chapter, has a modifying effect. We believe that the narrative form provides our authors with an ideal vehicle in which to convey their stories about the formation of their analytic identity.

Narrative: what is the story that wants to be told?

Narratives are our way of making sense of our lives. We favor narrative as it conveys the personal atmosphere, style and ideas of the author in a way that no other medium can. These narratives reveal the uniquely different paths followed by each analyst. At the same time the narratives show striking and surprising commonalities that we will explore in depth in Chapter 14.

The way that a patient tells us their story, its contents and the form it takes, is filled with meaning. According to Sherwood (1969, in Lipton 1977), one criterion of analytic success is that the patient develops a narrative. "By this he means the internally consistent, coherent, comprehensible and accurate account which emerges at the end of an analysis" (Sherwood in Lipton, 1977, p. 255). The form of the narrative as a teaching tool has a long, proud history, notably in the patient narratives of the Russian neuropsychologist, A. R. Luria (1969, 1971) and then Oliver Sacks (2015). Freud and Jung stressed its importance as a window into the patients mind, Freud through his method of Free Association (1904) and Jung (1963) in advocating for listening to the patients particular story. But what about the analyst's narrative as a way for the analyst to better understand who they are as a presence in the analysis of any given patient? And what about using it as a teaching tool for candidates, and as a companion for post-graduate analysts during their professional lifespan?

Narratives are always inaccurate or incomplete because of our human tendency to view all experience, including our own, through the lenses of our limited and biased vision. While narratives include knowledge about ourselves that is conscious ("the arrogance of consciousness") (Freud, 1910, p. 39), they leave out the unconscious, unformulated, dissociated, repressed, and the unthought known (Bollas, 2011), parts of ourselves. In addition, we also cannot see what someone else can see, even and sometimes especially, when it has to do with ourselves. There are also conscious constraints to what we express given the particular context and environment of that expression. And yet we persist with narrative because we desperately want meaning, consistency, and cohesiveness. We want to be known, heard, and we want to feel ownership of our own life history. Most importantly, we want a voice.

The recent rise in the popularity of the memoir as well as story telling (Moth and Future of Storytelling) in popular culture is striking and reveals a growing population of people who want to empower themselves to be known and heard. There is also a large audience, hungry to experience this sharing of personal truths. Our stories change or expand as self-reflection and awareness develop over a lifetime.

When a patient comes into our office, we want to hear their story. We start from there, noticing the inconsistencies, the contradictions, the lapses, the questions, as well as moments of clarity and authenticity. As we write about ourselves for this book, the same is true. You, the reader, may note the inconsistencies and the contradictions as we try to present a coherent narrative about our journey as analysts. We know the narrative is not complete. As Mitchell Wilson describes in his chapter, the very context of public exposure will cause us to edit our narratives in all sorts of ways: how we want to be seen, how much we want to reveal, how we present ourselves, and how we sound. So yes, we will hide, but at the same time, we want to be known and we want to understand. So we persist.

References

Bernardi, R. (1992). On pluralism in psychoanalysis. *Psychoanalytic Inquiry*, *12*, 506–525.

Bollas, C. (2011). Psychic genera. In C. Bollas, *The Chrisopher Bollas reader* (pp. 57–78). New York, NY: Routledge.

Davies, J. M. (1998). Between the disclosure and foreclosure of erotic transference–countertransference: Can psychoanalysis find a place for adult sexuality? *Psychoanalytic Dialogues, 8*, 747–766.

Eisold, K. (1994). The intolerance of diversity in psychoanalytic institutes. *International Journal of Psychoanalysis, 75*, 785–800.

Fogel, G. I., & Glick, R. A. (1991). The analyst's postgraduate development: Rereading Freud and working theory through. *Psychoanalytic Quarterly, 60*, 396–425.

Freud, S. (1904). Freud's psychoanalytic procedure. In J. Strachey (Ed. & Trans.), *The standard edition of the complete works of Sigmund Freud* (Vol. 7, pp. 249–256). London: Hogarth Press.

Freud, S. (1910). Five lectures on psychoanalysis. In J. Strachey (Ed. & Trans.), *The standard edition of the complete works of Sigmund Freud* (Vol. 11, pp. 1–56). London: Hogarth Press.

Freud, S. (1917). Mourning and melancholia. In J. Strachey (Ed. & Trans.), *The standard edition of the complete psychological works of Sigmund Freud* (Vol. 14, pp. 243–258). London: Hogarth Press.

Freud, S. (1925). An autobiographical study. In J. Strachey (Ed. & Trans.), *The standard edition of the complete works of Sigmund Freud* (Vol. 20). London: Hogarth Press.

Gilligan, C. (1982). *In a different voice: Psychological theory and women's development.* Cambridge, MA: Harvard University Press.

Jung, C. G. (1963). *Memories, dreams, reflections.* New York, NY: Random House.

Kite, J. V. (2016). The problem of the analyst as person and the ethical unknown. Paper presented at APsaA, Panel on the Ethics of Psychoanalysis, New York City.

Klauber, J. (1983). The identity of the psychoanalyst. In E. D. Joseph & D. Widlocher (Eds.), *The identity of the psychoanalyst* (pp. 41–50). New York, NY: International Universities Press.

Levine, S. S. (2007). Nothing but the truth: Self-disclosure, self-revelation, and the persona of the analyst. *Journal of American Psychoanalytic Association, 55*, 81–104.

Lipton, S. D. (1977). The advantages of Freud's technique as shown in his analysis of the rat man. *International Journal of Psychoanalysis, 58*, 255–273.

Luria, A. R. (1969). *The mind of a mnemonist.* Cambridge: Avon Books First Printing Edition.

Luria, A. R. (1971). *The man with a shattered world: A history of a brain wound.* Cambridge, MA: Harvard University Press.

Ogden, T. H. (1998). A question of voice in poetry and psychoanalysis. *Psychoanalytic Quarterly, 67*, 426–448.

Pine, F. (2006). If I knew then what I know now: Theme and variations. *Psychoanalytic Psychology, 23*, 1–7.

Sacks, O. (2015). *Gratitude.* New York, NY: Alfred A. Knopf.

Schafer, R. (1979). On becoming a psychoanalyst of one persuasion or another. *Contemporary Psychoanalysis, 15*, 345–360.

Smith, H. F. (2001). Hearing voices: The fate of the analyst's identifications. *Journal American Psychoanalytic Association, 49*, 781–812

Part I

Narratives

Chapter 2

All origins are suspect
Becoming a psychoanalyst

Francisco J. González

> "Now" is the moment when change erupts.
> —Anne Carson (1998)[1]

I don't remember when I heard it, but I have ever since been fond of the joke about the scientist and the old lady: after delivering a lecture on cosmology, the scientist is confronted by the elderly skeptic who refutes the scientist's claims, saying it's clear that the world actually sits on the back of a turtle. Flummoxed, the scientist wonders what the turtle would then possibly sit on; unfazed, she responds "you can't fool me, it's turtles all the way down." It's a satisfying joke for me; I like the paradox, the seeming resolution that only leads to the chasm. The old lady's answer is big bang aporia.

The satisfaction I get from turning over the question about when or how I decided to become an analyst derives from a similar kind of ungraspable.

I fell into my first analysis as a resident in psychiatry. I had little sense of what I was seeking in the treatment, other than some vague sort of grounding. I had moved to San Francisco a year earlier and had started a serious relationship: I was doubly *desubicado*.[2] My choice to come to San Francisco, rather than New York, was already deeply haunted by my family's immigration story, though I didn't recognize this at all at the time. That realization came to me years later, while acting as tour guide for an Irish friend who lived in London. We sat overlooking the city from a hilltop, and I recounted my very first visit to San Francisco, a family road trip my father had initiated in 1976. My father had visited the city for a convention the year before and fell in love with it immediately, its white stuccoed houses on a hill reminded him of Havana. The next summer he packed us all into the car and we went west, to see America with San Francisco as the organizing destination. I remembered joking to my mother as we passed Francisco Street on the way to the Golden Gate bridge, that one day I would live here, and on this street, and then my name could appear in every line of my address. It was a child's joke, the teenager emboldening himself for leaving home while affirming his narcissistic attachments to his mother. I recounted these memories those years later to my Irish friend sitting on the terrace at the San Francisco Art Institute. The whole story was an attempt to charm him, but it suddenly seemed clear to me, and in a way it had never been before, that my being in San Francisco had something to do with my father, as if he had chosen the city where I was to settle, to call home, without either of us knowing it. It was as if his nostalgic memory of Havana—a city to which he had sworn never to return—would become planted in my aspirations, only to bloom when it came time to choose the place I would live the bulk of my adult life. I was very attracted to this kind of thinking, the way meaning can move across places and times; ultimately, it came to seem to me that psychoanalysis had a particularly significant and beautiful way of conceptualizing and using this kind of reckoning. Though I hadn't come to that yet.

Apropos of this form of thinking, the recognition that my father's memories had something to do with my settling in San Francisco only arrived some years *after* my first analysis had ended, and I don't recall ever talking about it within the analysis, though I might well have. *Desubicación* did not exist for me as a concept either when I first sought out that therapy, but I think now that I was *desubicado* and, as I said, doubly so: first, by my move to San Francisco, which marked a definitive break from the place where my parents lived as immigrant Americans, but also a kind of hidden return to the place they and we had come from; and second, by the fact of having entered an important relationship, which provided me with a veneer of respectability in my young eyes, enough to allow myself contact with the flux and tumult that lay below it. These disorienting displacements set my balance off enough that I could be shaken loose from my usual moorings and fall into the analysis.

After a few months in the treatment, my therapist made a few remarks one day, seemingly simple re-descriptions of what I was relating to him about events in my residency training, about my fears and consternations, but some of the words he used ripped through the surface of my narrations, and set off a deep anxiety in me. I thought I was talking about one set of things, but they turned out to be animated by deep currents from my childhood, and suddenly I felt compelled to talk about things that I had never properly articulated to myself, let alone anyone else. The feeling was one of passionate agitation; I felt undone, but in a way that mattered very much to understand.

The analyst was Jungian and, among many other things, he taught me to listen to my dreams. Early on, I dreamt that I was led up a hill by an old man, a former neighbor, to a church; as we stood taking it in, there was an earthquake and the facade of the structure came crashing down all around us, but somehow as it fell, I was framed by an empty window and was left unscathed. It was a fecund dream, and we used it to organize other, more complex, processes throughout the treatment: the dismantling of aspects of my narcissism with its layers of camouflage; the waning of childhood religious beliefs and their evolution into deeper matters regarding faith and the unknown; and ultimately, the whole trajectory of the analysis, especially as it came to an end.

These were powerful experiences. Being able to think for the first time what I had long known but could not really think was generative, not only because in struggling to articulate something to my analyst I started to conceptualize it for myself, but also because it enlivened an inner current in me. On the one hand I could feel an inner expansion, as if I were incorporating parts of myself that had been rendered alien: I was annexing inner territory. And on the other, the process was profoundly de-territorializing and cataclysmic. If I had entered the analysis because I was *desubicado*, its undertaking was not a straightforward and linear path to feeling ever more located; it was as much a process of transposing that disorientation into other realms and different registers, of keeping it moving, rather than having it lodged and fixed.

Somewhere in the midst of all of that, a desire began to find it's way into my consciousness, at first in a vague and clouded way, and increasingly with reluctant conviction: I wanted to become a psychoanalyst.

This was hardly welcome. I resisted the press of it for two prominent reasons. First, I had expressly come to San Francisco and residency training in order to work in community mental health. In 1991, when I started my residency, the psychiatry department at San Francisco General Hospital operated under an innovative culturally focused model. Each of the locked in-patient units was inflected by a particular ethnocultural focus or identity. There were five such teams on the units: Latino, Asian, LGBT/HIV, Black, and Women. To be sure, this setup was haunted by the cultural reifications symptomatic of identity politics. Did an indigenous Central American civil war refugee have more in common with a white Argentinian of Italian descent than a Vietnamese refugee, just because they both spoke Spanish? What did it mean to have HIV status, sexual orientations, and gender "dyshporias" housed in one team (and one completely separate from the Women's team)? Was there something ghettoizing about constituting these teams in the first place—and especially on locked in-patient units, already highly complicated sites of power? There were a myriad of troubling questions, but they were intriguing ones to me, and certainly more so than ones asked in traditional psychiatric residencies with their increasing focus on positivistic science. However clumsily, here was a psychiatric training program that took up the cultural, and fostered an environment in which these problematics and the question of the social link in psychosis were front and center. I had spent a month doing a rotation on the Latino Focus Team during medical school: it was the first time in my medical education that I had the opportunity to work, learn, and train in Spanish. The milieu of the entire department was marked by multiple bilingualisms; I found resonance in their oscillations. I was mentored by a vibrant Puerto Rican psychiatrist—who danced in a samba collective and spoke Spanish with the Caribbean accents of my childhood (fast and lush, the "s's" dropped)—she practiced psychiatry with a passion that was infectious. Even in the midst of psychic catastrophes, she seemed to say, one could enjoy this hard work; there was pleasure in doing it, and the pleasure was in the process of it. After psychiatric training, I returned to San Francisco General as an attending psychiatrist, teaching residents and working with severely psychotic patients. Work there was a series of extraordinary encounters: conversations in radical otherness that cracked open language and inaugurated other kinds of multilingualism; forms of living a human life I hadn't imagined. I remember a man we dubbed Picky, under the influence of the gallows humor that made work there possible. Possessed by the spirit of James Dean, methamphetamines and other demons, he had picked away half of his scalp and one eyelid, leaving a whitish knob of withered sclera; and yet, he was as funny and beguiling as he was insane. Or a woman, profoundly narcissistic and brilliant and isolated, who let a breast tumor grow so large it couldn't be easily removed because of the hole it would leave in her chest wall. I would visit her on the medical floor, and as she talked I could feel myself being pulled into her psychic labyrinth, intrigued and then increasingly confused, losing my mental bearings, while I watched the fog roll over the hill through her window.

Work at the General had a quality of vibrant immediacy. It could be exhausting, but there was no question that it mattered. The idea of becoming a psychoanalyst, on the other hand, smacked of elitism and clinical distance; it felt like social disengagement, an ethical capitulation. I had not read the Freud of 1918, in his address to the Budapest Conference, where he called for free clinics, nor had I thought much about how all of Freud's later work was cultural critique. I knew nothing of the strong political impulse of Fenichel and others in the early analytic movement, or of how essential psychoanalysis was to the Frankfurt school, or the strong links between psychoanalysis and the social in Latin America.

These would come much later, and not directly through my analytic training, but rather through a network of affiliations with socially engaged analysts, community mental health workers and activists, social workers, and politically-minded friends. These interlocutors would help me to forge a creative synthesis between community mental health, sociopolitical critique, and conventional psychoanalysis. But back in my first analysis, such a synthesis was not easily imaginable. In my mind's eye, analysis occupied the domain of upper East Side ladies with poodles—a populist superiority in me made me recoil. What was becoming increasingly undeniable, however, was the strength of my uneasy attraction to it.

If the threat to my plans to become a socially conscious psychiatrist constituted one reason for the discontent I felt at these yearnings to become a psychoanalyst, it was not the most salient. Like the fox in the Aesop's fable, the grapes were judged sour simply due to my inability to reach them. For some time I felt quite convinced that even if I pursued my desire to become a psychoanalyst, no institute would take me. This was not without reason. I knew of no one who had applied to the local analytic institutes as an openly gay candidate, and I had no intention of returning to the closet. I had closed its door with great deliberation after living in Germany for almost 3 years with my "lover" (as we used to say then). When we returned in order for me to start medical school in Texas, I made a vow to myself to stop "coming out" to anyone: instead I would just *be* out, live out. In medical school I made no attempts to conceal my relationship, I spoke out politically at public assemblies, and helped establish a gay support group with another Latino man (we had to meet prospective members at a designated spot and escort them to the meeting room: people were afraid to come if we published the location). The self-determination I experienced in medical school was hard won. I could have used a therapist years earlier to help me sort out the confusion and shame that surrounded my sexuality, but—surprisingly to me now—it had never occurred to me to seek one out. Therapy was not practiced in my family. When I had come out to my father just after college, he asked me—to his credit, only once—if I wanted to see a psychiatrist. I simply said no. That had been the most extensive conversation I could recall on the subject of therapy in our family. I suppose if we thought of therapy at all, we probably thought of it as an American practice. The logic would have been: why pay a stranger to talk about your problems when there's family?

Like many of us who grew up in the 1960s and 1970s, I didn't have a word for the sense of difference I had felt since childhood for quite some time. Ironically, I remember the afternoon I first learned the word "homosexual." Was I 10 or 12 years old? I was sitting with my friend Patty who lived next door, on the back porch of their house. Her older sister Judy was sitting with us, flipping through a *Time* magazine; she giggled when she came across the word. She must have read us the passage. I had no idea what the word meant, and asked. I have no memory of what Judy told us; as far as I know, I did not retain the definition. But I remember learning the word itself. Years later, this story became a portal to my understanding of *Nachträglichkeit*, a concept I find to be one of the most captivating and original in psychoanalysis. Moments of a life can hold extraordinary densities of meaning, inscribed with future sense. With no conscious recognition that the word "homosexual" had anything whatsoever to do with me that summer afternoon, I stored the experience, charged with a significance that would become evident only a decade later.

And today sitting at my desk, writing, with a shelf of books within my easy reach, it's not difficult to thread the memory of that afternoon onto the same line of thought that leads to a passage I know lies waiting in a book by Foucault (1980, p. 43):

> The nineteenth-century homosexual became a personage, a past, a case history, and a childhood, in addition to being a type of life, a life form, and a morphology .... Homosexuality appeared as one of the forms of sexuality when it was transposed from the practice of sodomy onto a kind of interior androgyny, a hermaphroditism of the soul. The sodomite had been a temporary aberration; the homosexual was now a species.

It was to Saint Foucault—as David Halperin called him in his playful "hagiography"—and not to a therapist that I turned in those years of medical school and residency when I had decided never to come out again. And ironically enough it was through Foucault, who had little love for it, that the discipline of psychoanalysis first began to find me.

In that academic and rather dry passage from Foucault—somehow also still very memorable to me—I experienced a lightening crack of realization, simultaneously a recognition and a profound undoing. To say that the homosexual became a personage in the 19th century, one that now had a childhood and a psychology that could be formulated in a case history—that the homosexual was a species (!)—resonated with the kind of narrative I had constructed almost surreptitiously for much of my life, a story partly hidden even to myself, about that childhood, my own. But the mental explosion that Foucault made possible was not so much about my "finally" finding and consolidating my "gay identity," a term about which I always felt suspicious even as I embraced it politically; it was more about conceiving of these narratives and identity positions as something already radically mediated by the flows of history. Over the years, it had become increasingly, viscerally, painfully, clear that the given story of the family—a boy-meets-girl-marries-has-children story—was not the only way a life could be lived. The heterosexual imperative, I came to see, was an artifact of history. What Foucault helped me understand is that all forms of sexuality were inflected in this way; that sexuality itself—despite how raw and immediate and self-evident sex itself might feel—is always also a conversation with history. Here was a complex linkage to that afternoon when I discovered the word homosexual, and to the hours of clandestine searches in my father's medical textbooks for that same word: these were attempts to name something inarticulate but vital, to give form to desire, and by doing so to give desire a social place, to make it culturally intelligible. What I now also came to realize was that those names and forms had no inherent stability, that they too had their own restlessness and troubled histories. This opened onto heady terrain: there was something vertiginous about living into an identity not as solid ground, but as a contingency, as an effect rather than a foundation, as a necessary fiction. Recognizing and consolidating myself was simultaneously an invitation to coming further undone. But I liked this feeling of uncertainty: it felt like growing.

This was not unlike the passionate agitation I felt when my first analyst, a few years later, uttered those deceptively simple words that deeply troubled the way I thought about myself, and became a spur to refashioning the story of who I was. Were these first openings in that analysis an echo of the openings I felt reading Foucault, or is it only now that I thread them together, and link them back to that afternoon with neighbor friends when I learned the word homosexual? Where does any story really start, if not in the present?

When I say that I found psychoanalysis through Foucault, this isn't, of course, really true. "Foucault" is more like the name I give to a series of readings, conversations and processes, a semiconscious intellectual investigation that spanned many years, beginning in college and extending into the present. In one version of the story, I became a psychoanalyst because doing so allowed a continuation of this investigation, one that was interrupted by a foray to medical school. I had begun reading theory in college and graduate school: Sausurre and poststructuralist linguistics, Derrida, the reader response criticism of Wolfgang Iser and Stanley Fish, and later a whole line of queer theorists and historians, Eve Kosofsky Sedgwick, David Halperin, Jefferey Weeks, and later still, Judith Butler, Leo Bersani, Teresa de Lauretis, Elizabeth Grosz. The deconstructionist tendencies of these writers resonated deeply with me, and I now see them as formative to my analytic sensibility. They provided a backdoor entry to psychoanalysis, and in a multitude of ways. Theories of readership and literary criticism were, after all, theories of interpretation. How did one come to have a reading of a text? Did one stay within the frame of what was provided on the page? Situate it historically or as an effect of the writer's life? What was the association and communication between texts?

For a master's thesis in literature, I wrote on Jorge Luis Borges and Sir Thomas Browne, writers in two different languages, separated by a couple of centuries. I was taken by the idea that texts spoke to each other through the readings we give them. I was less concerned with the direct historical relationship of Borges' writing to Browne's; I cared more about the creative tensions that arose by the way they could be put in creative juxtaposition to each other in the mind of the reader. I can now see how strongly linked these ideas are to the ways I now understand association, reverie, and analytic interpretation.

But what I was really interested in was reading. Reading was an encounter and a transmission, a way of inhabiting the mind of another and of letting another mind inhabit yours. You had to suspend yourself in order to read deeply, to surrender to another's way of thinking. The transformative magic of that experience did not start with theory. I had always loved to read, ever since I was a child it had been something that brought me a great deal of pleasure. But when I went to college I quickly chose to pursue medicine and began the usual pre-med requirements in the sciences. One semester in my sophomore year, I was not able to get into the usual sequence of required English courses. Not wanting to fall behind on accumulating my credits, I took what was available: early American literature. We began with New England colonialist literature—works by Cotton Mather and blistering sermons by Jonathan Edwards, like "Sinners in the Hands of an Angry God." Concurrently, I was taking Physics 101. There, we were calculating coefficients of friction, sliding imaginary bricks down imaginary inclined planes. I was surprised to find that even the driest of Calvinist sermons stirred my imagination, presented me with a host of questions about the nature of god and history, belief, and the power of the word. On the other hand, I really didn't slide bricks down inclined planes. Practicality dictated I spend a few years reading.

I met with my parents the next time they came to visit and told them I was changing majors, to study literature rather than go to pursue a path to medical school. They did not much like this idea, anxious about the prospects for my future, but they were always supportive of my academic pursuits. Like most others at the time, they had been strong supporters of the revolution in Cuba, fleeing the country only when it became clear to them that there was little hope for democracy. They were middle-class professionals (my father a physician; my mother a pharmacist), and when they immigrated to the United States everything they possessed fit in a few suitcases. Their most valuable possession was their education: a value they transmitted through expectation and encouragement. My father, especially, would have liked to see me follow in his footsteps to medicine rather than study literature—a perfectly good avocation in his estimation, but hardly a career—but this disappointment was mitigated by my intentions to pursue graduate studies. For a number of years I studied literature, wrote, and enrolled in a Master's degree, lost my conviction to become a poet, and decided against becoming an academic, settled on returning to medical school but moved to Germany for a time and taught English composition, finished my master's thesis on Borges and Browne while taking post-baccalaureate science courses, and finally wended my way to medical school.

When I applied to residencies in psychiatry, I told the story that I only became interested in the specialty toward the end of my 4 years of medical school during my psychiatry rotation. Working on an inpatient unit, I met a young schizophrenic patient, a brilliant editor who had lost her job because of strange communications from beings who would come to her during the night and remove her uterus and other organs. These would be cut up and reassembled, only to be replaced before she woke. Conversations happened by means of her body: an ache in the knee, for example, was a reference to her friend Pat, since the knee is the patella. Often there were references to Greek mythology or characters from novels. There was urgency in the way she spoke to me: it was very important to her that I understand her. I had never had conversations like this before. She was speaking English but it was a cracked open language from some other realm: quite beautiful, but harrowing, enigmatic, and never what I expected. Applying for residencies in psychiatry I said I wanted to keep having conversations like these. It was a little like the feeling of reading poetry; my mind located in a similar place of associative reception. It was a poetry of awe and terror at times to be sure, a transmission from someone in need of help, but you had to be able to speak poetry back to help them. I think it is true that these experiences brought my desire to become a psychiatrist to clear consciousness, but it was only in retrospect that I recognized how much earlier my budding interest in psychiatry had actually manifested. The fact of the matter is that I had volunteered to be an ombudsman at the state psychiatric hospital 3 years before and I had done a psychiatric externship another summer with a beloved teacher and mentor. He showed an interest in me, felt I had an aptitude and that I had a facility for learning about these things. But I wasn't really planning a career in psychiatry. I was going to be an internist in the inner city at that time, working with the poor, working with gay men with AIDS.

This intellectual vagabonding of my early adulthood seems to me now a direct line to psychoanalysis, whose method aims for aimlessness while listening carefully for what emerges. My trajectory to becoming an psychoanalyst traces a kind of funneling shape of narrowing oscillations: from a childhood idea that I would be like my father and become a medical doctor, I found a path in young adulthood that turned away from that idea, only to return to it later, when it was more fully mine; following a path towards science, I left it to follow literature, only to become a physician, but one whose literary bent brought him to psychiatry, but a form of psychiatry inflected by an anthropological tendency, one that problematized the question of mental illness as culturally embedded rather than positivistically discovered, and a queer psychiatrist to boot, who came of age in a time when homosexuality was still a DSM diagnosis and who came out shortly before the AIDS crisis.

Association leads me to Freud's case of the homosexual woman. In that fascinating text he deconstructs the genesis of the nameless woman's sexuality, remarking towards the end that "the chain of causation can always be recognized with certainty if we follow the line of analysis, whereas to predict it along the line of synthesis is impossible" (1920/1955, p. 168). This reasoning extends well beyond the particularities of that distant case, to all constructions in psychoanalysis and perhaps even to any telling of a personal history. It is only looking backwards that we have much certainty, and even then it is little more than contingent on the organizing effects of the present. And as quickly as I think of this idea from Freud's case, I am reminded of a quotation from Borges, and find that I have used it at the end of my thesis, though I didn't quite remember I had. It obviously made a deep impression on me, and now strikes me as tremendously psychoanalytic:

> And yet, and yet ... To deny temporal succession, to deny the ego, to deny the astronomical universe, are apparent desperations and secret assuagements. Our destiny ... is not horrible because of its unreality; it is horrible because it is irreversible and ironbound. Time is the substance I am made of. Time is a river that carries me away, but I am the river; it is a tiger that mangles me, but I am the tiger; it is a fire which consumes me, but I am the fire. The world, alas, is real; I, alas, am Borges.
> (Borges, 1964, pp. 186–187)

This is the kind of story that comes to mind at present about how I finally came to make a choice that I wanted to train as a psychoanalyst, the kind of story in which the homosexual woman might be in conversation with Borges via Foucault. It is necessarily—because it is only in writing that I communicate with you now—a conversation between texts. But it is of course only a version of the full story and hardly any more true or convincing than any of a number of other versions that might otherwise come to mind.

And yet, and yet ... how could I tell a story of how I came to be an analyst, and not say that the seeds were planted very early indeed? Wasn't there some inchoate and potential desire in childhood? Like the pluripotential stem cells in the body that have the ability to develop into any number of tissue, wasn't there some early density of wanting to understand or of being understood, to make sense of the puzzles of the family, to figure out what was happening in and to my mind, to untangle the crooked paths to intimacy? Lacan is famous for his extended discourse on lack: it is what is missing in wanting that propels one forward, but only if one has the fortitude not to give up on desire while knowing that, by its very nature, desire will always go unfulfilled.

What then of the desire to become an analyst? It makes sense to devise explanatory mechanisms: not being understood must have been an engine for wanting to understand; being hurt must have been an impetus for seeking to heal. And what life doesn't have some version of these kinds of turns? Maybe my desire to become an analyst has something in common with the desire I had as a child to be a parent, to reproduce the conditions of childhood, to make new starts out of the old. A part of me, though, bristles at that characterization, as true as it is. I grew up in a three-generational, bilingual family: three of my grandparents died at home (my mother's mother died when she was only 6 years old). For the last many years of that setup, it was three kids, my parents, and the uncanny symmetry of my mother's father and my father's mother living under one roof. As I wrote in my application essay to psychoanalytic training: I grew up in an atmosphere of Oedipus squared. Undoubtedly many identifications and their repudiations, the deposits of unresolved family traumas, attempts to memorialize the loves or repair the empathic ruptures involving the most formative figures of this early life bent and shaped my trajectory towards becoming an psychoanalyst.

But today I want a different mythology beyond the ubiquitous triangle of the mother and the father and the child that has so completely colonized the analytic imagination. The story of my early individual influences, I leave to the shelter of my individual relationships—my intimate others, including my analysts. The individual story requires presence and a freer association. This essay is a different kind of communication: haunted by the absences of writing, carefully composed, addressed to you, an abstract and multiple other. It is a communication inherently inked on a social fabric. And so as regards the influences of childhood, I will mark two, social ones, without which I cannot imagine having become an analyst: growing up in an environment in which my sexuality was not socially recognized, and growing up as an immigrant in a bilingual family.

From within and without, otherness was recognizable in my childhood, and being recognized became constitutive. The doubling of consciousness that such otherness occasioned could of course be the source of consternation and pain, as W. E. B. Du Bois noted, though this was much more true of my sexuality than of my ethnicity. But it was also a generative and creative engine that powered imagination and provided perspective, akin to Bion's notion of binocular vision.

Betty Fuks (1999) has written beautifully about Freud's Jewishness. Exiling himself from the Jewish majority as godless nonbeliever, he nonetheless carried the mark of stigma as a German-speaking Jew in Vienna. In this way, Freud was the paradoxical and concurrent resident of both inside and outside. His genius lay in using this paradoxical position to find within his patients their own sense of the stranger within, their own status as exiles from the land of otherness, namely, the unconscious. As Fuks writes: "The analytic exile is a condition of *devenir* [becoming]: it allows the individual to search, through the word, for a designation of that which, coming from the outside, is in himself, although it is strange to him" (p. 10).

It is simplistic to say that my sexuality and my displacement as an immigrant constitute the provenance of my becoming a psychoanalyst, but there is no doubt this *coming from* and *coming to be*, have something profound to do with each other. The exquisite and generative dialogue of and with otherness that lies at the heart of the psychoanalytic endeavor, was a resonant match for a boy who grew up with one foot in, one foot out. Speaking two languages, being from somewhere else, knowing of a difference in my desire but not knowing what it might be named—this was all good soil for the germ of psychoanalysis. Once it found it's place within me, it caught and flowered.

When I entered my second analysis, I was keenly aware of my desire to become a psychoanalyst; it was the primary reason I sought the analysis out. Or at least so I thought at the time. A great deal unfolded over the course of that treatment that had little to do with the now explicit desire to become an analyst, though in another way, everything now had to do with that desire. Analysis became more of a snake that ate its own tail; yet another set of rearrangements and unsettlements. Among the transformations was a movement from *what* to *how*: I was less concerned with the content of what we unearthed in that second analysis, and more with the nuanced ways in which that content emerged and how it underwent multiple transformations. A part of my mind identified with my analyst, found exhilaration in surfing the waves of association. But who was this analyst, an impossible figure, the awesome Hydra who could turn from being a tender to a suffocating mother in the course of a couple of turns of phrase, who in turn, when vanquished, could suddenly reappear as the imperious and terrifying State, a child-father, caring friend, or queer lover? The experience of the transference was surprisingly richer than in my first analysis, despite or perhaps because of concurrent academic training at the institute. As I had found earlier while studying literature, in which learning about poetics and the tradition had only thickened my enjoyment of reading, emersion in psychoanalytic study now amplified my engagement with the lived experience of being in analysis. Borges has a metaphor I have always loved about the sphere of knowledge, an analogy he draws from geometric progression: as the sphere of knowledge expands, so much more does its surface come into contact with the unknown.

I am not the kind of analyst who believes that once we uncover some basic truths we solve the riddle of the Sphinx, finally decoding the rebus. I'm more the kind of analyst who believes it rebuses all the way down. On that slippery slope, I don't think of the technique of interpretation as something precious or particularly transformative. It's an everyday tool; less the royal road, more like a handrail for experience. And the practice of analysis is the setting in which that deep conversation with the stranger within one's self and others gets a good enough footing to keep creating new forms. This kind of conversation is difficult to achieve in a useful way; it is inherently confusing when horizons keep multiplying. As I keep trying to become the kind of analyst I think I want to be, it is my patients who are my greatest teachers and allies. They push me into places where I would not volunteer to go, and often compel me to find the transformations within myself that might allow me to remain in productive conversation with them. I do not always succeed in growing in the ways that would be helpful to them or to me. It is especially then, in my failing, when I most need the community of others who have taken up this practice. I do not mean the institute. While I am very fortunate to be part of a local institute that prizes collegiality, progressive thinking, innovation, and attention to group process, there is a great deal in the psychoanalytic establishment that is still in need of refreshment if psychoanalytic practice is to remain as vibrant and relevant in the 21st century as it was in the previous one. I mean a much looser affiliation of associates, clusters and networks of friends and colleagues, mentors and consultants, students, and co-workers in the trenches. These companions help keep the tensions open and help me see what I am missing; they help me recover again and again the pleasure of the work.

I remember now Marion Milner. After spending a lifetime reassembling the stuff of her diaries into theories of mind, restringing the beads of memories into new explorations in writing, she cut up a series of pictures she had made over the years and, towards the end of her life, recombined the cut-ups into new collages. The drama of analysis is at least as much one of constructing a new story out of the trappings of the old, as it is of the way the old story colonizes what appears to be a new present. Similarly, an an accounting of how one came to be an analyst might be more a story of now than of the past (though I probably can't tell how that is so, at least not just yet).

Notes

1 Reprinted as an epigraph here by kind permission of John O'Brien at Dalkey Archive Press.
2 *Desubicado* means confused or disoriented, but more immediately carries the notion of displacement, as in "dislocated." (Actually, the Greek origins which haunt the word "disoriented" carry a similar sense.)

References

Borges, J. L. (1964). *Other inquisitions (1937–1952)* (Ruth L. C. Sims, Trans.) Austin, TX: University of Texas Press.
Carson, A. (1998). *Eros the bittersweet.* Champaign, IL and London: Dalkey Archive Press.
Foucault, M. (1980). *The history of sexuality. Volume 1: An introduction* (R. Hurley Trans.). New York, NY: Vintage Books.
Freud, S. (1955). The psychogenesis of a case of homosexuality in a woman. In J. Strachey (Ed. & Trans.), *The standard edition of the complete works of Sigmund Freud* (Vol. 18, pp. 145–172). London: Hogarth Press. (Original work published 1920.)
Fuks, B. B. (1999). Vocation of exile: Psychoanalysis and Judaism. *International Forum of Psychoanalysis, 8*, 7–12.

Chapter 3

From Ebbets Field to 82nd Street
Finding my way

Ted Jacobs

One of my favorite teachers at the New York Psychoanalytic Institute was Bertram Lewin, an elfin-looking man with a mischievous smile who was known for his writings on sleep, dreaming, and the primitive mental phenomena that occur in dreams.

In one of our classes, Lewin was speaking of the fact that most analytic writers choose subjects that resonate deeply with their personal interests and concerns. "Take Franz Alexander," he said, "Alexander is a big man, an athlete and an action-oriented fellow. And he writes about action, about playing a role in treatment and deliberately acting in such a way as to counter the pathogenic influences of early relationships."

"As for me," Lewin added, "I like to sleep."

What is true for authors, applies, I believe, to analysts as well. Our theoretical preferences, our interests, our ways of working, and the colleagues we choose as mentors and friends, are determined by deep-seated, often unconscious forces that have their roots in childhood experiences and family life.

To talk meaningfully about my work as an analyst, it is necessary, therefore, to describe briefly the family environment in which I grew up, the various influences on me, and the wider cultural and social environment in which I was raised.

The West Side of Manhattan was my world as a child, a place that was filled with riches of all kinds. As a boy of 11 or 12, I was pretty much on my own, taking the subway or trolley car to the Capital Theatre for the double bill of a movie and stage show that it featured, to Madison Square Garden to see the Knicks or Rangers play, or to attend my favorite event, one of the world class track meets that, in the winter months, were held at the Garden.

A would-be athlete myself, I was part of a sports group that made the trip each Saturday to the upper reaches of Riverdale, to play competitive sports in the vast playground of Van Courtland Park.

I emphasize the considerable independence that I had as a youngster as an important factor in my upbringing as it fostered in me a tendency to go my own way and not be overly influenced by the particular environment in which I found myself; a quality that has strongly influenced my work and thinking as an analyst.

Judged by usual standards, I came from a middle-class family, but not one that was free from economic worry. My father, an embattled businessman whose firm knew little stability and regularly swung from prosperity to the brink of bankruptcy, suffered from depression that was due, in large measure, to his feeling trapped by having to earn a living at work that he thoroughly disliked and for which he was ill suited. He was, by inclination, a perennial student, a man who would read a book on history or politics and then entertain his family with his unique take on world events, a view of history that drew a good deal more on fiction than on fact.

My dad was an original and spellbinding storyteller, who, at the dinner table, would spin yarns about Jewish history—Rabbi Joshua, otherwise known as Jesus, was often his protagonist—that had us crying with laughter. His tales were interminable, however, and more often than not they exhausted his listeners who, weary with fatigue, would slowly drift away from the table until I, still transfixed by the power of my father's narrative, remained the sole member of his audience.

I, like my father, am a storyteller, his gift to me and one that I cherish. I have always felt that good clinical writing, writing that conveys the spirit and atmosphere of the work we do, as well as the facts of the case and the quality of the analytic relationship, draws heavily on storytelling. A case history is a story and to interest the reader, to grab him, as it were, that story must be told in a compelling way. If there is anything that characterizes my own analytic writing, it is my effort to do just that; to tell the story of an analytic journey as the adventure it is.

My mother, a high school teacher of English and Latin, had a strong interest in both literature and psychology. Although in many respects a shy and anxious person, she also had a flair for the dramatic. In her later years she became a book reviewer for women's groups and was known for her moving, at times memorable, presentations of works of contemporary fiction. She shared her interests with me and at home we had long conversations about books and authors, as well as political events.

My mother's circle of friends were mostly professionals who supported the Loyalists in the Spanish civil war, were advocates for the American Labor Party, and considered themselves, if not Communists, certainly forward-looking Socialists. The atmosphere of liberal thinking, support for unions and the workingman, and idealization of the social experiments in Soviet Russia filled our home.

It took sacrifice on both my parents' part to send me to private school. This was important to them as I carried the hope of the family, especially on the part of my mother, to have a son who was a success in the world.

I attended the Horace Mann School, an excellent, diversified school today but one that in the mid-1940s was an institution devoted to rote, textbook learning. The atmosphere fostered disciplined, task-oriented, and totally unimaginative learning. For the 6 years that I attended, H.M., as the school was known to everyone connected with it, I lived in a state of anxiety, more or less severe, according to the exam schedule of the week or the difficulty of the homework assignment. I found school to be one steady grind, the only relief being its extensive after-school sports program. I played three sports and very much enjoyed the camaraderie and good fellowship of my teammates. Even in this arena, however, anxiety was my constant companion as I worried a great deal about my performance on the diamond or the basketball court.

My greatest worry, however, fed by my mother's anxiety about my future, concerned my choice of vocation. Through my high school years I was quite uncertain as to what path to pursue, and I worried about whether I would choose wisely, and if I was capable of earning a decent living.

As an adolescent, my strongest interests were in the field of radio and journalism, especially writing about sports. I authored a weekly column for the school newspaper called *On the Bench*, a location I knew well as I was often relegated to it as a back up or substitute player. My ambition at the time was to be either a broadcaster or a journalist, so I made an effort in my senior year in high school to obtain some experience in both fields. Through family connections, I was able to land a job covering the Brooklyn Dodgers home games for the *Daily Worker*, the Communist newspaper that was quite popular with leftist families at the time. The sports page was minimal—sports was not a major interest of the politically engaged readership—but I got a chance to travel to Ebbets Field, storied home of the Dodgers, and a great place to watch baseball, and to report the exploits of Dodger greats—such as Jackie Robinson, Pee Wee Reese, Dixie Walker, and the feisty Dodger manager, Leo Durocher, who became the model for the protagonist in my novel, *The Year of Durocher*.

I learned a good deal about writing from this experience and also about the world of radio as the result of having a disc jockey show on a small FM station. The audience for this program, I suspect, consisted primarily of my mother, sister and a few adventurous souls who discovered the station at its remote place on the dial.

I learned, too, about the competitive nature both of the broadcasting industry and the world of journalism. I had seen highly skilled individuals in both fields relegated to writing for small town publications or working at radio stations not much larger than the one on which I had my show. I feared ending up in the sticks—some small mid-Western or Southern town and living my life as an also-ran.

A few years later, when I was considering becoming a college teacher of English—literature was in my blood—I feared something similar; that the only position I would be able to find would be as a teacher of freshman composition at some small college in a remote part of the country.

My anxiety about a choice of profession was such that in my college years I felt a need for help. Accordingly, I went to see the psychiatrist who had worked with my mother some years earlier.

Dr. E's willingness to see me, the son of a former patient, spoke to his unconventional approach to treatment and his independent, if not rebellious, personality.

Dr. E was a psychiatrist who had analytic training at a small prestigiousless institute but was known chiefly for his expertise in psychopharmacology. He was undoubtedly the last person an aspiring analyst today would choose as his therapist. And I would not have chosen him had I known about his specialty and his lack of well-recognized analytic training. Dr. E, however, was enormously helpful to me. Not only did he work effectively with the shy and insecure adolescent that I was, but he served as a model for me in many ways. He was an engaged, imaginative, and flexible therapist, respectful of traditional technique, but not bound by it in the way that later, I found, so many classically trained analysts to be.

Dr. E was a person who put therapeutic goals and the welfare of his patients first. In an original way, he employed a variety of techniques, including asking me in the middle of a session to sit up and face him when he thought I was using the couch to avoid dealing with an important issue. He also used metaphors, similes, illustrative stories, and humor to foster insight and understanding, knowing that patients can often grasp and appreciate aspects of their psychology more readily through these indirect means than through direct interpretations of their own psychology. He also made a point of being warm and responsive in his approach, often using his engaging personality to reach me when I had become defensive and withdrawn.

Dr. E's method of working was, by today's standards, not a strictly analytic approach. It was an effective mix of analytic and psychotherapeutic techniques, and, in that sense, anticipated the lowering of the boundaries between these two methods that many analysts today believe is necessary to obtain a therapeutic result in the case of the more guarded and disturbed patients.

In my work over the years, I have often recalled my treatment with Dr. E and how his inventive approach was helpful to a young person. He did not draw arbitrary or artificial distinctions between schools of thought, a tendency that has limited the effectiveness of many analysts. As a result, he was able to draw on ways of thinking and technique associated with a variety of perspectives to enhance his work. My treatment with Dr. E stimulated my interest in becoming a therapist and it was this experience, together with my reading of Freud's case histories, that were most influential in my decision to pursue a career as a psychoanalyst.

When I read Freud's case histories, I felt as though I had discovered someone who combined my interest in writing and psychology and who could use his insights, not simply to write scholarly papers, but in the service of helping people suffering from emotional illnesses.

Although this choice seemed a perfect match for me, there was one formidable problem. At that time it was necessary, I believed, to become a physician and a psychiatrist before undertaking analytic training. And for someone with no head for science, that was a major obstacle. With the encouragement of good friends, however, I decided to give pre-med studies a try. In my case, this meant taking a minimal number of courses that would qualify me for medial school. I did not do particularly well in this endeavor, and applied to medical schools without much hope of being accepted. The competition for admission was strong in those days and the more accomplished pre-med students stood leagues ahead of me.

To my surprise, I was admitted to the University of Chicago Medical School, an outstanding institution that was deeply committed to the education of its students.

I struggled through the first 2 years of basic science courses and were it not for my diverting myself by writing short stories—many abut the University of Chicago faculty—I am not sure that I would have made it through.

The clinical years were far more interesting, but difficult and constantly challenging, as we were required to do our own lab work on all patients and present the case, often without sleep, to an attending physician starting at 6 o'clock in the morning. I learned a tremendous amount, however, and medical training provided me not only with invaluable knowledge of physical illnesses and their effect on the mind, but imparted the caring, physicianly attitude that, I believe, lies at the heart of all effective psychotherapeutic work.

What was surprising in a leading medical school was that it had no Department of Psychiatry. At the University of Chicago, Psychiatry was a division of the Department of Medicine. This was because the faculty was composed primarily of research physicians, who devoted themselves to the pursuit of facts, data, and scientific evidence. In their minds, psychiatry was not a hard science and therefore did not have the same value as the other disciplines.

Fortunately, the part-time teachers that were employed in the Psychiatric Division were almost all analysts, and gifted ones at that.

I was fortunate in being able to do some electives with these analysts, most of whom were associated with the Chicago Institute, and found their teaching inspiring. This experience prepared me for that part of my internship that I spent on an in-patient psychiatric unit at Kings County Hospital and for my residency in the Psychiatry Department of the new Albert Einstein College of Medicine.

To be at Einstein in those days was a truly memorable experience. The Chairman of the Department, Milton Rosenbaum, was a unique individual. An analyst who practiced little analysis, he was nevertheless the best interviewer I have ever encountered. The Grand Rounds in which he interviewed an in-patient were lessons in how to elicit information in a skilled and empathic way. Rosenbaum was a superb clinician who could also teach and who inspired scores of residents to follow in his footsteps and learn the art of clinical psychiatry. He also had a talent for identifying unusually interesting and gifted individuals and bringing them into the Einstein family. Rarely in one department could one find such a variety of remarkable individuals. Because Rosenbaum welcomed individuals from widely diverse backgrounds, the staff included such unique and memorable characters as Edward Hornick, an analyst who was also an expert in community psychiatry, Mort Reiser, a premier researcher, who was to become Chairman of Psychiatry at Yale, Herbert Weiner, a scholar of international rank in the field of psychosomatic medicine, Israel Zwerling, a feisty and combative individual, also an analyst, who specialized in Social Psychiatry and José Barchelon, an analyst and literary scholar who conducted a seminar on great novels that was a superb liberal arts education in itself.

In those days, almost every resident who was interested in practicing therapy or had academic ambitions, sought analytic training and our Department of Psychiatry at Einstein became a prep school for the New York Psychoanalytic Institute.

When it came time for me to apply for training, I hoped to be admitted to that prestigious program with its array of world class analysts and its standing as the premier institute in the country. I did gain admission, although not easily. I learned later that my interviewers raised many questions about my analyzability and perhaps it was for that reason that I was assigned for my training analysis to Dr. Robert Bak. At that time, students who were not already in analysis were assigned to one of the training analysts. Bak was one of the leading figures at the Institute, but to my dismay, I learned that his specialties were schizophrenia and the perversions. In which category I fit, I was not quite sure.

My training analysis was almost the reverse of my experience with Dr. E. Dr. Bak was a partisan of the Isakower school of psychoanalysis, an approach that drew heavily on the topographic theory and viewed access to pre-conscious and unconscious thought and fantasy as the goal of the analytic endeavor. Little attention was paid to defense or character analysis. The aim of treatment was to identify and interpret those less than conscious thoughts, imaginations, fantasies, and dreams that contained and expressed core aspects of an individual's neurotic conflicts. To accomplish this, strict neutrality and anonymity had to be observed. Silent waiting for the emergence of the key unconscious-preconscious material was an essential part of the process. Accordingly, days and weeks would go by without my analyst uttering a word. He was waiting—in vain, I'm afraid, in my case—for the unconscious forces to surface.

The contrast with Dr. E was enormous, and, initially, I found the going tough in analysis. I was used to the give and take that characterized my former treatment and did not know what to make of this new and strange method. I duly free associated in sessions—or spoke as freely as I could—and did recognize some benefit from the abreaction that accompanied this steady outpouring. I also recognized the value of reliving my old and quite powerful fear of my father and its Oedipal roots. I also learned a good deal about the yearning for a father—the so-called father hunger—that is part of the young boy's psychology and that conflicts with, but is not extinguished by, the rivalry and hostility stemming from the inevitable comparisons and competitive strivings that are part of the young boy's development.

Transference, however, did not come in for as much attention and analysis as it does today, nor did the kind of detailed and careful analysis of defense and character problems that we currently emphasize. These were shortcomings in my training analysis, as I believe they were in the analyses of many candidates at the time.

Most wanting, however, in my opinion, was the kind of engagement between patient and analyst that I found so useful in my prior treatment and that I have come to value in my own work.

Part of what I missed, to be sure, was the gratification of contact, a not unimportant factor in treatment, but beyond that, also the greater learning experience and greater chance for working through core conflicts that comes with the use of confrontation, mutual exploration, active engagement, and the challenging of one's accustomed ways of thinking and reacting. This is not to say that there is not a place for quiet, attentive listening and for uninterrupted silence in analysis. This is an important and valuable part of technique.

What I learned from Dr. Bak and others of the Isakower school, is the immense value of giving a patient enough time and space, and enough latitude, to follow the twisting paths of their own thoughts and feelings, and for unconscious ideas and fantasies to become more accessible. For, as Christopher Bollas has so cogently reminded us, news from within comes in its own time.

The art of analytic technique, as I have come to understand it, lies in the analyst being able to utilize dual techniques, one that involves active engagement, and another that centers on quiet listening and the opening up of space for the patient. The art of the game lies in knowing when to employ each and how much of each to utilize. This is not something easily achieved, and to gain expertise in it requires much experience as well as a clear understanding of the principles and the methodology involved.

At the New York Institute I also learned important lessons about the interplay between warmth and restraint, spontaneity and discipline, lessons that I carry with me and use in practice every working day.

The New York Institute has always had a reputation as the bastion of classical psychoanalysis. In the popular mind and in the minds of some colleagues trained elsewhere, this has meant an approach to analysis characterized by distance, coolness, formality, adherence to the principles of neutrality and anonymity, and the centrality of interpretation as the agent of change.

In fact, there were some analysts at the New York Institute who fit that description quite well. Even Dr. Bak, as I have noted, utilized some of these principles in his work. Although he was not a cold person—I later came to appreciate his humanity and warmth—in some respects he typified the picture of the New York Institute analyst, one that increasingly came to be satirized in the popular media.

There was a group of analysts at the New York Institute, however, whose way of working was radically different from the formal, removed analyst. These were people who knew that a warm and positive relationship between patient and analyst was not only beneficial in itself, but it was a requisite for effective analytic work to take place. This did not mean leaning backwards to be friendly. It meant, rather, the conveying of a caring attitude, one of deep concern for the welfare of the patient, as well as maintaining a belief in his or her potential for growth and change.

A number of my teachers and supervisors, as well as Edith Jacobson, who I consulted for help at a time of crisis in my life, exemplified this attitude; one that I have found to be essential in analytic work. In my view, no truly therapeutic result can be achieved in the absence of an atmosphere of caring, dedication, and hope. This does not mean a lack of discipline. Quite the contrary. The people I am speaking of, Marianne Kris, Leo Stone, Edith Jacobson, Jay Schorr, Milton Jucovy, Mary O'Neil Hawkins, and Charles Fisher, among others, were highly disciplined analysts, well trained and devoted to sound analytic principles and techniques. But they combined a warm and responsive attitude with a disciplined and skilled approach, a combination that in my view, created the most effective way of working.

In the many years that I have been in practice, I have heard much that is positive about the relational approach. And I have admired the work of many colleagues and friends of mine who have been trained in that tradition.

Never, however, have I encountered a relational analyst who has exceeded, or perhaps even matched, the degree of relational engagement of these classical analysts of 60 and 70 years ago. They understood the relational foundation of the classical analytic method, as Freud did, and the importance of that dimension in achieving true therapeutic results.

I should mention another analyst, who, although a caring person, was quite different from these colleagues. Dr. Charles Brenner was as formal an individual as one can imagine, a man who worked in a way that prioritized insight and interpretation over the relationship between patient and analyst. In fact, in his theory, if not in practice, he minimized the relationship factor in the analytic process as he did the influence of transference and countertransference. Not that he regarded these aspects of analysis as unimportant, but he deplored their overemphasis in today's world, stressing instead the centrality of understanding and interpreting psychic conflict that has its roots in the age period 3½ to 6 when the child is struggling to find intrapsychic solutions to what he called the calamities of childhood. These included separation fear, fear of loss of love, castration anxiety, and anxiety over bodily injury, and fear of the power of self-criticism, that is, fear of the punitive superego.

Brenner's teachings were highly influential and he became a mentor to a number of younger colleagues. Although I disagreed with him on the importance of transference-countertransference interactions in analysis and, indeed, on his minimizing the relationship between patient and analyst in his view of therapeutic action, I found his basic message with its emphasis on psychic conflict and the enduring influence of the Oedipal stage of development to be valid and extremely useful. Over time, I have added, as others have, other elements to Brenner's formulation in an effort to make them more complete and therapeutically effective.

In my training, as opposed to today's curricula in many institutes, a good deal of emphasis was placed on the adolescent years. I welcomed the opportunity to study and discuss adolescent development as I have been impressed by the enduring impact of adolescence in all its phases, as well as the impact of the early adulthood, on later life. Many individuals are unable to move psychically beyond the later adolescent period, a time of intense experiences, both positive and negative, that not only arouse unresolved conflicts from earlier phases of development, but have a profound effect on the individual's sense of self. I have written a fair amount on this issue and would refer interested readers to the chapter entitled "On the Adolescent Neurosis" in my book *The Possible Profession: On the Analytic Process of Change* (2013).

Finally, I would like to say a few words about my writing in our field. As I have mentioned, writing has always been important to me as a way of expressing myself. At times I have found it to be a more accessible pathway than verbalization.

Writing has also been a way of gaining self-esteem since, from childhood on, I have always been praised for my ability as a writer.

It seemed natural, then, to want to write about the field in which I was intensely immersed. And what in the early 1970s I wanted to write about was my experience as a fledgling analyst. Central to these experiences were my encounters with countertransference issues, of which I had more than my share. I noticed that others did, too, but a peculiar silence seemed to surround the entire issue of countertransference. Everyone was contending with it and nobody was talking about it.

At the time I was treating several challenging patients and was struggling with disruptive feelings about them that were causing me a great deal of difficulty. Since I shared with my fellow students a good deal of apprehension about revealing these problems to supervisors and teachers, I thought that it might be useful to take some notes on the subjective reactions that I experienced in response to the patients' material. This seat of the pants project began to absorb me, and on the basis of what I learned about the varieties of countertransference reactions that one can develop—some so subtle as to be easily overlooked—I wrote a series of papers, which formed the basis of my first book, *The Possible Profession: On the Analytic Process of Change* (2013). My work on the topic of countertransference was greeted with a good deal of criticism on the part of the older, traditional analysts and I was labeled an exhibitionist, a narcissist, and as someone who had little understanding of the analytic situation.

These were not comfortable times for me at the New York Institute, but by the late 1970s, the winds of change were already being felt in America. The émigré analysts who were so close to Freud and so protective of him, were fading from the analytic scene and their place taken by younger colleagues who were interested in Klein, Winnicott, and the British object relations school. There was also interest in the relational analysts and in Heinrich Racker's work on countertransference. Quite a few analysts spoke of their dissatisfaction with their experiences in analysis with traditional Freudian analysts, especially those who kept themselves at a good deal of distance from their patients and who paid little attention to the interactive dimension of the analytic situation.

In 1986, I introduced the term, enactment, to analytic lexicon and this concept was quickly taken up and widely employed to designate the unconscious, mutually interacting behaviors of both patient and analyst. This concept was so widely utilized, I believe, because it coincided with the growing interest in intersubjectivity that was taking hold in this country.

In the last decade, this interest has expanded so greatly that in many parts of the world the transference-countertransference dimension of analysis is viewed as the heart of the process. This has led in some places, and among some analysts, to the virtual elimination of the inner world of the patient as the primary focus of psychoanalysis.

In my own work, I have also been keenly interested in the question of unconscious transmission between patient and analyst. My focus, however, has been on the use of the information obtained from the interplay of two psychologies for a single purpose: to enhance our understanding of the mind of the patient. I have pursued this interest in my clinical work and have tried to explore the many ways that such transmissions take place in analysis. At the same time, I have been strongly interested in adolescent development and the life-long impact of adolescence on the adult personality. My other major interest has been in comparing the creative process in artists, especially writers, with the creative process that takes place in the mind of the analyst.

My writing on these and related topics have been collected in my book, *The Possible Profession: On the Analytic Process of Change* (2013). In that volume I also speak of hope, both in the clinical situation and for the field. From what I have seen, psychoanalysis as well as analysis as a treatment will, in the future, interest only a small percentage of those patients who seek psychological help. But there will continue to be, I believe, a number of individuals who will need and who will seek out an in-depth approach. They will have learned, after trying other therapies, that analysis is the one treatment that can make an enormous difference in their lives. And there will also be, I believe, a small, but devoted, group of young people who will feel themselves drawn to the field of psychoanalysis, as many of us have, and who wish to devote their lives to the study and practice of this most fascinating of professions. These bright and able young people, many of whom are studying in our institutes today, are our hope for the future.

Reference

Jacobs, T. J. (2013). *The possible profession: On the analytic process of change*. New York, NY: Routledge.

Chapter 4

Psychoanalysis and me

Lissa Weinstein

The given task, to describe your development as an analyst, seemed deceptively easy; in practice the answer was elusive, shifting, impossible to pin down, often embarrassing. It was fairly simple to respond to the question of what led to my choice of analysis as a profession. Like all reconstructions, an answer was easy to formulate, convincing at the same time it was, at least partially, illusory. But the how, and the journey itself, the transformations and changes became like an internal version of Where's Waldo? Each time you thought you found him, he was off somewhere else. I was surprised to rediscover a piece I had written for a Funeral for Psychoanalysis, an event sponsored by *Cabinet* magazine in 2012 when I wrote as the mistress of psychoanalysis:

> How I loved you,
> Worshiped your absence that forced me to create you
> Over and Over
> Searched for you
> Day after day, year after year, lying on couches up and down Park Avenue
> Reading horrific prose in leather bound journals
> I believed in the unconscious
> And thought I'd never grow old
> But look at me. I've shrunk.
> And still I'm searching.
> Still you elude me
> You're probably not even in that coffin

And here yet again, trying to penetrate a process whose end twirls around to its beginning like a Mobius strip, but grateful for the opportunity to reflect on what has been learned. The chapter is titled after Jorge Luis Borges who documents the dissociation between his public and private self in Borges and I (1960/1998), claiming

> It's Borges, the other one, that things happen to. I walk though Buenos Aires and I pause—mechanically now, perhaps—to gaze at the arch of

an entryway and its inner door; news of Borges reaches me by mail, or I see his name on a list of academics or in some biographical dictionary.

(p. 324)

This is often how I have felt as Lissa Weinstein, PhD, when asked to give papers in public forums. Yet in the clinical practice of psychoanalysis, the self is intimately, gloriously, painfully involved in the process. To understand who I have become and who I am in the process of becoming as an analyst cannot sidestep an examination of personal history.

As Rapaport (1950/1965) suggested, reality is best known by way of a detour, thus my chapter will only superficially proceed from beginning to end in this admittedly formless essay; no final fixative will be sprayed over unruly charcoal, no pot of gold at the end of the rainbow. Instead, eras will be collapsed, scenes arranged by associative detail, topics will circle back on each other to begin again after they seem to have ended.

Thinking directly about the question provided few answers. Allowing the liberty of association, what occurred was far from rational—a pastiche of random scenes from childhood, moments with patients, snippets of songs, the sonorous voice of my analyst. Strangely, little directly from my coursework came to mind. I found it hard to remember anything from my 4 years of classes at the New York Psychoanalytic Institute, although I have no doubt that my time there was seminal for my work, and the manner in which analysis five times a week was truly valued and their allegiance to the unconscious was invaluable. But the classes were theoretical and other experiences seemed equally formative. I read voraciously and could name theorists that had influenced me, Rapaport, Hartmann, Jacobsen, Freud, of course, and later La Planche, Andre Green, and Ferro, but the most meaningful papers provided an articulation of something recognized from work with patients. Like Dorothy, who had the ruby slippers all along, but had to learn their magic for herself, no matter how much I read, the papers, by themselves, couldn't capture the poetry of psychoanalysis, the frustrations and despair it can engender, the profound hope it spurs and the deep understanding of what it is to be human. The vast majority were read and forgotten, however good their content.

As Bion did in his *Memoir of the Future* (1975), I will take license to express content through method rather than orderly exposition, to freely mix "actuality" and reverie. My assumption is that becoming an analyst is a journey that has no set end, a journey that is as characterized, like the transference, by deepening cycles of regression and resolution and by the recognition of loss and want. It is as much about absence as about presence, more about not knowing than knowing. The question of "What's missing?" will drive a quest to represent a process that is often intangible, a process where each new immersion in the transference/countertransference matrix impels a descent into 0, a regression to a "place" where thing presentations predominate over word presentations. Yet, with Freud who struggled again and again with the value and meaning of language, words are the best medium we have.

Beginnings

Secrets (profound and trivial)

My father sits in an overstuffed brocade chair, teal colored, its sturdy lions' feet carved of mahogany. He is wearing a navy V-neck sweater, its wool frayed and pilled and oil-stained pants, his "home outfit," so different from the single handmade suit he owns and wears everyday to work. His face is fleshy, his nose wide and large, the nose of an old Jew or a boxer. He does this often at night, sit by himself in the darkness, lit by the yellow of street lamps. He is staring out the window past Kissena Boulevard, past Norman's fish stand, the fruit store, and corner deli, past the highways. I imagine he is staring toward Europe, toward Poland, toward Bialystock, toward Sienkiwicza street where he grew up. I imagine its beauty, men and women walking arm in arm by castles and lakes, laughing easily in the sunlight, a moment when all things are possible. Why else would he be staring so intently? I have seen pictures of my father on the ski slopes of Europe. He is with a group of friends, their heads lean in to make the shot. The friends stayed behind, only dog-eared Polaroids remain.

As a child, I feel my father's sadness, his terror and his dread, know only a man who always heard the distant hooves of the Cossacks in the rumbling of the Third Avenue El, know that he will not speak any of the seven languages in which he is fluent to me, or explain the one in which he makes curvy odd shapes on paper. I know only that there are secrets that must be discovered and words decoded.

More secrets. My parents are committed leftists. It is the height of the McCarthy era. At school, my classmate draws anti-Krushchev pictures, pictures of a fat dictator destroying the world. My mother tells me "Don't tell anyone about what we talk about at dinner." I am learning about hiding, that people don't always reveal who they are, or what is important to them.

More secrets. My mother shows me a picture of a poster for the 1939 New York World's Fair, a tall building with a round egg-shaped structure next to it. "It's a phallic symbol," she says to me, winking conspiratorially. "A phallic symbol." I am 6 years old at the time. I have no idea what she is talking about, but I am very encouraged to find out.

More secrets. My parents are social people, they have many friends who come to our house; some have numbers on their arms. The ice clinks charmingly in glasses, an intense forced gaiety pervades these evenings. I watch the world of adults, admiring. The women dance together, lift their skirts to expose garters. The men pinch the women's fleshy behinds. When will I understand, be part of this magic?

Silence and noise

There is the silence of my father, a daily shroud. But there are other silences. My own. I have been told that I did not speak well into my fourth year of life. The family myth was that my mother told the clucking tongues at the nursery school that "Lissa will speak when she is ready." Ever the obedient child, I gratified her wish by speaking in full sentences at my first utterance. Whether this is true, or merely conjecture, a story told many times, I learned to take listening very seriously, recognizing that there are secrets in words. Underneath its ability to disseminate are rhythms that one must attend to, one must move past the content; there is an iconography, a hidden dictionary that exists beneath, around and over the words. A music of verbs and pronouns. I learned that words should not be wasted and through assiduous observation that people do things for other reasons than they say.

Psychoanalysts are born, not made. The secrets that surrounded me propelled a burning desire to know, the fears that I was slow as a non-talking child drove my needs to prove it wasn't so. Psychoanalysis beckoned, promising something behind closed doors: "Enter here." Like all things discovered in retrospect, it seemed an inevitable choice.

The ineffable middle

> The middle of things is less exciting than the beginning and less dramatic than the end.
> —Andrew Solomon, 2015

Often in psychoanalysis, the decoding of the "secret" is easy—we "know," or tell ourselves we know the reasons that the patient did that, made the choices they made. It's retrospective, easy to formulate a narrative that appears in hindsight like a straight line from here to there, ignoring transitions, false starts, the discontinuous and chaotic nature of development. So it was relatively easy to identify childhood roots of my interest in psychoanalysis, or to build an edifice of reconstruction. Harder to find the middle. Not why it happened, but how it happened, the telling detail.

Schoolings

My mother, a guidance counselor in a public high school, made frequent, premature attempts at interpretation that left me with little desire to ever study psychology. I graduated college without taking a single psychology course, majoring in European Intellectual History with a minor in labor studies. Marx, Commodity Fetishism, The Labor Theory of Value were what made the world go round; my senior thesis spelled out in agonizing detail why Freud and Marx had incompatible views of man. I planned on going to the University of Heidelberg. The best laid plans ... Instead I decided to come and study dance after college, an impractical enterprise for a 6-foot woman, 6' 2" in toe shoes. But as it had been in childhood, dance class was organizing, and it embodied the value of rigid structures and repetition that ultimately came to determine one central aspect of my view of technique. The ritual of the morning plié's, the soothing regularity of Chopin on the upright piano: dégagé front, dégagé side, dégagé back, dégagé side, front–side–back–side, front–side–back–side. Over, over and over, the sheer sameness of it. As the movements became automatic, a procedural memory, a movement into another space somewhere between this world and the world of dreams became possible. Aware of what's around you, you are thinking, but not in the same way as before. The piano sounds ... different, the sounds clearer, new. The swoosh of your shoe on the floor. The light coming through the studio window, the bustle of Broadway below. Of course, there is the masochism, the submitting to technique, and yet after years of that often boring, excruciating routine, at some point it becomes yours. The dégagé is no longer a movement of your feet, but rather a reaching towards one's first love, taking your first step away from a parent's hands into a new world, an amoeba pulling back to a place of safety. What has had no meaning, a rote physical act, becomes infused with meaning, now capable of bearing the weight of the symbolic. We joked that only girls who had gone to dance class five times a week could do classical analysis—the same rigidity, the intensity of the structure, the ritual nature of the postures as you stood from your chair and said "Our time is up for today" (just as your analyst had said it to you, incidentally). I learned in ballet class and at the New York Psychoanalytic Institute that the intense study of technique could free you as well as constrain you. Like all repetitions, technique can hold, bind, and open a potential space for new evolutions. It also makes you more aware of when you have departed from a rigid stance and forces you to examine what you have done, and why you have chosen to deviate (often successfully) from the path of convention. It is a far cry from the free for all, personal pastiche of a multitude of approaches and techniques, or a reliance only on the self and one's highly overvalued intuitions with which our students have to suffer today.

But I am ahead of myself. What changed? How did I ever get from tap lessons and typing for money to psychoanalysis? A year of being someone's secretary (official title: editorial assistant) at a publishing house convinced me that the inner life probably had some value. One day at the barre, a girl behind me started to cry during second position pliés. Perhaps it was an omen—I was already old for dance, having spent 4 years in college foregoing any training for politics. Perhaps I no longer had to defend so rigorously against identifying with my mother. It came to me in a flash that I wanted to get a PhD in clinical psychology. Why? Still no answer. Perhaps I was afraid to apply to a Comp Lit program. Perhaps at 22, as a woman, I wanted a sense of power and place. Perhaps all along, I had been saving the souls of my parents. I didn't like telling potential husbands that "I type for money." A good writer, I penned an application essay describing my college roommate, offered my theory about the Monkey's behavior in *Portnoy's Complaint*, and drew a parallel between history and psychoanalysis. I managed to talk my way into graduate school despite a shocking lack of any clinical experience and only one or two Post Bac courses in psychology.

In the 1970s and 1980s a psychoanalytic psychology doctoral program was not the anomaly it is today. We were allowed simply to learn, to take courses on Freud, object relations, pathology of the self, philosophy of science. We were taught to listen for underlying structures, not just get rid of symptoms. I had wonderful teachers, each of whom, in their own way, taught me what an analyst was, and helped me develop an analytic ego ideal. I. H. Paul told us not to ask questions, but simply to "speak when we had something useful to say," because he believed that the analysis should not be directed by our interests or our theory, but should come wholly from the patient, a process that truly embodied the aim of self-determination. Although I can no longer imagine conducting an analysis without asking questions, not being able to do so forced me to listen in a more intense way. In Steven J. Ellman's lab, introduced to research truly influenced by psychoanalytic thinking on drive I gained a faith that analytic concepts could be operationalized. Staying up all night, waking people up during REM sleep, asking what was going through their minds. Seeing the pens on the sleep records, quiescent during Stage 4 sleep, suddenly burst into phasic activity when the person went into REM sleep and waking them to record their mentation convinced me that the contribution of the physical body can never be forgotten in our wish to understand thought. My research has always followed my clinical interests. My fascination with language deepened as I spent hours listening to transcripts of psychoanalytic hours, thinking about what was a "good" interpretation, looking for signs of a process gone awry, and finding it in the types of repetition that patients would engage in when efforts to reach out to the other failed and they withdrew into themselves.

Personal analyses

Of course, the inquiry was unavoidable. Somewhere in the bowels of the Brill library at the New York Psychoanalytic Institute, there is a chart detailing the genealogy of analysts—who's analyst begot who, begot who. The question: How much were you/are you, as an analyst, influenced by your own analysis? There were two, the first in my early 20s with a deeply caring and gentle man. Several years into treatment, in the local Cuban Chinese restaurant, I saw my analyst and his wife, a rather beautiful, delicately featured and petite woman, sitting at the next table. Paralyzed, I watched transfixed as he and friends spoke excitedly in French, a language I had difficulty mastering, in part because of self-consciousness over a residual Queens accent. During my next hour, my analyst responded to my agony over this exclusion and my felt imperfection by asking why I assumed he didn't find me attractive, even if his wife looked so different? Granted that this memory is distorted by the conflicts involved, I report it because although I have no doubt that my analyst was attempting to be both genuine and supportive, my experience was of being mollified and of being told, subtly, that I was unrealistically angry. Inadvertently, his supportive remark preempted any exploration of psychic reality and prompted a spate of regressive acting out. Being both frightened by and guilty over vengeful wishes, I surely also welcomed a message to control myself, Although the treatment continued for several years after this incident, it was essentially over, leading me to conclude that support and genuineness are not inherent in the behavior of the analyst but, like beauty to the beholder, exist only in the eye of the patient.

My second analysis was with a renowned classical analyst, assigned to me when I became a candidate at the New York Psychoanalytic Institute. He was certainly not supportive in the traditional sense, and charged me for every hour I was in the hospital delivering my children; much time early in my analysis was spent bemoaning the fact that I needed a more Kohution treatment, where my feeling that I had been victimized by an unresponsive mother would be verified. He never once attempted to placate my anger, but his steadfast curiosity about my most murderous, perverse, shameful desires felt supportive, safe and containing. In 9 years of analysis 5 times a week, my analyst missed only two sessions.

I learned about love in analysis, its roots in the fearful and passionate pleasures of childhood, but also about the wish to defeat even an analyst one found helpful, or that one could be motivated to fail even because the help inspired a primitive envy. I learned about analytic integrity, that there was a special morality in being an analyst, a steadfastness and forthrightness about the work and that the analyst's regularity and predictability and his or her respect for the frame of the analysis was part of this. I learned that analysis was not about cloning yourself through your patients, particularly those in the field, but about providing a situation where someone could best become who they wanted, (a lesson my children would again teach me), as they defined it over and over again. I leaned that one couldn't possibly understand the depth of the regression unless one had experienced it for oneself. The behavior of the analyst, the regularity, the consistency, the provision of a space where the patient can create what needs to be created is the true wonder of analysis. Years later, I wrote a story about a woman in analysis. Her description of the setting as she walks to her morning hour conveys the mix of the ordinary and magical that is so central to psychoanalysis.

> A white room, a quiet room, empty save for a mahogany desk, a chair and ottoman. Bookcases filled with *The Standard Edition Volume I–XXV*, the *Quarterly*, and the *International Journal of Psychoanalysis*,

hard bound in dusty burgundy leather, the *Psychoanalytic Quarterly*. And the couch.

It was a crowded room filled with the nasal whines of her childhood, the skinned feet of chicken, blood dripping onto sawdust at the Kosher butcher, corsets and cracks in the plaster changing shape as lost continents emerged.

It is still a source of wonder that we can create so much with so little and find the strength to bear the unpredictable when we have brought the passions to light.

Five scenes from the analytic life

When I started this journey, I had no interest in helping other people. I was fascinated by how the mind worked (partly influenced by my experiments with psychedelics in college) and psychoanalysis seemed like the best, most humanistic way to explore the mind. It still does. Although it scares me to admit this in print, I believe that inadvertently the absence of a savior complex had some benefits. I didn't need my patients to get better, I was, in that way, without desire (if not without memory, as my thinking in the absence of any significant experience, was filled to the brim with theory). Lacking the pressure to "do good" or alternately, the inevitable correlate that they could hurt me by not doing better, my patients had an experience of being listened to, for some, their first such experience. I wanted only to find out what it was to be them, to see the world the way that they did, to formulate some giant Venn diagram with multiple three-dimensional structures where thoughts and passions interacted, where environment and fantasy melded, influenced each other, or retreated into the unknown. Accidentally, I had come upon something I was to learn again in another form from my analyst—that openness to any and all content in as much detail as the patient can muster is everything. When told that the patient wants to kill someone, the proper question is "How exactly were you planning on doing it?" When they mention a green purse in a dream, the question is "Why a green purse?" Only in this way can one begin to sense the truly multi-determined nature of thought.

But still, something was missing from this picture. The work was an intellectual exercise, one that didn't, couldn't, allow for a true understanding of the power or utility of transference. As Bird (1972) so eloquently pointed out, the transference is the hardest part of the analysis, the part of the analysis that every theoretical school has its own unique way of defending against. The transference requires not only decoding, but also experiencing; it demands an affective interpenetration between patient and analyst. In Bionian terms, it requires the analyst, in the hope of detoxifying those elements that have kept the patient from thinking, to share these inchoate emotions and to contain them. It was something more than just listening and thinking, it was the creation of a space that allowed what was unconscious to become brought to light, to be touched and worn away by the everyday, to join the stream of associative material that will mitigate its pathogenic impact.

So how did things change? When students ask how to write their first cases, I encourage them to sit down and without thinking describe five scenes between them and their patients. The story will emerge, their unconscious already knows the theme—you just have to trick your ordered way of thinking in order to find it. So …

The scenes have very little to do with my formal schooling, either as a graduate student or an analytic candidate. The address the question of how I came to believe. Believe what? What formed the core of my definition of the huge sprawling edifice that is psychoanalysis, what spawned the move from book learning to conviction, to the development of analytic hope? This faith came primarily from patients, from bright moments that stand out like screen memories. Strung together they tell a story, organize a chaotic field. But even the scenes are not static, my interpretation of them shifts as I grow, allowing for emendations and changes as my clinical work evolves. I present them loosely in chronological order, as they build upon each other. Each of the "truths" revealed, like the Declaration of Independence, are held to be self evident, and in that way commonplace, intuitively obvious. But each one, when discovered, felt like a revelation. Our patients are our true teachers.

One

At the clinic where I trained, it was commonplace for child clinicians to make the child a party before we left for vacation. I bypass the local Bodega and buy Brownies from the Eclair bakeshop for Kevin, a 10-year-old boy whose dark skinned father left while he was 2 years old to fight a war and did not return. Instead, his mother found a new husband and thinking the boy wouldn't remember said "Here's your father, back from the war." The new father, unlike Kevin, was light skinned. Kevin builds unstable houses that rest on "secret" blocks of alphabet letters. This July afternoon, I proudly dole out the goodies, scooping an extra large helping of Ben and Jerry's vanilla ice cream over his brownie. I am a good person, a giving person. This is "fun." For me. Kevin takes my offering, dumps the brownie and ice cream on the floor and says "Let this be a lesson to you." I would never after that experience try to mollify someone's pain, to pretend that it is not there. The idea that by being a "good" and "giving" person I could make the pain disappear was disrespectful, not to mention useless. It would be a while before I understood the necessity of feeling that pain.

Two

One of my first patients, a young college student, molests women on the subway, often on the way uptown to his sessions. Only when the subway car is crowded and people are sandwiched in like sardines, only when he is unable to move except for his arms, he touches from behind, searching, with great excitement for what is between the woman's legs. Years later, he tells me that up until the time he was 7 years old, he slept in his parent's bedroom in a leather harness, a not uncommon enough practice in the late 1950s to keep children from falling out of the crib or carriage. While there are many lessons here, among them the relentless, demonic power of repetition, at the time it was the realization that everyone is doing exactly as well as they possibly can, and that even the most seemingly bizarre or perverse behaviors are not beyond the reach of empathy.

Three

Carolyn, a 7-year-old girl, has lost her 27-year-old father to cancer after numerous unsuccessful operations. She asks me to bring her many things. A stapler, nice magic markers, a radio so that we can listen to songs together. When I bring these things, there is always something wrong with them. The stapler is too small, the markers are the wrong color, the Play Doh is dried out.

When the treatment begins, I expect she will talk about losing her father. Yet in 3 years, that never happens. Instead, she locks me in closets, screams to my colleagues that "Lissa Weinstein doesn't understand children," and makes up my face as an ugly clown. I often feel stupid and repulsive. One day we are making paper butterflies. She tells me they have hurt their wings; the wings must be cut off. She continues to cut away the bad parts, cutting and cutting until on the floor there are piles of paper. "There's nothing left," she tells me. It becomes clear that the entire treatment has been about the unmentioned father. His absence fills the room. The most powerful parts of the treatment it turns out are not necessarily when talking directly, but about experiences in the present tense that can be rewritten in the context of another.

Four

The sounds of silence. My child case is happy with treatment twice a week, but I am certain that analysis is the only possible solution to this gifted child's profoundly phobic behavior. His parents support the decision. For his part, the child takes his stance, and decides never to talk to me again. He agrees only to write. This is his way of maintaining control, sadistically asserting himself against a overbearing mother while also expressing through quiet and deadness, his fears of the excitement of the primal scene. Each week, when I present in my supervision group, my fellow analyst ask "Have you gotten him to talk yet?" I begin to hate this child, murderously, a mere 7-year-old, as he comes into the office and once again refuses to talk. This hatred is not acceptable to me, but the feeling is unavoidable. Over time, his writing becomes more and more excited, its initial defensive utility coming more and more to encompass the underlying desires. My supervisor supports my decision. "Analysis is not about how the child behaves, it is about his inner life," she tells me in her charming, authoritative Viennese accent, giving me the strength to continue in this unorthodox fashion. My patient and I begin to create a story together, the writing a record of our time, bridging a gap. I learn, slowly, to tolerate my affect and to talk to him about hatred, learn that these intense and seemingly unacceptable feelings were the key to this child, what he needed to extrude. It was imperative to recreate through his behavior something in me that he could not symbolize, much less voice. This was far different that the distant and measured stance I had been used to. Not that there were no feelings before, but not ones that felt intense and disorganizing. Eventually, I came to feel that I knew this child in his silence better than any other child I had treated before.

Five

An adolescent patient who I have not seen for over 2 years emails telling me that he has been diagnosed with a chronic and ultimately fatal illness. He wishes me well, and although he realizes it might be a good idea to talk, makes it clear that he will not be doing so. He just wants to let me know. This young man, who was erratic (at best) in his attendance and rarely called to say he would not be able to make it to our session time, once told me that he didn't call because he thought that I wouldn't remember if he didn't show up. My amazement at this statement must have been palpable, and the implications of not feeling held in someone else's mind became a center of the work. My dilemma—how to respond to this latest communication. Paradoxically, I had recently been thinking about this patient, wondering what he was doing now that he must have finished college, reviewing our time together. I remember a movie he had asked me to watch whose central theme was the importance of creating a story with others in order to make the unbearable, if not beautiful, tolerable. While I would always have acknowledged the letter, I would not in the past have written that I had been thinking about him, or communicated that I was honored that he thought to write to me. I certainly would not have written about the movie he had once shown me. The change was an awareness that interpretation, at times or perhaps often, is superfluous, that for some patients to know that they exist in your mind, and having the courage to communicate this to the patient is a part of the process that must scaffold all other work.

Writing and, of course, life

I had always written analytic papers, dry and dessicated, they filled the literature unread, like so many others. When my son was diagnosed with severe dyslexia, I decided to write a book about our experience for other parents. The first draft was deadly, more a textbook than a memoir. In order to honor my son's experience, I had to be honest, actively undoing everything I had learned as a writer of analytic papers. I had to get under the words, stop theorizing and show, don't tell (something that is still hard for me). I had to how to describe and learn how to create characters, more accurately how to find characters. This involved listening, looking, and hearing in new ways, not what it *means*, but what it look like, feels like, smells like, how it tastes to the mind. Detail, detail, detail. This immersion in characters, in story and how it is told transformed my analytic work. No longer in a rush to understand, I began to allow myself to be open to what needs to be experienced. Theory is still there, but ever more so, the search for characters, an awareness of how characters are created and why we have chosen to write the stories we write about our lives. In addition, the writing process, with its necessity of tolerating not knowing, as well as the shame, and the fear of exposure it engenders mimic the process of analysis. When you write, it is useless to try and steal an image or a phrase from some other writer—the only evocative images must come from your own life, your memories, however transformed. In analysis too, we contact the patient through allowing their stories to touch ours, giving us access to parts of our own lives that may have remained hidden. In short, we meet the patient through reverie, just as when we write.

The end, or more accurately, the conclusion (circa 2016)

Always be on the lookout for the presence of wonder.
—E. B. White, 1952

Like Freud, every clinician is on a journey, facing some of the same pitfalls and taking the same trajectories. First, the wish to be powerful and helpful to our patients, the feeling that we have a privileged understanding in our thrilling discovery of the unconscious, the secret and seductive world of meaning. Then, the limitations of relying on authority, narrowly defined through the hypnotic method, or on its modern guise, the positive transference, and the wish to call on the patient's cooperation, to cajole them to uncover their secrets, the failure of conscious cooperation and even the wish on the patient's part not to get better, to defeat us in our efforts. But to allow the patient to manifest what they need to, one must be without desire, and yet not without emotion, in fact that ability to feel what needs to be contained, transformed and detoxified exists prior to an effort to decode the unconscious meaning. And the ability to do this is a form of love. And so, while in no way do I believe that analysis is love, or that we cure our patients through love, or reparenting, or being a good object, I do believe that being an analyst has to do with one's capacity to love, and all that happens on the long and unending path that takes you there—love of children, love of an idea, love of colleagues and mentors, the capacity to give yourself fully over to your own experience, and to tolerate the experience of another, the capacity to bear loss. Love as a resolution to the Oedipal phase, where the other object exists, at least in one iteration, as separate from the self. And like one's capacity to love, becoming an analyst is a never ending journey, an ideal to which we strive, no more reachable than the elusive O, a mystical state that we perhaps touch once and can only in partial iterations communicate to others. This is the long distance journey of an analyst, perhaps it is why we write so much about a work that is often lonely and internal. If I had to characterize this incomplete journey, I would say it was an increasing ability to allow the full flowering of the transference.

At its best moments, psychoanalysis brings a mystical feel to the ordinary and yet those moments are fleeting at the same time that they are structuring. So we keep writing and analyzing and writing about analyzing, hoping to capture the ineffable in ourselves and our patients and somehow force it into the shape of words, as imperfect as these inevitably are.

References

Bion, W. (1975). *A memoir of the future*. London: Karnac Books.

Bird, B. (1972). Notes on transference: Universal phenomenon and hardest part of analysis. Journal of the American Psychoanalytic Association, *20*, 267–301.

Borges, J. L., & Hurley, A. (1998). *Jorges Luis Borges: Collected fictions*. New York, NY: Viking Press. (Original work published 1960).

Parsons M. (2000). *The dove that returns, the dove that vanishes: Paradox and creativity in psychoanalysis*. New York, NY: Routledge.

Rappaport, D. (1965). *The organization and pathology of thought: selected sources*. New York, NY: Columbia University Press. (Original work published 1950)

Solomon, A. (2015, March 11). The middle of things: Advice for young writers. Retrieved from www.newyorker.com/books/page-turner/the-middle-of-things-advice-for-young-writers/.latest_citation_text.

White, E. B. (1952). *Charlotte's web*. New York, NY: Harper & Row.

Chapter 5

The voice endures

Mitchell Wilson

Dear Reader:

Let me be frank. I will say what comes to mind. The First Amendment underwrites my speaking my thoughts freely as they occur to me in consciousness. (It is of interest that I need the State to guarantee this right.)[1] I'll do the best that I can.

But no. I will not do the best that I can. I will not say everything that comes to mind, all that occurs to me. The Second Amendment guarantees my right to bear arms—my right, that is, to my own defense, my right *not* to speak.

And so it goes with the psychoanalytic project: the hope to speak freely, my desire to bare all, within the limits imposed by external structure and internal worry—the mechanisms, as Anna Freud long ago described, of defense.

Let's talk … so said the late Joan Rivers.

Let's talk, then, about the external structure first: I am to contribute to a volume on the psychoanalyst's development. It's something like an autobiographical project: why did I decide to become a psychoanalyst? How did I develop my psychoanalytic "voice"? Who influenced me? What events and people in my life conspired to make me who I am and led me to be a psychoanalyst? And the like.

These are good questions. They are also impossible questions to answer truthfully, especially for a psychoanalyst. We psychoanalysts do know some things (we disclaim knowledge of many other things). One of the things we know is that any kind of self-representation offered in a public forum (such as the book to which this essay is contributing), or in a private office (such as to a psychoanalyst), is an *invested offer*, neither pure fiction nor hard fact. I choose to tell you some things and not others, all rendered in a particular way. So what follows is a complex rhetorical gesture meant, inevitably, to persuade or move you. At the same time whatever effects I evoke are largely outside of my conscious control and are difficult for me to anticipate … what you will think, or how you find yourself responding to what I have written. Whatever my manifest gesture amounts to or is constituted by, it is in some measure a *false gesture*.

Let's talk, next, about the internal constraints. Which, upon even cursory reflection, relate intimately to the external conditions I just summarized.

These internal worries have to do with what can be revealed—what to say from a personal point of view. And what it is *possible* to say from a personal point of view. I have a worry about what will happen with my words as they make their way to other people's eyes and ears. What about my analysands? Do I have a duty to protect them, in that I would wish their analyses to be relatively unencumbered by my "over-sharing"? What about my family? My wife? And what about me? I have, as I said before, a duty to protect myself ... from myself.

In short, we know as psychoanalysts, intimately and perhaps more than most, about this *so-called* freedom of speech—the seeming imperative of the fundamental rule of psychoanalysis: it is constrained by the frames (both external and internal) in which the subject is imagined to speak so freely.

Even so (i.e., in spite of all I have said in what you have just read), in the end I must take responsibility for how I articulate what I articulate. It's an ethical project, this effort at self-representation, this giving an account of oneself. And it's an *ongoing* project, a performative becoming, not simply (or perhaps not at all) a *re*-presentation of an already existing set of historical circumstances, beliefs, desires. Charles Altieri, the literary scholar, says this:

> For ultimately articulation is not simply a modification in language, it involves a modification in selves who have to interpret why they find satisfaction in it and who have to indicate what consequences might follow from that act of identification.
>
> (1996, p. 84)

In other words, we assume ("that act of identification") that which we say and how we say it in a process of becoming ("modification of selves"), and in the process of moving into the future ("what consequences might follow"). There is satisfaction in this kind of self-making articulation. If psychoanalysis is worthwhile, it is worthwhile because of this project of articulation and emergence of self within the context—no ... the *constraint*, of the analytic relationship.

We speak of "voice." Not only the "who" of speaking, or the "what" of speaking, but the *sound* of the speaking itself: the voice. To articulate is to speak in a unique fashion. The voice endures. Bodies change. Relationships evolve ... some continue ... others end. Fortunes are made and lost. Time ... waits for no one. But the voice ... its weird particularity, the unique way in which each of us pushes air past the thin reeds of the larynx, is the very signature of subjectivity.

The voice articulates. In the end, in spite of everything, as a person, or psychoanalyst, or analysand, one does the best one can.

It was 2005. I was at a high school reunion. The sun was setting on the Pacific Ocean as a large crowd of middle-aged former yuppies caught up with old friends and vaguely familiar acquaintances in Santa Monica. It was crowded. At some point in the evening I noticed a very, very large man—morbidly obese—talking with an old pal of mine. His face did not ring any bells. When I approached the two of them I saw on the nametag of the very large man: John Cossette. I had not seen John in many years. And I could not believe what I saw: he was totally unrecognizable. His face had none of the features of the face I remembered. How could this possibly be? Of course I didn't let John know I couldn't believe it, that he was totally unrecognizable. I said "Hi," and after handshakes and pleasantries, John started to talk. All the indentifying features of his voice were instantaneously present: its mid-range timbre and lively cadence, words dancing within the music of sentences often interrupted by his high-pitched laugh. I was filled with that sense of pleasure one gets from the immediacy of recognition of something both familiar and wonderful, and I thought to myself: "Oh yes. This is the mark of a person. The voice."

John was completely transformed from the assured and brainy athlete I had played baseball with and against for a good decade in our youth. Now he was unrecognizable. But that spry and spirited voice—and his wry wit, his willingness to tell the off-color, politically-incorrect joke—all of it was exactly the same.

Jacques Lacan spent his entire psychoanalytic career theorizing the signifier. If "in the beginning was the word," and if psychoanalysis is a "talking cure," the pivotal question must be: how does talking cure? This was Lacan's urgent preoccupation. He married the early Freud of the *Joke Book* and the *Interpretation of Dreams* with structural linguistics to create his version of psychoanalysis. Regarding the voice: it became, in Lacan's middle phase of theory-building, one of the five "object causes" of desire. The voice, along with the gaze, and the oral, anal, and genital zones, were remnants in the real. These are ways the body lives on, and calls us, de-centers us, because it can't be completely domesticated by symbolic processes. So we find ourselves drawn to certain people who have a particular look or voice. We can't explain it; we are just so drawn (as I was to John's voice). The voice gives voice to the symbolic but can never be totally subsumed by it. It endures in the real.[2]

I think Lacan is right here, and these ideas are helpful clinically. But he missed something fundamental regarding the voice. It not only calls the other in ways the other can't control (this is the voice as cause of desire in the other). More importantly, the voice is the positive stamp of the indelibility of the subject, the speaker. To put it crudely: the voice doesn't gain huge amounts of weight. Nor does it become gradually more feeble or infirm. Moles don't grow on its skin, because it has no skin. Its organs don't fail, because it has no organs. In the end, of course, the very end, the voice stops, but not because of it's own foundering. While entirely dependent on the body, the voice lives almost entirely *independent* of it.

I loved John Cossette. We met in the fifth grade at Brentwood Elementary School (only blocks from where, 25 years later, O. J. Simpson would murder Nicole Brown Simpson and Ronald Goldman). John and I played baseball against each other in Little League, Pony League, and high school. We both had professional baseball ambitions. But he came from a much more stable and successful family than I did. And he had a natural and easy-going confidence I both lacked and could only admire. His father was a well-known Hollywood producer who started the Grammy Awards. My father was an alcoholic who worked in the post-office in Westwood Village and delivered mail to the wealthy who lived near by. John's parents were married and had a big home in a ritzy part of Brentwood. My parents were divorced and we lived in a small two-bedroom ranch house near the San Diego Freeway. He came from French-Canadian stock and had an unassuming sophistication. (As an example: John appreciated early on the brilliance of the TV show "All in the Family." I had never heard of the show until he told me about it.) I was a product of the co-mingling of two entirely different worlds: my mother's side was from Jewish middle-Europe and arrived in the United States permanently in 1938, and my father's side came to this country in the mid-18th century from England and Scotland. One descended from the Bal-Shem Tov, the other from Alexander Hamilton and James Wilson. You might think that such an origin would lead to something like sophistication; in me, it led mostly to a feeling of disquiet, insecurity, and doubt.

By the time I was 5 years old my mother had divorced my father. By the time I was 9 I had decided, on my own, to not see my father any more because he drank during visitation time and got into fights. He felt easily slighted by other men, and routine interactions could lead to violent conflict. Course epithets tumbled unprovoked from his mouth, in a voice whose qualities now feel distant and inaccessible, but whose rage-filled content is easy to recall.

My father was an outlier of substantial proportions, so much so that I could establish, out of emotional necessity, a kind of psychic distance the lasting effects of which became clear to me only in my 20s. But I also had a few things going my way that helped me effect this distance, a mapping that allowed me some sense of safety: I had an uncle and a grandfather who were both on my side and dedicated to me. I had a mother who was pretty tough in the face of adversity, and was committed to raising my brother and me. And I had baseball. I was exceptionally good at baseball. Better than John Cossette, who was pretty good himself.

I played organized baseball from the time I was 8 years old until my junior year in college. I was especially serious about hitting. I collected broken bats from the teams (Semi-Pro, American Legion, and UCLA) that played baseball at Sawtell Field near my house. I'd practice my swing every day in my back yard in front of the big living room sliding-glass door—every day for 10 years. I read Ted Williams *The Science of Hitting* and knew it backwards and forwards. Williams was brash and cocky and wanted to be known as the best hitter who ever lived. In front of that big sliding-glass door I slowly but surely perfected my swing.

My first coach was Forrest Casterline, who went by "Cas." Cas was a middle-aged welder from Culver City. Totally working class. He was gruff, stern, and did not play favorites. He commanded great respect from both the kids and their parents.

Here are some of the things Cas would say:

> "You should have had that ball in your hip pocket." (When a player botched an easy ground ball.)
>
> "It only takes one. Hang in there." (When a batter, with less than two strikes, took a strike or swung through a pitch. This is counsel that is generalizable to many life-situations.)
>
> "Wait on the pitch. Let it come deep. Then be quick with the bat." (A crucial bit of advice that not only applies to hitting a baseball well.)

One time when I was 12 years old and the best hitter in the league, I had a game when I went hitless, the only game out of 20 I did not have at least one base hit. I was oh-for-three and hoping in my last at bat to get a hit, but it was not to be. Given that my home life was riven and sad, and my father was a bad actor and I continued not to see him in any official visitation way (he would show up unannounced at a neighbor's house and drink, and at my ball games sometimes and stand off to the side, away from the other parents), to be really good at something, in this case baseball, had by that time taken on great urgency. So when I grounded out weakly to second base to make it oh-for-four, I was very upset. I veered off the baseline, not even trying to make it to first. I came back to the dugout, threw my helmet against the fence, and started to cry. Cas would have none of it. He said to me, in front of everyone:

> Son, stop this nonsense right now. I will not have you acting like a baby on my team. You are 12 years old, not 5. And if you continue on like this, I will sit you down for the rest of the game and have someone else take your place.

His voice was gritty and gravelly, authoritative, and true. I said I was sorry, wiped the tears from my face, picked up my hat and glove and went back out onto the field.

It will not come as a surprise, perhaps, given the out-sized importance baseball had for me in my growing up, that I stumbled badly in high school. Though I had considerable talent, I had more than considerable anxiety. This anxiety I denied, rationalized, made excuses for. I found myself consciously hoping for rain-outs, or that the opposing team's bus would break down.

Though I was a 3-year varsity starter, and had some success, by my senior year I had played my way onto the bench.

Psychoanalysis is a peculiar practice in many respects. Perhaps the most peculiar aspect is the way an analyst goes about listening. We listen, roughly speaking, for the "other"—that which is unsaid, half-said, weirdly said, alluded to, implied by, inferred from, imagined about, metaphorized and simile'd, day-dreamed, scene-irized, stumbled upon. In other words, there is almost always an *in other words*, a more to say, a more to imagine, to feel, and to speak to, again, furthering the analytic dialogue. In psychoanalysis, the straightforward, declarative sentence, while still important, has a minority status amid the myriad other voices spoken and heard.

But when it comes to a lived life outside the consulting room, and the voices whose uttered words meant or mean the most to us, we don't listen for the "other" in the discourse. We are hit directly, effectively, unequivocally (as in my moment of truth with Cas). We don't say: "I remember the opaque manner in which my uncle gave me that crucial piece of advice when I was 18. He was so brilliantly allusive." Instead we say:

> When I was 18, after my first quarter at Berkeley, during Christmas break, my uncle Art, a child psychiatrist, casually asked me what I was planning on majoring in and doing after undergrad. I told him I was going to be a clinical psychologist. At this point Art became quite serious. He took me up to his study and spent the next 45 minutes telling me why I should go to medical school. "You can do this," he said directly, after I voiced understandable doubt. "You can still be a psychotherapist, or a psychoanalyst. And you will have more flexibility in terms of job choice, you'll have a more comfortable income, and you'll have more authority within the mental health field. Most importantly, you'll learn how to care for the sick, something that is precious and can't be learned in the same way in any other field."

This was the single most important conversation I had in my young life, because it was literally life-changing. I had great respect for Art Sorosky. He was a dedicated psychiatrist, always studying or working on a project. He was the first person to do research on, and write a book about, the sealed-record controversy in adoptions. The book was called *The Adoption Triangle* (1979). I can't say his voice was distinctive, but his words were, to me. I am sure if I heard Art's voice again I would recognize it immediately. But that won't ever happen: he died of a glio blastoma in 2001.

By the time I decided to take the necessary classes to apply to medical school, John Cossette and I had fallen out of touch. He went to USC and was not good enough to make the baseball team. I went to Berkeley and made the team as a "walk-on." I only played through my sophomore year. But around that time, during summer, I called John to see if he wanted to meet at Sawtell Field where he and I had played together on a semi-pro team before high school, and against each other in high school.[3] There was a batting cage down the left-field line where, over the years, we had spent many hours throwing batting practice to each other. I suggested we get together for old-times' sake, take some cuts in the cage, and then go have lunch. I had an old collection of baseballs and several bats we could use. It was great to see him. He was his light-hearted self and in good baseball shape. We mixed fastballs with curves as we pitched to each other, took our cuts, and then went to the Apple Pan for lunch (a classic Los Angeles diner where you can get great burgers and banana cream pie). As we said goodbye John gave me a book about "Murphy's Law": Whatever can go wrong will go wrong. It was supposed to be a joke, a book of humor. I'm not sure I ever cracked the cover. The next time I saw John was at the reunion in 2005.

Medical school, it turned out, was not for me, or at least that was how it felt at times. The first 2 years were a hard and painful slog. I had depressing dreams of being wrapped in the same thick, translucent plastic in which the anatomy lab cadavers were wrapped as they lay stiffly in the Medical Sciences building at UCSF. I was a humanities and social sciences person (which is what I had said to Uncle Art during that fateful conversation: "I can't do well in chemistry and physics. I haven't taken a science class since biology in the 10th grade"). This is how I thought of myself, and though I did well in my pre-med science courses, once at UCSF I felt out of place in a radical kind of way. The old anxieties and insecurities returned. I had no business going straight from undergrad to medical school with no break, no journey, no risk. After 2 years I petitioned the UCSF Dean to take a year off and go back to Berkeley to study English literature.

At this point in my life—age 24—a number of voices claimed the main stage. And, for the most part, I was "all ears." I wanted to know what they knew. I wanted to know how they knew what they knew. I wanted to know how they thought. I wanted to know how they put their thoughts into words. And I wanted their help.

Imagine a cherubic, round-faced, short-limbed, stubby-fingered professor of English with a sparkle in his eye and a gift for conveying what felt like the true significance, the "what is at stake," in a literary text. The voice was mischievous, playful, even roguish, but always informed by an ethical sensibility. When Ralph Rader was reciting verse or describing the role of Providence in the actions of the early novels, such as *Tom Jones*, he captivated the room. I remember his delivering the opening lines of Browning's "My Last Duchess," a dramatic monologue in which the speaker gradually reveals to his guest his having murdered the woman in the portrait they are admiring. Rader's performance, as he fully inhabited the weirdly detached voice of the narrator, was cold-blooded:

> That's my last duchess painted on the wall,
> Looking as if she were alive. I call that piece
> A wonder now: Fra Pandolf's hands
> Worked busily a day, and there she stands.
> Will't please you sit and look at her?
> (Browning, 1842/1993)

Rader was a neo-Aristotelian, which means he was very old-school as far as literary theory went at the time. While he read texts using basic concepts like "author," "intention," "action and plot," "character," "genre," and believed we all (at least implicitly) read texts with these categories in mind,[4] the rest of the department was being swept up by Deconstruction and Lacanian ideas. Michel Foucault (1977) wrote an influential essay titled: "What is an author?" (Answer: a socio-cultural construction that puts a limit on what a text might mean and how it might otherwise "proliferate.") Roland Barthes (1977) developed the idea that a literary "work" is importantly different from a literary "text." (The former is a product—circumscribed, denotative, finished, complete. The latter is open and unfinished, connotative, a site of uncertain meanings that borrow and inform a network of texts, other sites of meaning.) These voices were of an entirely different order than Ralph Rader's.

And reading Lacan was like going to the Oracle at Delphi: possessed of a burning question wanting of a revelatory answer, one instead encountered the ceaseless mystery of ecstatic speech, a perpetual circling around an imagined object of desire, in this case something like "knowledge," or "truth." Ralph Rader (a mid-Westerner from Indiana) thought this stuff was *nuts*— needlessly hysterical and obscure, evasive, even sadistically provocative. But I was taken with Lacan's voice, the moments of hesitation and worry you can hear amid all the pronouncements and presumed authority. Lacan was, also, a gifted reader of texts of all kinds and an equally trenchant critic of trends in psychoanalysis he thought were deeply problematic. These trends— ego psychology, the reliance on affect as a primary signifier of meaning, the appeal of/to the maternal—left him, as he said many times, with a feeling of "abjection." Abjection—a powerful affect indeed.

The psychoanalyst, while a listener for the "other," is also a practitioner of the symbolic order. We are like Levi-Strauss' *bricoleur*: we analysts take what is available to us in the cultural surround, the symbolic tools ready-to-hand as we listen to our patients and make sense of how they are situated in relation to their important objects. As we listen we learn about the central signifiers and stories that they use to represent themselves to us, the way, as Altieri says, they give shape to themselves in the process of articulation. And as we learn more, we associate what we are hearing to images, metaphors, tales and myths, and artifacts of the culture in which the patient (and we) lives. "What you are saying reminds me of ... " is not an uncommon way of offering a "furthering idea" to a patient, a building of something symbolically meaningful brick by brick.

But, of crucial importance is this: that for all of us, including our patients, there must be places of *dis-order* within this symbolic world, and it is in these places in which the "other" can be found. My parents and their parents came from radically different worlds. My mother divorced my father when I was 5. My father didn't fit, easily, anywhere. And within each of these moments of dis-order can be found countless smaller moments (things said, actions taken, feelings felt and forgotten, fantasies imagined, desires dashed) in which the "other" might be found through a kind of "filling in," a kind of ordering of these shards and rents of disorder, through the process of psychoanalysis.

Winnicott, of course, described this area of analytic work best with his idea of transitional objects and transitional phenomena. Winnicott's is a picture of the very beginnings of culture as the child and parent transform the concrete object into an affectively significant one, the ownership of which is not a question that has relevance within such a space. That the psychoanalyst is a practitioner of the symbolic order is why the analyst ought to read widely, be curious about many things, and, most importantly, be curious about what he or she doesn't know. I remember well my Uncle Art's studying the lyrics of a rock album one of his patients had spoken to him about. He wanted to know, in detail, what his patient had found so meaningful there.

But ... I needed help, not just interesting ways to read texts and think about the world. I suffered from a bitter-sweet melancholy a lot of the time (more bitter, perhaps, than sweet). I had recurrent dreams about baseball. These dreams, which seemed to go on for days and plagued me throughout my 20s, were populated with the guys I'd played ball with, including John Cossette, and often staged in some way an impossibility: I can't find my cleats, or bat, or glove, as if I were re-living my high school nightmare over and over again. And my father was back in the picture as well. He had been sober for a while, and would visit San Francisco occasionally; but he was just as insecure and ineffectual as ever. He was subtlely competitive with me and unable to evince any sense of pride in my accomplishments. During my year back at Berkeley I started seeing a psychoanalyst, and once I returned to UCSF I began an analysis, four times a week, which lasted 7 years.

"Psychoanalysis is hard enough work as it is without making it harder by your building up a large debt to me." The words of my first analyst, Gordon Baumbacher, a psychiatrist and a candidate at the time at the San Francisco Psychoanalytic Institute. This he said to me early on, when we were figuring out how to arrange meeting times and set a fee. I had suggested that I could owe him money, because I was in medical school and had none. His response so impressed me I never forgot it, especially the "hard enough work" part. I took it as a warning and a challenge.

My analysis with Baumbacher was crucial in my emerging into something that resembled a person who was more than simply self-sufficient, judgmental, and flippant (all words friends of mine, in choice moments, had used to describe me). His voice, in spite of the declarative mode of his "hard work" comment, was often halting, hesitant. He struggled with a stammer, and at times would get stuck on a word. Though he might have appeared wavering and wobbly, in fact he was rock solid when it counted. We'd fight too, at times. I hated it when he'd answer his phone during sessions, or ask me "How have you been?" upon my return from a vacation break. I thought he tended to interpret too generically: "You're afraid of intimacy," types of comments. I was not easy, as I struggled with an enduring sense of disappointment that was masked by a pseudo-independent, cavalier exterior.

Complaints aside, Gordon said some things to me that seemed exactly right: "You came into analysis as much to cure your father as to cure yourself." This he said to me after I had a dream in which my father was walking up the steps of the Medical Sciences Building, as if he were a medical student going to class. Or, "You're afraid that [girlfriend's] natural enthusiasm and excitement will go off the rails, that she'll get crazy like your father did so many times, when he'd completely lose it." And, "When I stammer you worry I'm not reliable, can't be trusted. That I'm going to fall apart, and you'll be responsible for it." Obviously, someone who can speak to the possibility of his falling apart is not going to fall apart.

Baumbacher was trained during a time when American psychoanalysts found a way to speak their minds in an unadorned idiom, with pith and intention, and without undue fear. Jacob Arlow used to say that we should speak with patients the same way we might talk with a taxi driver. Perhaps this might seem strange, because the people I have in mind— Owen Renik, Jacob Arlow, Vic Calef, Adrienne Applegarth, Joseph Weiss, among others—were "ego psychologists." And though the "one-person psychology" that most people associate with American psychoanalysis back in the 1970s and 1980s may have been problematic in some ways, the analysts I mention here were able to speak in direct fashion to their patients in a way that did not blame the patient or imply that the patient was up to something suspicious. I think of it as a kind of street talk. The interventions we typically read about now, or hear about in case conferences—a kind of formal, nearly arch way of speaking to a patient, as if proper sentence structure and diction relate directly to how a person's mind ought to "properly" function—were anathema to the analysts I am thinking of. They were not interested in protecting themselves, ruminating in the dense forest of their "countertransference"; they wanted to speak to the truth of what they saw in the patient as best they could, and go from there. Each of them inhabited a voice that can only be called "their self," or "who they are." They often used sarcasm or a joke; at other times paradox or confrontation. All rendered with nothing if not something like psychoanalytic love. These analysts are among the lost voices of American psychoanalysis. Or perhaps, to make a larger point, American psychoanalysis has lost a *particular way of speaking* to patients.

Between 2005 and 2010 Facebook went from a small Cambridge, Mass. phenomenon to a global one. Over those 5 years nearly all of the guys I had played ball with and had all those dreams about managed to reconnect with each other on Facebook. John Cossette was among them, though his Facebook page was notably pictureless. The pleasure we all got from catching up and reminiscing about old times was felt, I am sure, by every one of us. In 2010 we decided to have a Pony League all-star reunion down in Los Angeles, where all the best players from that era would get together, play some softball, and have a party. And so we did.

John and I had had some phone conversations since 2005, and I knew by the 2010 gathering that he was seriously considering leaving his wife as he had fallen back in love with a woman he'd first met in high school. At the reunion he watched the ball game (such as it was) from the sidelines because he was simply too big to swing a bat or throw a ball. At the party afterwards he and I talked about some serious stuff (along with the usual cracking of risqué jokes): his brother's drug addiction and my father's untreated prostate cancer and recent death. The old connection was still there. Ever the Hollywood kid, he said to me: "When I saw you back in 2005 after 30 years it was straight out of *Field of Dreams*."

Early in the next year John left his wife. In April we spoke by phone. He had lost 50 pounds with a goal of losing another 100. He had accomplished this, he told me, with the help of a gastric stapling surgery he had undergone a month earlier. He was in an optimistic mood, feeling chipper, and his voice had that light and lilting quality I remembered when he was on top of the world years before. Two weeks later John was dead. I never heard a cause of death, but it was likely an embolism as he had complained about fairly severe right leg pain on the morning of his death. Pain he had probably ignored.

Dear Reader:

I will leave it to you to cobble together, like a *bricoleur*, what I have offered here into something that might answer, if partially, the question of how a person such as I became a psychoanalyst. But anxious that I have not offered enough, I give one further story—another reunion story of sorts. It also serves as a parting story, from me to you. In this regard I am reminded of the Robert Hunter lyric: "The story-teller makes no choice/soon you will not hear his voice. His job is to shed light/not to master."

Around the time I was a senior in college I had been rummaging through my mother's files (unbeknown to her). There I found an old letter my father had written to my mother's attorney in 1962, in the middle of their acrimonious divorce proceedings. The three-page letter, to my filial and literary ear, was a marvel. Here was my U.S. Postal Service employee father, aping lawyerly language, rebutting every scurrilous accusation that had been leveled against him by my mother, via her attorney. Never mind that all the accusations were no doubt true. The letter was a masterly mixture of style, wit, sarcasm, and brash courage. I finally had something about my father I could point to and say: this is amazing. So I wrote *him* a letter, telling him what I had found and that I thought it showed not only chutzpah, but great promise. Maybe he could do something more with his life, be a writer, or a teacher perhaps? Upon receipt of my letter he called me, and the first thing he said was, "I always knew you'd come back to me."

Notes

1 I am indebted to Celeste Langan for this idea.
2 Lacan in the mid-1950s conceptualized the voice as hallucinated, a "*positive index* of the hidden truth of the subject" (Lagaay 2008, p. 54, italics in original). Later, in his seminar on Anxiety, 1962–1963, Lacan theorizes a more complex set of part-objects, such as the voice and the gaze—objects that the subject experiences from the outside, as *other*, but that Lacan insists are more absent than present (1962–1963/2014). We might understand this idea by considering how alien one's own voice sounds when listened to on a recording: "That's how I sound?! It can't be."
3 For those paying close attention, the reunion of 2005 I attended was not my high school's, but our main rival high school's reunion. I knew many of those people from elementary school and junior high, including John, and wanted to see them again after so many years.
4 See Radar (1974) as an example.

References

Altieri, C. (1996). The values of articulation: Aesthetics after the aesthetic ideology. In R. Eldridge (Ed.), *Beyond representation: Philosophy and poetic imagination* (pp. 66–89). Cambridge: Cambridge University Press.
Barthes, R. (1977). From work to text. In R. Barthes, *Image–music–text* (pp. 155–164). London: Fontana.
Browning, R. (1993). *My last duchess and other poems*. Mineola, NY: Dover. (Original work published 1842).
Foucault, M. (1977). What is an author? In M. Foucault, *Language, counter-memory, practice* (pp. 113–138). Ithaca, NY: Cornell University Press.
Lacan, J. (2014). *Anxiety: The seminar of Jacques Lacan, Book X* (J.-A. Miller, Ed., A. R. Price, Trans.). Cambridge: Polity Press. (Original work published 1962–1963)
Lagaay, A. (2008). Between sound and silence: voice in the history of psychoanalysis. *e-pisteme*, *1*(1), 53–62.
Rader, R. (1974). Fact, theory, and literary explanation. *Critical Inquiry*, December, *1*(2), 245–272.
Sorosky, A. D., Baran, A., & Pannor, R. (1979). *The adoption triangle: Sealed or open records and how they affect adoptees, birth parents, and adoptive parents*. Ann Arbor, MI: Anchor Press.

Chapter 6

Becoming myself
Resuming a derailed adolescence

Therese Rosenblatt

My conscious thinking and fantasizing about my analytic identity began when I was a teenager. I had become acquainted with Freud through my mother's admiration of him, and then in twelfth grade through a course I took. I fell in love with the field of psychoanalysis as soon as I discovered it. I was lucky to find such an abiding passion at a young age. This early passion became a part of my identity as a way to make sense of external events and internal feelings. I felt at sea in my family, and psychoanalytic thinking provided me with a way to navigate my inner turbulence. It became a kind of mental hard wiring, an internal regulator. It made me feel stronger. It became a good friend who was always there and kept giving—usually a source of nourishment, though occasionally an intrusive tyrant. I have gone back to these feelings many times when I have doubted myself as an analyst. They have served as my touchstone when I have questioned matters of technique or theory or who I am as an analyst. In those times of self doubt I remind myself that I am doing this work for reasons that began at a time early in childhood when I experienced the first stirrings of what felt like a calling. Contact with that original wellspring of interest provides me with a sense of authentic and alive connection to myself and who I am with a patient. I have come to realize that within that source is also a repository of traumas experienced but not fully appreciated by caregivers and ancestors and absorbed into me. This reservoir fuels my empathy and creativity. Driven to peer into other people's minds, the role of psychotherapist has always felt natural. I have found that my own ease and interest comforts others.

Background

As a young child I spent endless hours listening to my mother discuss the characters who peopled her life in her personal edition of "armchair analysis." She and I spent many hours together—best friends, sort of. I accompanied her driving to errands, visiting her friends, sitting at home over the numerous cups of tea she required. I wanted to connect with her in any way that I could. I was a good listener. My mother did most of the talking. In fact she rarely stopped. But I was fascinated by this charismatic creature who was my mother and my interest brought out her warmth. Other than being a man, listening to my mother was the most reliable way to win her love and I was hungry for it. Her effusive stories were filled with colorful detail and idealization of the characters she described. She spoke of ancestors, childhood neighbors in Palestine (all Hitler's refugees), the newly independent state of Israel, relatives who were casualties of the new state, her own mother, childhood friends, her navy service, teachers, and more. Her ruminations about them fascinated me. I was a curious child and eager to please. In part, she presented her stories as an investigation into what made these people tick. It seemed to me we were like two detectives involved in a project together.

"Come Tessie. Come to Safeway with me. Make me a cup of tea first and then we'll go. Maybe I'll see if we can visit my friend Tamara afterwards. Come Sweetie." Nothing seemed more compelling than that invitation into my mother's inner sanctum of mysterious, beautiful, and worldly women. These femmes fatales were an exotic and seductive blend of Israel, the Middle East, and Europe. Sitting in the front passenger seat of the car with the warm sun shining down on me, I was transported beyond the tensions and demands of the world and all the people who absorbed my mother's attentions—my father, my brothers, her friends, and a galaxy of admirers. That meant not only listening and advising but also sharing my personal life and choosing to spend my free time with her. It felt safe, passive and cocoon like. For those moments, I was the special object of her affection and attention. Once drawn in, she would say "the best and most important thing in the world is for the two of us to be best friends. I preferred being with my own mother over anything in the world," she would say. "We are conspirators together. We can tell each other secrets and have more fun together than anyone." She, ever the foreigner—an only child and the sun in her mother's life—had left her beloved and vulnerable homeland and her traumatized, immigrant parents behind, at age nineteen. She experienced herself as a deserter.

Once we were on our way, my mother would embark on her daily musing about whomever and whatever was on her mind for that day. More and more as the years of my childhood wore on, that topic became one of my brothers.

My mother was consumed with one of my brothers. I remember him as a happy if stubborn and oppositional young boy who sank into an angry and isolated depression the older he got. He seemed to pine for my very reserved father but wouldn't ask for him. My father himself was bereft, having lost his mother at age fourteen, after seven years of illness. I felt that my brother longed for acceptance, approval, limits, and calm containment, something that my taciturn father and fragile mother found difficult to provide. Instead they idealized his masculinity, aggression, and intellect. He would say something openly defiant. My mother would fly into a helpless rage. Though at other times, his defiant behavior elicited giggles from my mother. Mother and son could not live with or without each other. They were tied together in a passionate but stormy bond.

Increasingly the lovely hours alone listening to my mother became ruminations about why my brother did what he did. It was important to her not only that I listen but increasingly that I help her figure out what was wrong, to spin some theory. I took this task extremely seriously. But when I offered my suggestions—"He's fine. He shouldn't feel as if something is wrong. Set limits. Let him know calmly that his behavior is unacceptable. He feels like an outsider in his school. He needs more attention from our father"—nothing was of use to her. She preferred her own magical and sometimes shocking theories. When I cast doubt on her theories about his depression, withdrawal, and anger, she paid no attention. I felt I had no impact. Undoubtedly, one part of my motivation in being an analyst is to recreate that therapist role, this time to be heard and to make a difference.

As I got older she brought Freud into the picture, giving her version of his psychoanalytic method. Just as she had regaled me with stories about the people from her childhood, her current friends, my brother, she would refer to Freud—tidbits about his life, his clinical work, and the unconscious. My mother idealized Freud and through my identification with her, so did I. Little did I realize until I was older, the enactment that was taking place—that her preoccupation with psychoanalysis, a communication of her pain, engaged an urgent calling in me to respond to her need and make sense of her mind. She unwittingly used me as her therapist as she sought my opinion on the people who captured her interest, in particular, herself and the brother that worried her so. The therapist aspect of myself, which was both pleasurable and oppressive, was getting overdeveloped and over applied in my relationships. Unconsciously I felt compelled to suppress anything other than that therapist voice. Consequently, for a while after college I resisted entering the field of psychology, feeling that I wanted a period of fun without too much reflection. At that time I didn't understand that I could be both serious and lighthearted. My development became stalled. I was sacrificing too many pieces of my core self.

The finding of my mature voice as an analyst began in a formal sense, at the beginning of my analytic training at The New York University Postdoctoral Program in Psychoanalysis and Psychotherapy (Postdoc). When I graduated from training I felt simultaneously abandoned and comfortably ready to be an analyst. I believe that the blossoming of my voice as an analyst was part of an extended developmental process, which took place formally over the ten years it took me to go through training, but that had it's roots early in childhood and became intertwined with the emergence of my True Self—the fount of my productivity and creativity. The ten years unfolded in the context of several facilitating environments (Winnicott, 1965), starting with my institute, extending through my analyses with three different analysts and within the setting of a supportive marriage. That these environments took place in turn within the context of my personal life history, was equally influential. The 10 years of training in a non-authoritarian environment helped to release me from an over reliance on "complying with externality" (Mitchell, 1993, p. 23), enabled me to develop my independent voice as an analyst, and to feel organically and fully identified as one.

My family's educated, sophisticated, and liberal values masked a pronounced authoritarianism, which led to a prolonged internal struggle between my compliant tendencies and my strong need to be my own person. In my upbringing, there was one God so to speak, and one way for everything. Even those messages were confusing. For example, I was enrolled in Episcopalian and Quaker schools, but was expected to lead a Jewish life. Non compliance— even for misdemeanors like going out two consecutive weekend evenings— meant a withdrawal of love. The dialectic between these two currents—of traditionalism and originality—helped shape my development as an analyst and a person.

During my years of analytic training, I came to realize that ecumenical aspects of my program that I was initially skeptical of, such as the lack of a required, sequenced, uni-theoretical curriculum, while sometimes posing challenges, were wonderfully freeing in allowing me to integrate different theoretical and clinical perspectives with who I am as a person.

Formal training

I chose NYU Postdoc for analytic training. Postdoc is organized around a track system in which there are four different theoretical orientations, each of which offers courses, supervision, training analyses, symposia, and events. This system, while creating certain tensions in the program, generates a vibrant, intellectual atmosphere that, by its very existence, lets candidates know that there are at least four ways to think about analysis; Contemporary Freudian, Relational, Interpersonal—Humanistic, and Independent. When I started at Postdoc I was involved in what I felt was an effective analysis with a traditional Freudian. My satisfaction with this analysis led me to affiliate with the Contemporary Freudian Track. As I became more disillusioned with the analysis, I became more appreciative of Relational points of view and ultimately synthesized an orientation that was considerably left-leaning Freudian. Having the luxury to be influenced by divergent points of view has allowed and encouraged me to find my voice as opposed to the "right" voice.

As a mother raising three young children and married to a man who worked very long hours and traveled a lot, I could not have been more delighted to find in Postdoc an intellectually rigorous program that offered a part-time option. This felt like some version of a well-attuned and empathic parent who could recognize my needs, desires, and challenges as someone who valued rigorous training and mental stimulation, yet prioritized the raising of children. Second, here was a program that offered choice, freedom, minimized infantilization, all without sacrificing quality. This felt like an exciting new prospect but risky as such. As I deliberated on my choice of an institute I wondered if Postdoc would be a program that would offer enough space to thrive without giving me so much rope that I would hang myself. Could this parent have boundaries, standards, and high enough expectations? Did this parent have the omniscience necessary for proper guidance and education or would I feel as so many of my adolescent and young adult patients do as they step out into the world, that they are cut off from the mother ship and alone in a void? I became very conflicted for a while in my choice between Postdoc and another institute that offered a single, cohesive, traditional program but that was highly authoritarian in its stance. This choice was mirroring and stirring an internal conflict between my loyalty to my historical roots and my longing for something new and freer.

In addition, the freedom and the choices offered by Postdoc, elicited a transference wish for forbidden fruit. The fruit was the possibility of autonomy, and the realization of my True Self (Winnicott, 1965). I longed to feel secure in my independent thinking. Paradoxically, while choosing freedom broke with the values of those who inhabited my mind so loaded and charged, and a subsequent risk of their abandonment, real and internal, it also expressed a covert message from my father, which could be summed up in the following example. As a young adult I once delighted my father by expressing my opinion that if I was pressed for time, I would prefer to read the hard news stories in the newspaper rather than the opinion pieces because I could form my own opinions but first would need to get the news on which to base my opinion. My father applauded my independent thinking and deductive reasoning. He represented the parent of separation, cognition, and worldliness, even though my independence threatened our family system and in reality caused me to be isolated and censured. Part of the complex dynamic that was included in my wish to try and taste new fruits was the danger of outdoing my mother by going out into the world and freely exploring possibilities that would enhance my growth in addition to the growth of those for whom I cared. Symbolically that meant joining my father and brothers and the world of powerful men.

The institute that I considered but did not choose, tempted me with what felt like the familiar. It was an establishment kind of place with an authoritarian structure—much like my family of origin. When that institute accepted me, I felt tapped for an exclusive club. I felt like one of the chosen, a derivative of my wish to be welcomed into the mysterious orbit of my Oedipal parents. I felt accepted into "the group" and redeemed from the lifelong albatross of feeling like a perpetual "other." It offered a sense of safety and familiarity and seemed to guarantee that I would learn the "right" things in the "right" way. This knowledge might function like a good self object that would enhance my self esteem and show that I was "ok", not damaged goods. During the course of negotiations with this institute in which I presented my case to keep my then analyst, I learned a lot about the organization that I found disconcerting and that felt like a repetition of past experiences. My choice became clear. The impulse to avoid being re-traumatized by training led me fearfully at first, to choose Postdoc, an institute that was founded and organized along principles that were refreshingly non-authoritarian. I thrived in this atmosphere in spite of the inevitable shortfalls and deficits of training in a four-track program. I started psychoanalytic training at the age of forty-four. I had earned my PhD, was well into my second career as a psychologist (the first was radio and media and before that intensive ballet training) a longish marriage with three children and numerous other responsibilities. I was in no mood to be infantilized.

I had an immediate, primarily positive transference to my institute-family, though some ambivalence lingered, stemming from my conflict in choosing between the two institutes. In this atmosphere of free choice, which contained many different analytic parents and siblings, I could observe, try on, and imagine different identities, much like an adolescent does as she separates from parents and family to discover who she is and to find her place in the world. The diversity and liberal, free choice of the program forced me to struggle actively to make my own choices, discover my preferences, and ultimately, to forge my identity. I was forming and refining my ego ideal, the standard to which I aspired to hold myself, a process that had ossified and then derailed sometime in early adolescence.

Early in my career my tendency toward rule-following prevailed and my outlook bore the stamp of academic psychoanalysis. My vision of myself as a professional had come to match strict standards of practice, which at times came close to representing a certain well-known caricature of American psychoanalysis. It also fit with unattainable standards and judgments that I had internalized from my upbringing and that so well matched an illusion that they would provide some kind of internal order. I imagine that at that point some of my patients must have found me to be cold and/or rigid. I remember with shame one patient who was very nervous about the impending birth of her baby and didn't know what to do about the unpredictability of her due date and the interruption of our sessions. Using the excuse to myself about upholding the frame, I did nothing to help work out a creative and flexible arrangement with her. We had had a very good rapport and worked well together but the work ended around her due date. I believe it was because I was no help in working out a mutually suitable arrangement. But as my analytic training, my personal analyses, and my life progressed, I developed a much more open, flexible, tolerant attitude and became more responsive to the needs of patients rather than to theory. I came to see that in psychoanalysis, as in life in general, there are many truths or maybe none at all. I came to trust my clinical judgment and to know that the guiding principles of theory have their limits and have to be tempered by experience. They cannot always provide answers to many clinical situations. It is often in those moments of doubt, uncertainty, and aloneness that I invoke Sullivan's famous comment, "we are all more simply human than otherwise" (2012, p. 7) as my guiding principle.

Like a good enough parent, Postdoc provided a defined space in which I tested out the perspectives offered by the various theoretical orientations. At times the existence of the tracks felt like having amicably divorced parents but they also enabled me to discover and refine my own beliefs and aspirations. My biggest challenge during this time was to figure out how to integrate my belief in a consistent, intrapsychic core with the clear validity of a two-person psychology. I worried that I would not master the Freudian position and, instead, would become a dilettante of several perspectives. My worries were mostly of a clinical nature like how much of myself and my own intuition could I bring into my work with patients? Nonetheless, authoritarianism was minimal and candidates had the opportunity to become autonomously functioning analysts. In this environment I felt like someone had opened a window and let air into a musty room. I could breathe. I had hope that I could become comfortable in my own analytic skin.

Teachers

In my family, tremendous cachet was accorded to intellectual and professional prowess, to the point of brinksmanship. But it was not until graduate school when I joyfully performed at the very top of my class, that I began to perceive that my family met my accomplishments with silence, exhorting me to transfer to an MSW program as an easier road to travel, and surprisingly, outright denigration of the profession. Though confusing and demoralizing, this reaction strengthened my resolve to develop as a psychologist. In graduate school I found an intellectual home and a place where my zeal to understand what makes people tick was a plus, not an oddity. I was excited by the material I was studying in my clinically focused Developmental program. I thrived there and received recognition and encouragement from my teachers and mentors. I grew into myself with a sense of relief and optimism.

Over the course of my training, there were several teachers whose clinical and analytic sensibilities I absorbed and metabolized into my voice. My dissertation mentor, Beatrice Beebe, provided empirical evidence and data to buttress and dramatize what seemed intuitively true. The infant's early capacities and relationship with caregivers reverberates into adulthood and becomes part of character structure. I was spellbound by Beatrice's world of frame by frame analysis of videos of the interaction between mother and baby. I decided I had to do my dissertation in this arduous area of research. I felt like I was watching the key to human behavior. Traces of these early origins seemed so evident in the behavior of adult patients, communicated often through their non-verbal communications and the analyst's countertransference. With certain patients one gets a palpable sense of aspects of their infant life, which can shed light on current adult experiences. In addition, watching the way the infant brings his genetic temperament and self regulatory system to bear on the interaction with the caregiver and is then influenced by that interaction, has confirmed my conviction that both one and two person psychologies are at work in treatment as in life (Mitchell, 1993). The clinical application of such work and the metaphors derived from mother/infant observations, have proven enormously mutative and comforting to some of my patients. These insights have developed my radar for sensing and articulating formative, pre-verbal experiences in patients. For example, I have two patients who felt held and understood when I told them that it seemed they wanted to be swaddled like infants. Both patients had experienced severe deficits in their earliest mothering. Another patient was struggling to communicate an affect being expressed in her transference to me. I remarked that her experience was that of a crawling baby who needed to visually check in with her mother/analyst in order to get the encouragement she so sorely needed in order to continue her explorations. This interpretation resonated with her and brought a palpable sense of relief.

Through Shelly Bach's teachings at Postdoc, I sharpened my ability to observe analytically with reference, especially, to pre-Oedipal experience. I came to trust the patient as a communicator of her history and needs, and the importance of giving her the space to let the "transference blossom" as Shelly would say. I became more attuned to the broad picture of the patient's process and core challenges. Through Martin Bergmann I came to relish, rather than feel ashamed, of my independent thinking. I sharpened the rigor of my analytic thought and curiosity, and mostly gained confidence in the joy of trusting and valuing my own mind, not to mention understanding Freud in a fresh, critical, and intimate way. In admonishing against the dangers of "the overly silent analyst," Martin affirmed my growing belief that the analyst's passivity can be harmful and can leave the patient stuck in her own pathology. Steve Solow and Carolyn Ellman were instrumental in helping me grow my body of clinical knowledge, by imparting their own considerable knowledge, but also by their confidence in my work and by giving me the mirroring and encouragement necessary to build trust and confidence in my clinical skills and style. Gil Katz convinced me of the power and ubiquity of enactments and how to recognize and understand them. Marsha Levy Warren extended my developmental knowledge into the adolescent stages and sensitized me to the relevance of those issues throughout the lifespan.

Those ten years of training at Postdoc provided a space in which development could occur and an incubator in which I could fantasize, trying on different styles of the analyst I might become.

Analyses

With my first analyst I experienced an ambivalent transference in that she was a woman who provided a needed and admired alternative to the way my mother functioned. Reminiscent of my father, she was contained, academic, and methodical. She was ambitious in her efforts to master psychoanalytic knowledge. Like my father she was perfectionistic and formal. She was enormously successful in helping me make sense of, and separate from, my mother who still loomed large in my head. A highly intelligent woman, my first analyst was all intellect, clinging with brittle rigor to her analytic rules and authority, most of which were camouflage for her withdrawn and fearful tendencies. We stuck mostly to maternal narratives and a positive paternal transference. But when I moved into later conflicts and transferences, Oedipal and those of separation and autonomy, we reached an impasse. These issues were ignored, giving rise to negative maternal and paternal transferences. Although her scholarship melded with my image of my father and became part of my ego ideal, ultimately my feeling that she just did not much like me became undeniable. I came to realize how right Freud was when he said that there is no cure without love. I would aspire to be an analyst who could offer patients analytic rigor, understanding, and analytic love.

Three years later, after repeated attempts to discuss the possibility of my leaving this analysis, I faced a life-altering and life-saving surgery for an abdominal tumor. The surgery produced a complete cure and I now enjoy excellent health, but the recovery period was arduous and lasted many months. Four months after the surgery, when I was ready to go back to treatment, I knew I could not resume with my analyst. In the period of time between surgery and finding a new analyst, thoughts, feelings, and fantasies, which had been brewing for many years, suddenly crystallized into the clear knowledge that I had to find an analyst who was kinder, softer, warmer, and not arrogant. It had to be someone who would speak to me as one human to the next but still have more knowledge then me—true authority according to Fromm (1969). I needed to be able to challenge her authority and beliefs as a healthy adolescent would, to be outspoken about my opinions and doubts and face thoughts and feelings that shamed and scared me. I needed the opportunity to be oppositional as a way to find and solidify my own mind. I needed to find a guide who was not afraid of the rugged terrain that I or any analysand would need to traverse. I needed to be able to make the analysis work for me. I knew this meant that I might need to face a turbulent and infantile regression, something I had never safely experienced.

I wanted my next analyst to be someone who incorporated newer theories and techniques and not be doctrinaire—a man with core beliefs that were grounded in a one person psychology and incorporated aspects of a two person psychology. The preservation of the centrality of the intrapsychic, the balance between an internal core process and interaction with the interpersonal field has always felt very much like a variation on my ballet background. A dancer needs to re-find her core body placement as she executes creative movements, which pull the body off its center. In the ballet model as in psychoanalysis, the classical core is the discipline and language underlying creativity, flexibility, experimentation, and freedom of expression. Ballet inculcated in me a strong sense of discipline, a resolve towards steely strength and an appreciation for the language and meaning of the body and its movements. Appreciating a guiding discipline in my work and recognizing the beauty inherent in that discipline is an intrinsic part of who I am and how I practice. Attunement to a patient's style of moving, body placement, awareness, and control, has become an automatic tool, which adds nuance to my understanding of my patients' inner lives. There is a wealth of information in non-verbal communication. For example, a patient who doesn't look at me or answer my goodbye when she leaves the session, used to leave me with the impression that she was haughty and dismissive. And yet this impression does not fit with other information she has given me about herself. I came to realize that this behavior was an expression of her shame over her expectation that she is unimportant and unloveable to me and in general. I don't know if I would have gotten to this insight if I had waited for her verbal expression of it. I have developed a sort of body empathy, which is present when I work. I had taken this mode of expression for granted because it was such a part of me. It wasn't until conversations with an actor highlighted the significance of body language and physicality in acting, that I realized I needed an awareness and a language for this aspect of my analytic work. I think many people have this kind of intuition, though it remains out of their awareness. The next analyst would need to be flexible, intuitive and warm, disciplined and scholarly, with an ability to cut to the core issues, but above all be human. That was my new ego ideal.

Analyst number two was a kind person, a man with whom I had an immediate rapport. We liked each other from the start. I was quickly drawn into the full blown paternal transference I had been so ready for but unable to attain in my last analysis. He was instrumental in helping me emerge from a major depression, post surgery. But when we shifted into a more analytic mode as the depression lifted, things went awry. This analyst's practice was self admittedly orthodox in style. He agreed to consider and incorporate newer techniques—an interesting proposition in itself. I overlooked his orthodox approach in spite of my wish for something new, because of my unconscious desire for a warm and accessible kind of father/analyst. His fondness of me confused me into imagining that things would turn out differently and that he would provide something new. As someone who came from the blended family of Postdoc and now felt myself to be a considerably left-leaning Contemporary Freudian, I was immediately positioned to challenge this person and challenge I did. The result was fireworks, both the good and bad kind, otherwise understood as an increasingly frequent series of barely analyzed transference/countertransference enactments. Trauma ensued as the analysis spun out of control and I found myself experiencing an intense regression that was proceeding unmanaged in the treatment. The entire analysis became an enactment in which troubling dynamics of my relationship with my father were continually replicated without analysis, causing me to feel re-traumatized.

When I finally left this analysis 2½ years after it started, I had to sort through the wreckage but my analytic ideals were brought into sharp relief. They took on a new meaning in the most personal way, a way one learns only through the transferential re-living of trauma. It induced in me a new sense of responsibility for, and appreciation of, my patients' vulnerabilities, dependencies, and need for humanness, availability, and authentic caring. My strengthened appreciation for these dynamics was brought to life by a contemporaneous experience with an intensely vulnerable and regressed patient of mine who begged me for love and intimacy in the most concrete way. In trying to understand our transference/countertransference dynamics, I was forced to confront my own fears and longings for intimacy. As a consequence, my thinking about the analytic principles and practices that I had been studying and considering for years, gained strength. The "failed" analysis with my second analyst turned out to be one of the most powerful and illuminating experiences of my life. What I learned from it informed and transformed my work. The positive regard he felt for me as a patient had colored the enactments in a way that made them mutative in spite of mismanagement. I now understood and valued the necessity of "loving" a patient in an alive and convincing way. Without this "analytic love" I would not have been able to let myself experience a full regression that, although it felt disorganizing at times, was also a necessary luxury not experienced during my childhood and adolescence and that led to growth and maturity. I also gained a sense of the true power of enactments both positive and negative, to provide the kind of insight that is experienced affectively with the analyst and leads to change.

My third analyst illuminated the road out of my quagmire. His perceptive grasp of the problem, expressed in a forthright manner in which he treated me as an equal, combined with his compassion towards me, and my admiration for his clinical work, made me realize that he embodied most of my new analytic ideals. He bore some similarity to good experiences I had had with caregivers but mostly provided an enlivening alternative to what I had known. He offered a refreshingly flexible yet solid frame. He expressed a kind of commitment to me that was therapeutic but also something that would have scared me as too unfamiliar, as little as a year earlier. He had authority with humility. He had traits I didn't like but that felt tolerable to me, as I was now able to accept this analyst as a whole person, separate and imperfect. As we worked together we sorted through the shards of the previous analysis and tied them into the bigger picture of who I was. Many aspects of my life and my True Self emerged with a new clarity and bittersweetness. I came to accept and appreciate aspects of myself that I had previously not recognized or rejected for being different from the person I wanted to be, including my sense of being perpetually other. The years of development, experimenting, and fantasy solidified into a strong sense of identity as a person and an analyst. My work became characterized by a new confidence, creativity, and a consistent and individual style of my own.

Most notable to me was the way this analysis unleashed my creativity. The analysis and the analyst, felt original and unstereotyped. I felt safely held. The analyst held a vision of me that was just slightly ahead of my self-concept and projected a sense of me that was suffused with permission, approval, and belief in me in a Loewaldian sense (1960). He was able to collaborate with me to create a safe analytic space in which I could make meaningful links with my unconscious. He was able to truly hear me and possibly even more importantly, to passionately want to hear me, to withstand my anger and try again when initially he had resisted hearing. He recognized broad but deep themes in me and my environment that had never been articulated before. This dynamic proved to be the recipe for new and creative thinking.

Clinical experiences

Encouraged by the new feelings of freedom and separation from my internal demons facilitated by this new analysis, I felt inspired to express independent ideas about how to work more creatively, incorporating the use of the self. I was scared and excited to be more creative. I began to accept that analytic work is creative, a kind of interpersonal art. In analysis as in art, the therapist must use her very self. In the end she has no choice since the analyst's personality ultimately asserts itself. Transference manifests itself in the analyst's practice of analysis as well as in the patient. I am an inveterate responder. Occasionally I have to remind myself to *not* respond to a patient in the interest of giving her the space to make contact with her own process and to follow her associations.

Creativity does not come without anxiety, however. Often when I do or consider doing something creative, something not in the canon of psychoanalytic technique, I fear abandonment and feel lost and alone in outer space, anxious that the road home is forever gone. The idea of the intuition, flexibility, and creativity demanded by analytic work had once threatened my identification with my rigorously, scholarly father (as well as that of the culture). I feared merger with those very characteristics that I found so terrifying in my emotionally expressive and more creative mother

A patient was grieving heavily over the tragic death of her daughter, feeling bitter guilt over her inability to hug her one last time at bedtime, when she had called out, gravely ill, from her bed on the night before she died. Her imminent death had been sensed but not known to the two of them. I had been completely absorbed in the experience of reliving this moment with my patient with all of its bitterness, empathizing deeply and trying to make sense of it's meaning with the patient. The patient was leaving my office sobbing at the end of this painfully emotional session. It was one in which the two of us were deeply engaged. I was not to see her for the next three weeks while she was overseas on vacation. She held out her arms halfway for a hug, then dropped them and said, "I wish I could hug you." I promptly opened my arms and hugged her. I questioned myself for a while, conflicted over whether I did the "right" thing by gratifying her. When I reflect back on it, I believe I did.

As I gained experience and confidence in who I was as an analyst I sometimes look back with regret and occasionally with horror at my experiences with several patients whom I would have treated differently had I held the views that I do now. One patient with whom I worked for six years, was a borderline schizophrenic woman who needed the kind of support and availability that I withheld for "analytic" reasons. I would be able to provide that to her now that I trust my judgment in responding to her paranoia, lack of a stable, internal structure, and inability to sustain emotional object constancy. I would have answered certain questions directly. I would have occasionally offered the encouragement that she was seeking, albeit in analytic style. Observations to a patient about their positive and adaptive tendencies are every bit as important as interpretations of their problems and sometimes more powerful than those that reflect their conflicts. Another patient was so paralyzed with anxiety and inhibitions that communicating her fears and trauma was too excruciatingly painful for her. She and I were attached and liked each other. Together we did try many things to ease her ability to communicate and sense of exposure, but in the end, with eyes brimming with tears, she left the treatment, leaving me with a feeling of so near and yet so far. I realized after the fact that she needed me to alter my approach, to share more of myself in order to instill a reassuring sense of transparency. Mostly I would have chatted about "non-analytic" topics like the movies, art, and daily life that this patient so enjoyed. She had implied that this was the way to soften her dread of me as a judgmental authority figure and her own dread of what "psychic truths" (Ogden, 2015, p. 305) would be revealed. I "heard" these clues but resisted them out of my own fear of judgment by the psychoanalytic establishment and my own psychic truths. But my analytic models and my analytic superego at the time prevented me from offering that to her.

Gratifying my patients this way would have satisfied a way in which patients need to use the therapist much the way Fonagy and Target (1996) describe children need to use the parent during the Psychic Equivalent Stage. They use them as a prop in their fantasy play. Does this advocate for the offering of a Corrective Emotional Experience (Alexander and French, 1946)? I think in truth that analysis and therapy are *in part* corrective emotional experiences, but what separates analytic therapy from that which employs other theories or follows other principles, is that ultimately these acts and what they symbolize, are discussed and their meanings explored by patient and analyst.

Through the pleasure and the tumult of this work, I have learned some of what is positive and mutative in analysis, as well as what doesn't work. My analytic experiences were illuminating, and at times, painful. On one hand, rigid adherence to theory and emotional constriction can lead to impasse and lack of progress. But problems arise when the analyst gets so caught up in the transference-countertransference matrix that he loses his observing ego. Dale Boesky (1990) summed up the need for the balance between analytic rigor and human, emotional involvement when he said "If the analyst does not get emotionally involved sooner or later in a manner that he had not intended, the analysis will not proceed to a successful conclusion" (p. 573). Yet he adds that "serious countertransference can destroy an analysis or stalemate it. All analysts must monitor their work throughout their careers with this in mind" (p. 573). In order to achieve this balance the psychoanalyst must draw heavily from both her intellect and her emotional life. That is the challenge and the pleasure of the work.

Postcript

Writing and time change a person and her perceptions. If I was starting to write this chapter now, it would be different even though what I have written here is authentic. I am a little farther from training. My voice is a little different. My views and self-concept have evolved. The process of writing this book has helped me to learn about myself differently from psychoanalysis in which the vehicle of change is the relationship with the analyst. With writing the relationship is with aspects of oneself and one's written words on the page. This writing project facilitated an authorship of my own narrative similar to analysis. The editing provided a next step in allowing me to observe and reduce a defensive formality in parts of my writing. The editorial process creates an illusion of control, though it is therapeutic for just that reason.

I was surprised to discover that several of our authors put great emphasis on the influence of reading on their psychoanalytic identities. In writing this chapter I have realized that while much of what I have read in my life and education, from psychology and psychoanalytic theory to great novels, has been extremely enlightening or moving, little of it has consciously become part of my voice and identity in the way that people have. Many psychoanalytic theorists have been invaluable and compelling to me in terms of learning theory and technique but in a more intellectualized and less vivid way.

I am transfixed by people—watching and listening to them. I am compelled by my interactions with them. I feel honored and privileged to be privy to the internal worlds of my patients. I have been told that I am particularly sentient in my orientation, which explains why ideas transmitted by people become animated and real to me in a way that reading sometimes does not. My work nourishes my lifelong fascination with human development.

A small number of writers prove the exception. These writers drew me into their worlds, minds, and ambience, affectively and vividly. Some notable ones are the writings of the psychoanalysts Freud, Ogden, Renik, Bach, and Ted

Jacobs, the neurosurgeon Paul Kalanithi, the philosophy of scientist Frank Sulloway, the economist Sylvia Hewlett, as well as the novelists Henry James, Jane Austen, and Jhumpa Lahiri. I am sure there are others that escape my mind right now. I remember the sensation of "living" in the worlds of certain books while reading them, going way back. I seek experiences and a sense of being fully alive that comes from purposeful human connection, heightened awareness and spontaneity in the world. I find that in psychoanalysis.

References

Alexander, F., & French, T. M. (1946). *Psychoanalytic therapy: Principles and application.* New York, NY: Ronald Press.

Boesky, D. (1990). The psychoanalytic process and its components. *Psychoanalytic Quarterly, 59,* 550–584.

Fonagy, P., & Target, M. (1996). Playing with reality: 1. Theory of mind and the normal development of psychic reality. *International Journal of Psychoanalysis, 77,* 217–233.

Fromm, E. (1969). *Escape from freedom.* New York, NY: Holt & Co.

Loewald, H. W. (1960). On the therapeutic action of psycho-analysis. *International Journal Psychoanalysis, 41,* 16–33.

Mitchell, S. A. (1993). *Hope and dread in psychoanalysis.* New York, NY: Basic Books.

Ogden, T. H. (2015). Intuiting the truth of what's happening: On Bion's "Notes on memory and desire." *Psychoanalytic Quarterly, 84,* 285–306.

Sullivan, H. S. (2012). Conceptions of modern psychiatry in The First William Alanson White Memorial Lectures 1940. Psychiatry, 75(1), 1–2.

Winnicott, D. W. (1965). *The maturational processes and the facilitating environment: Studies in the theory of emotional development.* New York, NY: International Universities Press.

Chapter 7

Becoming a psychoanalyst

Jack Drescher

Why did I become an analyst? My own training has made me skeptical about psychoanalysis' ability to answer "why questions." Instead, what follows is a personal account of *how* I became a psychoanalyst.

As I begin writing this chapter, it is Christmas eve in Paris and our plans for this evening, to spend the holiday with my partner's French-Armenian cousins, have been cancelled. A grandmother from the French (as opposed to Armenian) side of the family passed away a few days ago; her funeral was yesterday and consequently tonight's anticipated event with extended family was called off.

Instead, we are by ourselves in our hotel room in the Saint Germain des Pres *arrondissement*. Paris is in mourning following the terrorist attacks last month, reminding me of New York after September 11. I am also in mourning. One of my patients, someone I'd been seeing for 11 years, often twice a week, recently passed away in his sleep.

I feel anger, sadness, and the unfairness of it all. His passing at age 49 reminds me of too many tragic early deaths of friends, acquaintances, colleagues, and patients in the early years of the AIDS epidemic. I feel re-traumatized by this new loss, although I am grateful my patient appeared to have died in his sleep peacefully, book in hand. An avid reader, he was always making book recommendations. A self-identified "romantic," he loved Jane Austen; his endorsement led me outside my science fiction and fantasy comfort zone to read her books.

When I first decided to become a psychoanalyst, I had no idea losing a patient would affect me this way. Rationally, it makes sense. I don't spend anywhere near as much time talking and listening to close relatives and friends as I do talking and listening to patients. In fact, other than my patients, my partner, and—before she passed away in 2016—my elderly mother in Florida, I can't think of anyone with whom I exchange many words, thoughts, and feelings on a weekly basis. For patients I see more than once a week, the relationship becomes even more intense. This exposure to the inner world of others and the relationships we create with them is one meaning of what it means *to be* an analyst.

When I was young, I never thought of becoming a physician because, frankly, I could not stand the sight of blood. I had no physician role models as a child and yet I became the first person in my family to practice medicine. The family doctor of my childhood was not particularly warm or nurturing, certainly not a role model; nor did I particularly care for the shots he dispensed or his office's medicinal smell.

On the other hand, I have anecdotal experiences supporting the notion that the desire to repair one's early experiences of trauma often serves as a motivating force for people entering the health care professions. Early in my career, interviewing medical school applicants, I found the most compelling prospects among those who recalled some early experience in which they helplessly watched a close family member or friend get ill. To these young people, a physician's intervention, curative or not, offered an adaptive template: compassionate engagement in medical (or helping) activity as a defense against feelings of helplessness. Altruism serving both selfish and interpersonal purposes.

So what led me down this path? Before responding, I suggest keeping in mind Freud's caveat about psychoanalytic theories of causality:

> So long as we trace the development from its final outcome backwards, the chain of events appears continuous, and we feel we have gained an insight which is completely satisfactory or even exhaustive. But if we proceed the reverse way, if we start from the premises inferred from the analysis and try to follow these up to the final result, then we no longer get the impression of an inevitable sequence of events which could not have been otherwise determined ... The synthesis is thus not so satisfactory as the analysis; in other words, from a knowledge of the premises we could not have foretold the nature of the result.
>
> (Freud, 1920/1955, p. 167)

The family matrix

My parents were born in Poland, my father in 1911 and my mother in 1925. The Nazis invaded Poland in September 1939. My father lost his parents, his two sisters, and innumerable relatives in the concentration camps. My mother was luckier. When the Nazis invaded her small village, frightened by their appearance and behavior, she urged her family to leave. Although only 14, a child by today's standards, she was listened to as an adult. Consequently, everyone in the extended family who did leave avoided the Nazi death camps. Those left behind were lost in the Holocaust.

Escape was not a picnic. Both parents were among hundreds of thousands of Poles who left western, German-occupied territory for the eastern, Soviet-occupied Poland, now part of Ukraine, in October, 1939. A 2007 documentary film called "Saved by Deportation" (www.logtv.com/films/deportation)

tells how Stalin's forced relocation of 200,000 Polish Jews saved their lives. It spared them from capture and probable death following the German invasion of Russia in December 1941. My parents, who were yet to meet, were among those arrested in May 1940 and sent to Siberian slave labor camps. They each spent more than a year there.

After Germany's invasion, Russia joined the allies, and my parents were relocated from Siberia to Soviet Central Asia in the summer of 1941. They were sent to Bukhara, Uzbekistan, where they first met. They married after the war in April 1946 and left Bukhara a month later. After being returned to Poland, the entire extended family decided to pick up again as Poles were killing Jews returning to claim their lands, belongings, and homes. They bribed their way across the Czechoslovakian and Austrian borders, making their way to a refugee transit camp in Linz. From there, American occupying forces transferred them to a displaced persons (DP) camp in Ulm, Bavaria, in fall 1946. They lived in that DP camp, where my older brother was born in 1947, for 3 years.

After the 1948 creation of Israel, my parents and my mother's extended family were slated to emigrate there; but at departure time, my father became ill. The extended family left for Israel but my parents and older brother stayed behind, expected to follow shortly. However while my father convalesced, a cousin who had gone to the States before the war discovered he was alive and initiated arrangements to bring my parents and brother to the United States. They arrived in New York City in October 1949. HIAS, the Hebrew Immigrant Aid Society sent them to a shelter in Greenwich Village for 6 months and helped them find an apartment in Williamsburg, Brooklyn. I was born in in 1951, my younger brother in 1953 and my parents became American citizens in 1954. In 1956 we moved to Bensonhurst, a mixed Jewish and Italian neighborhood where I grew up, attended public school and *talmud torah* and later college until leaving home at age 21.

The major trauma of my childhood could be described as intergenerational, my parents' Holocaust experience transmitted to me (Bergmann & Jucovy, 1982; Kuriloff, 2014). I have a strong, recurrent visual memory of being 7 or 8 years old with the entire family seated in front of the television watching a Channel 13 documentary about the Holocaust. My parents insisting adamantly, "Sit, watch, and learn." In my mind's eye, I still see an image of splayed naked, dead bodies piled up inside a gas chamber. However, it could not have happened as I remember it: I see what had to be black and white television images as yellowed ones, like old photographs or newspaper clippings.

I compare this unsettling "screen memory" with the experience of visiting Washington DC's Holocaust Museum together with my extended family shortly after it opened in the 1990s. My brother's twin boys, then 10 years old, were not permitted in the main museum where minimum entry age was 12. I remember a light bulb going off: *age-appropriate learning!* Not a concept with which my parents or their cohort of survivors were familiar when I was growing up.

As a child, I learned to manage others' anxiety, perhaps an early training ground for my later ability to therapeutically monitor and reduce patient anxiety. My parents found it difficult to react proportionately to mundane childhood problems. Small incidents could be infused with anxiety levels of catastrophic proportions. If any of their children had a problem with a teacher, the teacher was always right, even when she was wrong. So it was better not to have problems with teachers or other authority figures at all, because in the end, it was going to be interpreted as our fault. That typically led to working out problems ourselves rather than bringing them to our parents. To reduce parental anxieties, we were to make no waves, do well in school, do as we were told, become good Jews, successful professionals, marry Jewish girls (ideally with Polish parents as well), be fruitful and multiply and replenish the world with Jews to replace those lost in the Holocaust—and for whom we were all named.

On the other hand, my parents taught me a thing or two about duty and responsibility. They also taught us how to deal with the anti-Semitic comments I first encountered as a child. After years of playing together without incident, my Italian Catholic friends began their catechism lessons at around age 8. This was before Vatican II and some of them, having been dutifully instructed by the priests of St. Finbar's, asked, "Why did the Jews kill Christ?" I had never heard this accusation before and so I went to my parents to ask them about it. They said, "You go back and tell them the Romans killed Christ." Which I did.

Medical school

I did not enter Brooklyn College thinking I wanted to be a doctor and, in retrospect, I chose to become pre-med in my junior year because of pressure from friends and family and feeling I had to choose a career. High school had not been very challenging. I achieved good grades without studying hard and won a Regents Scholarship. However, my college grades did not reflect a very determined drive to enter medical school. With competition so intense in those years, I was not accepted into an American school. After taking a year off, I decided to go to Italy in 1973, certain I wanted to go abroad, although not so certain I wanted to be a physician. Like my parents, I found myself in a foreign country with little knowledge of the language. However, unlike my parents, I was not a refugee, the accommodations were civilized, and I had a return ticket home any time I wished.

After a summer studying Italian in Rome, I went to Padova (Padua) to begin medical school. Italians start medical school after high school in what is officially a 6-year program; in reality, it usually takes longer, with 7 or 8 years often the norm. However I was in no hurry, not hurrying being just one aspect of the Italian lifestyle to which I would become accustomed. As an added and unexpected benefit, I also received an education in foreign languages, European history and politics, religion, art history, postmodernism, enology, and gastronomy while I was there.

It was only after a couple of years of Italian university life, mostly retaking premed courses in Italian, did I feel more determined to seriously pursue a career in medicine. Having made that decision, I diligently worked to transfer back to a US school. In 1978, after 5 years in Italy, I transferred into the third-year medical school class at the University of Michigan.

There I had my first contact with my future vocation at the Ann Arbor VA Hospital, doing a 4-week, required psychiatry rotation on an inpatient unit. My assigned patient was a married, Vietnam War veteran my own age. He had sought voluntary hospital admission after experiencing an ego-dystonic impulse to hit his infant daughter one day when she wouldn't stop crying.

Today my patient might have been diagnosed with PTSD, but in 1978 that diagnosis was not yet in the DSM-II. I presented him at a weekly case conference to a visiting psychiatrist, pretty certain this was the first psychoanalyst I ever met. He did not believe people developed PTSD symptoms without predisposing characterological traits. I experienced the analyst's theory as contemptuous of my patient's character. It sounded like patient-blaming. The analyst communicated disdain for anyone in the room who thought external circumstances mattered more than development in the first 3–5 years of life. Although not yet interested in training in psychiatry at the time, and knowing nothing about longstanding theoretical debates in psychoanalysis, I already had the sensibility of an interpersonal/relational analyst skeptical of the arrogant certainty I came to associate with practitioners of one-person psychologies.

Nevertheless, I had an analytic experience that did have an impact on me. On my last day walking out of the hospital, a sudden thought popped into my head, accompanied by a strong sense of accomplishment and relief: "I didn't catch anything." I never knew I had a fear of mental illness being contagious, although in retrospect it was not unsurprising. I believe this was my first awareness of having an unconscious.

Events that followed shortly after led to my decision to become a psychiatrist. At my next rotation, internal medicine, I met Faith Fitzgerald, a preceptor who lived and breathed a passion for medicine. Although I didn't know it at the time, she would become a role model for a level of professional excellence to which I subsequently aspired.

The problem I discovered during that rotation was that I didn't live and breathe medicine. However, I did like listening to patients. University of Michigan Hospital was a tertiary care center and I had several very ill patients transferred from small Michigan towns for treatment of complicated, chronic illnesses. I found myself drawn to conversation and commiseration with them.

As a student, all I could offer them was a sympathetic ear and hopefully a painless phlebotomy.

Faith, accompanying me every week on our preceptor/student rounds, saw my patients brighten as we entered their rooms. At least that's what she told me in my evaluation, saying I had a "genuine therapeutic effect" on patients. I still remember a strangely odd feeling of pleasurable astonishment at her words. I had never gotten feedback like that before. Of course I knew nothing about the work of Heinz Kohut at the time. However if Faith, never one to hold back frank criticism, said I made people feel better, then perhaps I did.

The following year, having matched in a psychiatry internship in Manhattan, I felt more secure about coming out in professional settings. A stylist friend persuaded me to let her perm my hair. Sporting my new curls for the first time in the hospital, I encountered Faith rushing by me in the corridor. Without stopping, she turned back, smiling to face me, ran her hand through her own shock of natural, ample curls, remarking, "nice haircut."

Psychiatric training

In 1980, I began my psychiatry internship at St. Vincent's Hospital in New York's Greenwich Village. However, I found the training's primary focus on patient management (excellent management, for the record) less intellectually stimulating than what I wanted. Also, while five of the eight psychiatry interns were gay (four men and one woman), there was a, "don't ask, don't tell" atmosphere permeating the hospital environment and we did not feel particularly open about discussing personal lives in public settings. Not that other Manhattan programs at the time were much better. As I discuss below, many were deeply committed to keeping openly gay psychiatrists out of psychiatric training.

I transferred in my second year of residency to SUNY-Downstate in Brooklyn. At the time, academic psychiatric training in many New York City programs was a "lite" version of psychoanalytic training. Many of the analysts who taught at Downstate were orthodox Freudians whose preferred pedagogical methods included (1) deriding any non-analytic ideas offered by residents and (2) interpreting resident disagreement as "resistance." For several fellow residents, exposure to individuals I today think of as mediocre analysts bred antipathy to psychoanalysis in general.

On the other hand, I met notable exceptions who increased my curiosity about analytic thinking. As a third-year resident, I was supervised by Lucy LaFarge on my first outpatient case of psychoanalytically informed psychotherapy. That year, I also began a sensitive supervision on my required child psychotherapy case with John Munder Ross. Donald Moss and the late Barry Opatow, in addition to teaching a third-year course on Freud, taught a fourth-year class on object relations theory, a perspective that still informs my clinical thinking.

In 1981, I started a personal therapy with Stuart Nichols, then one of two or three openly gay psychiatrists in New York City (Ashley, 2002). He was not an analyst but he was a good therapist. During my residency, I became actively involved in a group called Gay Psychiatrists of New York (later Gay and Lesbian Psychiatrists of New York or GLPNY). Gay and lesbian psychiatric residents like myself, dealing with the prejudices of psychoanalytic teachers, supervisors, and even personal therapists, found GLPNY a safe space and an oasis of sanity and common sense. There I met the late Bertram H. Schaffner, who had trained as a psychoanalyst at the William Alanson White Institute and who would become my friend and mentor. Bert was unlike any analyst I encountered in my residency training. He was not dogmatic, he eschewed using jargon in clinical discussions, and he didn't think of psychoanalysis as a narrow field but rather as one that could be fruitfully cross-fertilized with others (Drescher, 2010; Goldman, 1995).

Upon completing residency in 1984, I had no plans to become an analyst. For one thing, most programs would not accept the openly gay psychiatrist I had become. I took a position leading a treatment team on the teaching unit at Downstate's University Hospital. Nursing station 52 had a high staff/patient ratio and was mostly staffed by psychiatrists, psychologists, and social workers with a psychodynamic bent. Community meetings were extraordinary examples of group communication and process (Katz, 1983).

I started a small private evening practice in 1985. After 2 years, hospital work began to feel repetitive and unchallenging. I left the hospital tired and depleted; after seeing patients in the evening I felt more awake. This led me to seriously consider psychoanalytic training, although how to go about that presented challenges.

Historical interlude

In 1973, the American Psychiatric Association (APA) removed homosexuality from its list of mental disorders, the DSM-II (Bayer, 1981; Drescher & Merlino, 2007). I was just 22 years old, had just started medical school in Italy and only come out a year earlier. It was uplifting to read I was cured without yet having seen a psychiatrist. It was only years later, first when I decided to become a psychiatrist and then later a psychoanalyst, that I would come up against almost a century of analytic theorizing about gay people, which eventually led to my professional study and writing about those experiences (Drescher, 1995a, 1996, 1997, 1998, 2002, 2007, 2008).

I learned the modern history of homosexuality usually begins in the mid-19th century, most notably with the work of Karl Heinrich Ulrichs (1864/1994) who hypothesized that gay men and women constituted a *third sex* for whom homosexuality was normal. In contrast, 20 years later Richard von Krafft-Ebing labeled homosexuality a "degenerative" disorder. His *Psychopathia Sexualis* (1886/1965) was influential in disseminating among the medical and scientific communities both the term "homosexual" as well as his view that homosexuality is psychopathological. In contrast, Magnus Hirschfeld (1914/2000), an openly homosexual psychiatrist and standard bearer of that era's third sex theories, offered a normative view.

Sigmund Freud (1905/1953), however, begged to differ. He believed everyone has bisexual instincts and that expressions of homosexuality are a normal phase of heterosexual development. As innate bisexuality did not allow for the existence of a third sex, Freud rejected Hirschfeld's normal variation theory: "Psychoanalytic research is most decidedly opposed to any attempt at separating off homosexuals from the rest of mankind as a group of special character" (p. 145n). He also refuted Krafft-Ebing's theory of pathology, claiming homosexuality could not be a "degenerative condition" as it was "found in people whose efficiency is unimpaired, and who are indeed distinguished by specially high intellectual development and ethical culture" (p. 139).

Instead, Freud offered a third perspective, a theory of immaturity that saw expressions of adult homosexual behavior as caused by "arrested" psychosexual development. Towards the end of his life, he wrote, "Homosexuality is assuredly no advantage, but it is nothing to be ashamed of, no vice, no degradation; it cannot be classified as an illness; we consider it to be a variation of the sexual function, produced by a certain arrest of sexual development" (Freud, 1935/1960, p. 423).

Yet after Freud's death in 1939, most psychoanalysts of the next generation labeled homosexuality as pathological. Their views were in part based on theories of Sandor Rado (1940), founder of the Columbia Psychoanalytic Institute, who had a significant impact on mid-20th-century psychiatry and psychoanalysis. Rado, refuting Freud, claimed innate bisexuality did not exist. Heterosexuality was the biological norm and homosexuality a "phobic" avoidance of the other sex caused by inadequate parenting.

Yet at this time in the mid-20th century, while psychoanalysts "treated" homosexuality, sexologists conducted field studies. They recruited large numbers of non-patient subjects in the general population, the most important study being the Kinsey reports (Kinsey, Pomeroy, & Martin, 1948; Kinsey, Pomeroy, Martin, & Gebhard, 1953). Kinsey surveyed thousands of non-patients, finding homosexuality more common in the general population than was generally believed. This finding challenged psychiatric claims of the time that homosexuality was rare in the general population. Ford and Beach (1951) studied diverse cultures and animal behaviors, confirming Kinsey's view that homosexuality was more common than psychiatry maintained and was found regularly in nature. Evelyn Hooker (1957) compared psychological test results of 30 gay men with 30 heterosexual controls, all non-patients. She found no greater signs of psychological disturbances in gay men, refuting psychoanalytic beliefs of her time that *all* gay men had severe psychological disturbances. Psychoanalysts mostly ignored this growing body of sex research and, in Kinsey's case, expressed extreme hostility to findings that contradicted their own theories (Lewes, 1988).

It was gay activist groups who brought modern sexology research to the attention of the mental health mainstream. Believing psychoanalytically informed psychiatric theories were major contributors to antihomosexual social stigma, they disrupted APA's 1970 and 1971 annual meetings. Their protests led to unprecedented educational panels at APA's following two annual meetings. In 1972, John Fryer, MD, appearing as Dr. H Anonymous, a "homosexual psychiatrist," who, given the realistic fear of adverse professional consequences for coming out at that time, disguised his true identity from the audience and spoke of the discrimination gay psychiatrists faced in their own profession (Bayer, 1981; Drescher and Merlino, 2007).

APA also engaged in an internal deliberative process about the homosexuality diagnosis. Robert Spitzer (1981), who chaired a subcommittee looking into the issue,

> reviewed the characteristics of the various mental disorders and concluded that, with the exception of homosexuality and perhaps some of the other "sexual deviations," they all regularly caused subjective distress or were associated with generalized impairment in social effectiveness of functioning.
>
> (p. 211)

Using this novel definition of mental disorder, his Nomenclature Committee agreed homosexuality per se was not one. Several other APA committees and deliberative bodies then reviewed and accepted their work and recommendations. As a result, in December 1973, APA's Board of Trustees (BOT) voted to remove homosexuality from DSM-II.

Psychoanalytic psychiatrists, however, objected. They petitioned APA to hold a membership referendum to vote either in support of or against the BOT decision. The BOT decision was upheld by a 58% majority of 10,000 voting members. However, it should be noted that psychiatrists did *not* vote, as reported in the popular press, on whether homosexuality was an illness. What APA members voted on was to either "favor" or "oppose" the APA Board of Trustees decision and, by extension, the scientific process they had set up to make the determination (Bayer, 1981, p. 148). Further, psychoanalytic opponents of the 1973 removal repeatedly tried discrediting the referendum's outcome by declaring, "science cannot be decided by a vote" (Gadpaille, 1989). They usually neglect to mention they were the ones who petitioned for a vote in the first place. In any event, in 2006 the International Astronomical Union voted on whether Pluto was a planet (Zachar & Kendler, 2012), demonstrating that even in the hardest of sciences, interpretation of facts are filtered through human subjectivities.

Psychoanalytic training

Psychoanalytic opposition to the diagnostic change did not end with the vote. One implication of depathologizing homosexuality—nondiscrimination in the selection of openly lesbian and gay analytic candidates—was not officially accepted by the American Psychoanalytic Association (APsaA) until 1991 (Roughton, 1995). I experienced this opposition directly when I sought psychiatric training in 1980, and then psychoanalytic training in 1988. I discovered that some of my future colleagues saw gay people as mentally disordered. As a consequence of that belief, and because I was not temperamentally suited to wearing a Dr. Anonymous disguise, I learned I did not have the same rights to train as a psychiatrist and analyst as my heterosexual peers.

Surprisingly as it may seem today, in New York during the 1980s a psychoanalytic myth informed by mundane prejudices thrived. It went something like this: "Homosexuals," which is what analysts called gay and lesbian people back then, are developmentally arrested, regressed, or phobic. They were restricted to compulsive, immature sexual practices. They were believed to be incapable of forming meaningful, long-term relationships. Furthermore, gay people could not become competent analysts, because they were believed to be sexually impulsive, presenting a danger to patients. Lesbians and gay men seeking analytic training were regarded as sociopaths if they tried to conceal their homosexuality from institute interviewers. Given that institutes were willing to provide them with the opportunity to undergo a psychoanalytic conversion, refusing to accept the heterosexual terms of admission was seen as evidence of impudence, moral turpitude, exhibitionism, or some other form of psychopathology.

This was no mere academic exercise. It was a painful reality leading to enactments deeply affecting gay men and women seeking to advance their professional identities and careers. Ellis Perlswig, for example, was accepted at an American-affiliated institute in the 1960s. On the first day of his training analysis, he told his analyst he was gay. Apparently the issue had not come up during the screening process. The analyst, having already told the patient to sit up, said this information would have to be reported to the training committee and abruptly terminated the session. Within a week, the candidate withdrew from the institute at a time when psychoanalytic training was a major step of advancement in academic psychiatry and psychology (Blechner, 2005). It comes as no surprise that lesbian and gay mental health professionals in psychoanalytic training in the 1960s and 1970s kept their actual lives a secret from their own analysts to protect their professional advancement. By saying "she," when he meant "he," something many gay people learn to do at an early age, a gay person in analytic training could avoid a fate like the one that befell Perlswig.

Alternatively, some gay men and women had a different kind of experience. One institute training director told a colleague of mine who sought a consultation with her in the 1960s that as a "homosexual" he would not be accepted for training. However, she said he was fortunate. Not getting into her institute meant he could have a "real analysis" with her, by which she meant a non-reporting analysis. One colleague, 40 years my senior, first told me this story as an illustration of his analyst's kindness, as have others who told me similar stories. While I have no reason to doubt their kindness, I always wondered, and still do, what ethical principles informed analysts' decisions to affiliate with institutions practicing discriminatory policies with which they disagreed? Of course, this entirely begs the question of what one should make of analytic training directors who thought "real analysis" was only practiced outside their institutes.

When I started thinking seriously about analytic training in 1986, the general consensus in my professional circles was that psychiatrists should consider only four institutes in Manhattan: Columbia, New York Psychoanalytic, the former Downstate (now Institute for Psychoanalytic Education at NYU), and White. I did inquire about applying to the APsaA-affiliated institutes. One former supervisor, at the time a candidate at the Downstate Institute, said being gay would make admission in any of the institutes of APsaA unlikely. Another former supervisor training at Columbia confirmed this. Ironically, this was happening at a time when applications by psychiatrists for psychoanalytic training were on the decline.

Another colleague training at the New York Psychoanalytic Institute asked if I was applying there. I said her institute did not accept gay people and she did not believe me. So she asked her training analyst who confirmed it was true, explaining, "Blind people should be entitled to all the rights and privileges of sighted people, but you don't want them to fly a plane." This was an example of what I later came to define as "psychoanalytic coyness" (Drescher, 1995a). These coy responses usually result from a conflict between unconscious disdain and an analyst's self-representations as a caring and tolerant individual. Overt expressions of psychoanalytic coyness can be provoked by drawing attention to an analyst's prejudices, as my colleague did when she directly asked hers a question. Coyness emerges as a clever analogy, an intellectualization, or a rationalization intended to cover up the analyst's true feelings or intentions.

While many APsaA-affiliated Institutes openly discriminated in the mid-1980s, some began adopting an informal "don't ask, don't tell" policy. An openly gay psychologist on the West Coast was supervised by an analyst with an important position at her institute. She liked him and admired his clinical work. She offered to arrange admission interviews with three analysts who would not bring up his sexual orientation if he would not mention it either. If accepted for admission, he was not to speak openly about his homosexuality during the entire course of training, either in classes or in supervision. He was, however, free to discuss his sexuality in his non-reporting training analysis. He declined her offer and trained outside APsaA at NYU's Postdoctoral program where he was accepted as an openly gay man and co-organized a groundbreaking conference on homosexuality for that institute (Domenici and Lesser, 1995). Maggie Magee and Diana Miller (1997), have further documented their own experience with "don't ask, don't tell" policies at their Los Angeles institute during the 1980s.

As I was in my late 30s and "out" for more than a decade, I declined to participate in "don't ask, don't tell." I decided the White Institute, which had a decades-long reputation for quietly accepting openly gay candidates (Goldman, 1995), was my only New York option and I consulted with one of their training analysts before applying. I felt there was no sense in exposing myself to the admissions process before I knew what analysis would be like. I further needed reassurances that a heterosexual training analyst could be trusted to deal with my being gay in an open and safe way. Of course, the analyst would have to be heterosexual, since even at the White Institute, openly gay training analysts were rare as hen's teeth.

I found an analyst, Raul Ludmer, and our work together was enormously helpful. In fact, my experience with my two therapists sensitized me to how a patient's knowledge of the sexual orientation of a therapist can have an impact on treatment. In my first therapy, I needed someone I believed was like me (a gay psychiatrist) to learn how to accept myself. In my analysis, on the other hand, the work with someone who I thought was not like me provided me a way of accepting otherness and differences, both in others and in myself.

In 1987, a year into my analysis, I applied to the White Institute where I was interviewed by three training analysts. Two of them made no issue of my sexuality and both went out of their way to make me feel welcome; I later chose them as analytic supervisors. My third interview with the Institute's Director at the time was a different experience. He questioned me extensively about heterosexual experiences from years earlier, asking questions about my orgasms and those of my female partner. As for my life partner of 35 years—at the time we had been together for 6—he asked what was it he did for a living and when I tried to talk about the most important relationship of my life, he abruptly changed the subject.

At the end of the interview, sensing his discomfort, I asked how being gay would affect my application. He retorted disdainfully that I had asked "a false question." I told him I did not know what a false question was. He said I asked a false question because had I had been a heterosexual applicant, I would not automatically be accepted for admission. Recognizing psychoanalytic coyness when I heard it, I said it was not a false question as I was sure he was aware of other institutes that did not accept gay people. He testily responded, "It will neither help nor hurt you." Apparently not and I was accepted for training in the fall of 1988. However, I did not go into supervision with him.

At White, I found an Institute that idolized one of its founders, Harry Stack Sullivan. Sullivan was an openly gay man who lived with Jimmy Sullivan, a younger man he legally adopted and made his heir. Although his official biographer, Helen Swick Perry (1982), alludes to their intimate relationship, she never clearly defines it, unlike Blechner (2005) and Wake (2011) who do. Further obscuring matters, Perry repeats a rumor that Jimmy had been a young catatonic street urchin delivered into Sullivan's care by a friend, reflecting attitudes within the White Institute where being gay seemed more discomfiting than being psychotic (Drescher, 2017).

Yet to this day, I value my supervisors and teachers at White. Anna Antonowsky was my first supervisor. Having been denied access to more conservative institutes—wanting what one cannot have—I wanted exposure to a conservative approach to analysis. In the 3½ years we worked together, she provided a traditional, non-disclosing treatment approach with which I now respectfully disagree (Drescher, 2013). My next supervisor, the late John Fiscalini, taught an interpersonal self-psychological approach that showed how to help patients with low self-esteem. The late Marcia Rosen taught empathic listening. Amnon Isaacharoff, my third and perhaps one of my most influential supervisors, taught me how to use countertransference in listening to patients. My final supervisor was the late Steve Mitchell who supervised the case I would eventually present to become a training analyst and who, years later, wrote a blurb endorsing my first book (Drescher, 1998). I was also fortunate to attend classes taught by Phillip Bromberg, Don Stern, Jay Greenberg, Larry Epstein, and Nat Stockhamer—all of whom influenced my thinking, sometimes directly and other times unconsciously.

Post-analytic training

In 1989, a year into analytic training, I left a full time position on the psychiatric inpatient unit in Brooklyn for a part-time position in the outpatient department. This gave me the flexibility to see more analytic patients in Manhattan during the day as well as go to supervision. After completing training in 1992, my private practice had grown and I left Downstate in 1993 for full-time private practice.

One of the many positive changes resulting from my personal analysis was the emergence of my writing self. Although I had worked in a university center for the previous 9 years, I had done no academic writing. In 1992–1993, I wrote two analytically oriented papers. The first, "Psychotherapy, medication and belief" (Drescher, 1995b) reflected my ongoing interest in treating patients with combined medication and psychotherapy.

I submitted the second paper, "From preoedipal to postmodern: Changing psychoanalytic attitudes toward homosexuality" (Drescher, 1997) for White's Lawrence W. Kaufmann Award, a prize for a publishable paper written by a recent graduate. I won the award and the $1000 cash prize (now $500 according to the Institute's website: http://goo.gl/uDDQ4F). Yet in an unprecedented turn of events, the Institute would not publish the paper in its journal, *Contemporary Psychoanalysis*. One editor and former teacher called it "too political." Another editorial board member and former teacher agreed. It was no small irony that both had written interpersonal/relational papers considered "too political" by others at the time. After complaining to the Institute Director, I was told rather coyly, "We say the award is for a publishable paper, we don't say that we publish it." I told the Director that if that was the case, I expected the Institute to retract a recently published puff piece about me in its promotional newsletter, *The Record*. That profile created the false impression that the Institute was open to diversity. Later that day, I was informed the paper would be published but having had my fill of Institute coyness, I chose to publish it elsewhere (Drescher, 1997).

In retrospect, I believe my capacity to directly confront the Director's behavior grew out of my Bensonhurst upbringing where a general attitude of "don't take no bull***t from nobody" prevailed. It was also an example of what I began learning in my psychiatric residency: bullies in professional settings can only operate with impunity if the people they bully withdraw, hiding the facts out of a sense of shame or a sense that one bears the blame for being bullied.

In 1994, I met John Kerr, then an editor at *The Analytic Press*. He and publisher Paul Stepansky helped and encouraged me through the 4-year process of writing my book, *Psychoanalytic Therapy and the Gay Man* (1998). In 1997, I became the Editor of the *Journal of Gay and Lesbian Psychotherapy* (now renamed the *Journal of Gay and Lesbian Mental Health*), a then-moribund journal I shepherded through 10 volumes. The *Journal* is still going strong and is in its 21st volume.

I was appointed a Supervising Analyst at White in 1999 along with Mark Blechner. In 2001 we were both appointed Training Analysts. To my knowledge we are the only two openly gay Training Analysts in the New York City area. In 2006, I was invited by my colleague Ann D'Ercole to teach at the NYU Postdoctoral Program in Psychotherapy and Psychoanalysis where I am now an Adjunct Professor and Clinical Supervisor. At the time of this writing, I am in the process of being appointed a faculty member at the Columbia University Center for Psychoanalytic Training and Research.

Concluding reflections

My psychiatric and psychoanalytic training coincided with the most devastating years of the AIDS epidemic, a time before effective treatments became available. I lost my first close friend, a psychiatrist, in 1987, just as I was beginning my analysis. The three other gay men with whom I interned at St. Vincent's died between 1990 and 1992. There were too many deaths to count. Although my own health was okay, one important lesson I learned from losing so many people so young is that no one knows how much time they have left. Consequently, I have tried to live my personal and professional lives cognizant of that reality. These experiences sharpened my awareness of an unfortunate side effect of our field's veneration of its older members and their wisdom: a seniority system that all too often infantilizes and ignores contributions from younger colleagues, simply because they are younger.

Having become an openly gay psychoanalyst in a field that for many years denigrated or rendered gay people invisible, I faced several challenges. These included: (1) where and how to say what I needed to say, (2) whether I would have enough time to say what needed being said, and (3) whether anyone in the field's older generations would listen to what I had to say. Having survived into my 60s, I find I'm old enough so that older analysts now listen. If there are lessons to transmit to the next generation of analysts, they include follow your own instincts and find your own voice. While an older generation of psychoanalysts may not be listening to the important things you may have to say, there is a good chance that the next generation will pay attention.

References

Ashley, K. (2002). An interview with Stuart E. Nichols, Jr., MD. *Journal of Gay & Lesbian Psychotherapy*, 6(4), 55–71.

Bayer, R. (1981). *Homosexuality and American psychiatry: The politics of diagnosis.* New York, NY: Basic Books.

Bergmann, M., & Jucovy, M. (Eds.) (1982). *Generations of the Holocaust.* New York, NY: Basic Books.

Blechner, M. J. (2005). The gay Harry Stack Sullivan: Interactions between his life, clinical work and theory. *Contemporary Psychoanalysis*, 45(1), 1–19.

Domenici, T., & Lesser, R. C. (Eds.) (1995). *Disorienting sexuality: Psychoanalytic reappraisals of sexual identities.* New York, NY: Routledge.

Drescher, J. (1995a). Anti-homosexual bias in training. In T. Domenici & R. C. Lesser (Eds.), *Disorienting sexuality: Psychoanalytic reappraisals of sexual identities* (pp. 227–241). New York, NY: Routledge.

Drescher, J. (1995b). Psychotherapy, medication and belief. *Issues in Psychoanalytic Psychology*, 17(1), 7–28.

Drescher, J. (1996). A discussion across sexual orientation and gender boundaries: Reflections of a gay male analyst to a heterosexual female analyst. *Gender & Psychoanalysis*, 1(2), 223–237.

Drescher, J. (1997). From preoedipal to postmodern: Changing psychoanalytic attitudes toward homosexuality. *Gender & Psychoanalysis*, 2(2), 203–216.

Drescher, J. (1998). *Psychoanalytic therapy and the gay man.* New York, NY and London: Routledge.

Drescher, J. (2002). Don't ask, don't tell: A gay man's perspective on the psychoanalytic training experience between 1973 and 1991. *Journal of Gay & Lesbian Psychotherapy*, 6(1), 45–55.

Drescher, J. (2007). From bisexuality to intersexuality: Rethinking gender categories. *Contemporary Psychoanalysis*, 43(2), 204–228.

Drescher, J. (2008). A history of homosexuality and organized psychoanalysis. *Journal of American Academy of Psychoanalysis & Dynamic Psychiatry*, 36(3), 443–460.

Drescher, J. (2010). In memoriam: Bertram H. Schaffner, MD. *Journal of Gay & Lesbian Mental Health, 14*(3), 251–256.

Drescher, J. (2013). Ghosts in the consulting room: A discussion of Anson's "Ghosts in the Dressing Room." *Journal of Gay & Lesbian Mental Health, 17*(1), 112–120.

Drescher, J. (2017). Smoke gets in your eyes: Discussion of "When Harry met Jimmie." Psychoanalytic Perspectives, 14(1), 31–39.

Drescher, J., & Merlino, J. P. (Eds.) (2007). *American psychiatry and homosexuality: An oral history*. New York, NY: Routledge.

Ford, C. S., & Beach, F. A. (1951). *Patterns of sexual behavior*. New York, NY: Harper & Row.

Freud, S. (1953). Three essays on the theory of sexuality. In J. Strachey (Ed. & Trans.), *The standard edition of the complete works of Sigmund Freud* (Vol. 7, pp. 123–246). London: Hogarth Press. (Original work published 1905)

Freud, S. (1955). The psychogenesis of a case of homosexuality in a woman. In J. Strachey (Ed. & Trans.), *The standard edition of the complete works of Sigmund Freud* (Vol. 18, pp. 145–172). London: Hogarth Press. (Original work published 1920)

Freud, S. (1960). Anonymous (letter to an American mother). In E. Freud (Ed.), *The letters of Sigmund Freud* (pp. 423–424). New York, NY: Basic Books. (Original work published 1935)

Gadpaille, W. (1989). Homosexuality. In H. Kaplan & B. J. Sadock (Eds.), *Comprehensive textbook of psychiatry, fifth edition* (pp. 1086–1096). Baltimore, MD: Williams & Wilkins.

Goldman, S. (1995). The difficulty of being a gay psychoanalyst during the last fifty years: An interview with Dr. Bertram Schaffner. In T. Domenici & R. C. Lesser (Eds.), *Disorienting sexuality: Psychoanalytic reappraisals of sexual identities* (pp. 243–254). New York, NY: Routledge.

Hirschfeld, M. (2000). *The Homosexuality of men and women* (M. Lombardi-Nash, Trans.). Buffalo, NY: Prometheus Books. (Original work published 1914)

Hooker, E. A. (1957). The adjustment of the male overt homosexual. *Journal of Projective Techniques, 21*, 18–31.

Katz, G. A. (1983). The noninterpretation of metaphors in psychiatric hospital groups. *International Journal of Group Psychotherapy, 33*(1), 53–67.

Kinsey, A. C., Pomeroy, W. B., & Martin C. E. (1948). *Sexual behavior in the human male*. Philadelphiam, PA: W. B. Saunders.

Kinsey, A. C., Pomeroy, W. B., Martin, C. E., & Gebhard, P. (1953). *Sexual behavior in the human female*. Philadelphia, PA: Saunders.

Krafft-Ebing, R. von (1965). *Psychopathia sexualis* (H. Wedeck, Trans.). New York, NY: Putnam. (Original work published 1886)

Kuriloff, E. A. (2014). *Contemporary psychoanalysis and the legacy of the Third Reich: History, memory, tradition*. New York, NY and London: Routledge.

Lewes, K. (1988). *The psychoanalytic theory of male homosexuality*. New York, NY: Simon & Schuster.

Magee, M., & Miller, D. (1997). *Lesbian lives: Psychoanalytic narratives old and new*. New York, NY: Routledge.

Perry, H. S. (1982). *Psychiatrist of America: The life of Harry Stack Sullivan*. Cambridge, MA: Harvard Press.

Rado, S. (1940). A critical examination of the concept of bisexuality. *Psychosomatic Medicine, 2*, 459–467.

Roughton, R. (1995). Overcoming antihomosexual bias: A progress report. *The American Psychoanalyst*, *29*(4), 15–16.

Spitzer, R. L. (1981). The diagnostic status of homosexuality in *DSM-III*: A reformulation of the issues. *American Journal of Psychiatry*, *138*(2), 210–215.

Ulrichs, K. (1994). *The riddle of "man-manly" love* (M. Lombardi-Nash, Trans.). Buffalo, NY: Prometheus Books. (Original work published 1864)

Wake, N. (2011). *Private practices: Harry Stack Sullivan, the science of homosexuality, and American liberalism*. New Brunswick, NJ: Rutgers University Press.

Zachar, P., & Kendler, K. S. (2012). The removal of Pluto from the class of planets and homosexuality from the class of psychiatric disorders: A comparison. *Philosophy, Ethics, & Humanities in Medicine*, *7*, 4–10.

Chapter 8

Hiding in plain sight

Linda Hillman

Up river

Freud lured me in. Having spurned the largely experimental psychology course offerings as an undergraduate at Brandeis, I chose to immerse myself in literature, poetry, and creative writing as an English major. In my last year in college, I entered a small seminar on literature and psychoanalysis taught by the Dean of the College, Richard Onorato.

What is a transformative moment? While we can't predict such a moment, we recognize it when it's happening, just as we recognize a good psychoanalytic session when it is happening. Something feels both enlivening and unsettling, as if recognition and shifting are happening at the same time. You start to realize how many threads were leading to this moment without your having had the slightest conscious clue. All of that contributes to the sense of inevitability you have as it is happening.

Onorato was one of those exceptional teachers who affirmed me but didn't hesitate to seriously challenge my writing and thinking, pushing me to think critically and work harder than I was used to working. Some of my former mentors were glowing with their praise as long as I echoed their voices—and I was an expert mimic.

I considered the paper that I wrote for the Onorato seminar as the first that was *in my own voice*. For his course in literature and psychoanalysis, I chose Joseph Conrad's *Heart of Darkness* and started my journey up the Congo River and into Kurtz's and my hidden world—the world of the unconscious and the savagery/cruelty within us. The plot, character, and structure of the novel lent itself to psychoanalytic interpretation and the journey into psychoanalytic thought hooked me. In those days psychoanalytic literary criticism (Holland, 1968) was based on an exacting and literal reading of Freudian theory making it overly technical and reductionist. Despite this, reading Freud was like finding a new language, one that resonated more deeply than my native tongue. With the idea of the unconscious, the world fell into place—like the colors in the Rubik's Cube lining up. At the same time, the idea stirred me, creating what Martha Graham has called "a blessed unrest" (De Mille, 1991). I fell in love with these ideas though it would take years to understand and find my way to psychoanalysis and even more years to create my own vision, place, and voice in the field, a process still very much underway.

Career choices

All of us are so young when we are expected to choose our direction in life. Adolescents prone to rebelliousness, idealizations, splitting, and binary thinking, we create dichotomies that soon prove to be, if not false, overly simplistic like *follow your passion but be practical and make a living, greed vs. service to others, big life vs. small life.*

I had planned—as much as one can plan in college—to become an English teacher (*practical*) who would write (*passion*) or at least brood (*neurotic*) with romantic longings to write creatively. But I came to realize somewhere along the way that despite these plans, I was already changing lanes, moving towards psychology, and with hindsight, into the process of becoming a psychoanalyst. There have been times in my life—long periods of time—when I have looked back and viewed both the choices of "English teacher" and "psychologist/psychoanalyst" as failures of courage. What I considered a bolder choice, becoming a writer, would have been a more perilous path that felt too daunting to my unformed adolescent self.

Other times I have viewed the decision to become a therapist as a way for me to work myself into a substantial and long-term therapy with hopes of curing the anxiety and inhibitions that so limited my life. Just as often, I have seen it as the natural outgrowth of the role I played in my family. I spent much of my childhood trying to regulate my mother's unhappiness, trying to stabilize my parents' failing marriage and to minimize its impact on my younger brother and myself.

Reflecting on my own storyline, I recognize how we love creating narratives, and of course, they are all true at any moment in time. We are constantly creating self-narratives that change over time. They each have some piece of the truth in them, but are missing other often-unconscious pieces. They can be like multiple self-states in which we are severed from parts of ourselves or they can take on a more integrated shape involving increasing awareness.

As I get older, I view the decision to pursue psychology as many life threads coming together. What I couldn't see then was a longing, a desire embedded in the choice as well. Yes, I wanted to understand human development and conflict—especially the hidden parts, just what had steered me to literature. But I was in a passionate or perhaps desperate search to feel at ease in taking up space in the world. There was a longing as well as a fear of being seen and a desire for love and intimacy. That search was intellectual, theoretical, but most of all deeply personal.

Imaginative play and a masters degree

My friends were my lifeline in early childhood, and imaginative play filled all our free time. The storyline of three sisters who were all princesses, all named some version of Aurora (powerful and never ignored) turned my spacious backyard into a perpetual kingdom. A large rock at the periphery of our school field was our palace, our transitional space (Winnicott, 1975), and our antidote to the mundaneness of everyday reality. Later, we played school and house and rehearsed for life as teachers and mothers using dolls and little brothers as props. Children of the 1950s, we were under the full sway of gender stereotypes. And while I never pretended to be an astronaut, I did run in all school elections including for school president at a time when there were few female candidates. In fourth grade, I gained momentary infamy by organizing an all-day filibuster in response to a teacher's excessive punishment of our class.

The imaginative play turned to writing plays and performing them for our families and still later in my 20s to a job facilitating roleplaying (psychodrama, though I would not have called it that then) with young children at the Children's Aid Society on the lower east side.

Right after college, I wanted to make my way into the field of psychology and in hindsight, the path I chose linked together several childhood passions. I entered the Teachers College, Columbia University masters program in Educational and Developmental Psychology. Teaching, educational policy and thinking about how learning happens was already of deep interest to me, and that interest has threaded itself through my adult life through a long volunteer career culminating with serving on and becoming President of the Board of Education in the town where we raised our children.

On entering Teacher's College, I learned that one of my professors was the inspirational Brian Sutton-Smith, a New Zealander who spent his career and life exploring the meanings of "play." Sutton-Smith extended the definition of play to include adult play including games (sports, gambling) as well as play through the arts. According to Sutton-Smith, play contained "an excitement within a person's own spontaneity" (2008, p. 95). He wrote that play "makes it possible to live more fully in the world" (p. 95). His work encompassed the role of surprise (creating empathy and flexibility), the role of teasing (play aimed at helping parents socialize children), the roots of play in folklore, and the cultural context of play. Through play children learn about ordinary social objectivity as well as personal subjective intentions; the differences and the importance of both. The kingdoms of my childhood took on meanings and purposes I had never considered—and my interest in "play" deepened.

Training

I chose to do a doctorate in clinical psychology and went through hoops to get myself the opportunity to pursue it. But the minute I got there, I felt that

I needed to argue with everyone and constantly remain skeptical. Although I attended City University Graduate Program in Clinical Psychology, one of the few psychoanalytically oriented training programs (much fewer now), I bristled in reaction to what seemed to me to be an overly simplified and pathologizing way of talking about people. Case presentations seemed artificial and reductionistic. Human development seemed infinitely more complex than any one theory or explanation. The revolutionary writings of Freud that had exploded my world in college later became a prison of theories cast in orthodoxy, a lesson in how social context and time could change a narrative so completely. I was busy defining myself against the norms, yet I loved the work and I knew that I would have to find my own integration of ideas and practice.

After graduate school and several years of working in an in-patient hospital setting with psychotic patients and maintaining a private practice on the side, I began NYU Postdoc, a psychoanalytic training program that allowed a great deal of freedom and individual choice. The course options, flexibility in scheduling as well as less centralized authority were aspects of the program that suited me very well. When we begin training as psychoanalysts, we borrow from whatever model we can. Like a driver in training, I grasped at rules and tried to copy role models. My responses were sometimes stock and inhibited, a repertoire I put together from my readings, classes and supervisors. Like with my earlier mentors, I swallowed my identifications and theory whole. Too often, I wound up basing my comments/interpretations about patients more on theory than on what was going on in the session, becoming a caricature of an analyst. Many years would pass before I was working in a more authentic and relaxed manner, really listening, and knowing the structure and frame viscerally.

By the time I finished psychoanalytic training I felt removed from the academic, professional aspects of the field. Psychoanalytic theory held less and less intellectual interest for me. I bristled when I read case studies that presented linear, overly simplified explanations for behavior, often in what seemed to me like a pejorative tone, objectifying the patient. My distaste for the rigidity or what felt like an assumed moral superiority of the ego psychologists of the day presented a dilemma for my integrating theory and practice. I dealt with that tension by keeping the two separate, holding them apart in my mind for a long time. I never had that feeling of disaffection about my practice. Holding the theoretical orthodoxy at some distance allowed my clinical practice to thrive and feel increasingly more alive and creative. I was able to experience and preserve those things I loved about the practice of psychoanalysis.

Some of this frustration with the profession had to do with the rigid and narrow "classical" approach to psychoanalysis that was the state of the art when I was in training in the 1980s. If I were in training now, with the way psychoanalysis is exploding with wide-ranging and creative re-imaginings, I suspect I would have had a different experience. Nowadays, I feel an organic flow between what I read and what I do clinically. Of course, I am drawn to read about those things that already pique my interest and focus on theories that feel enlivening to me.

Separate from my struggle with the theory of the time, I was also young, insecure and not as able to take in the positive as I might have been. In retrospect, I had some remarkable formative experiences with teachers, classes, and peers. Classical training in the Freudian Track at NYU grounded me in a very deep way, but left me struggling to turn down the volume on some powerful voices from the past, as I tried to integrate new ideas and points of view with my own evolving perceptions and beliefs.

It is inevitable that we attribute power and influence to our teachers and mentors even at an institute that is flexible and allows multiple perspectives. Because they do understandably exercise so much power over our young minds, our institutes need to pay more attention to the development of the person who is the analyst and provide a safe environment for personal and professional development, while fostering the accumulation of knowledge and technique.

Poetry, listening, and voice

College again. As a freshman I wrote a paper on the poet George Herbert for my 17th-century religious poetry teacher, Allan Grossman, a brilliant poet and scholar.

In his class, I would sit quietly cowering in the back of a tiered lecture hall, hiding in plain sight. Suddenly, he bellowed out my name. He had a loud and distinctive voice, a combination of irreverent affectation, a poet's enunciation, and god—I can still hear him roaring my name. He then read my paper on Herbert to the class. I had written that paper in his voice, imitating his thinking, and perhaps that is why he liked me. Flattered, I followed him around like a shadow for 3 years, through remarkable literature courses and a small hand-picked seminar on Milton. He was deeply disappointed in my choice to pursue psychology when I graduated and insisted I write him a 10-page letter about why I was making that choice. I sent him a 20-page letter, and he responded with a note that said "No. That's not it."

I never spoke with him after that. Recently, some 40 years later, after I published my first collection of poetry, I wanted to send it to him with a note of thanks for his being able to imagine me as a writer well before I could, but before I could write the note, I saw his obituary in the *New York Times*.

I believe that reading and writing poetry have been the most formative influence on the development of my psychoanalytic voice, or simply, my voice. Along with imaginary play and writing plays, I wrote poetry as a child. I stopped for many years and picked it up seriously after the birth of my children. I was fortunate to have the time and space to immerse myself in writing while maintaining a small practice and raising my children. The pulls and stresses of my late adolescence and early adulthood (normal stresses as well as a shattering of my family) had led to a dampening of my creative longings and an inability to envision a future. I couldn't imagine and dream my future the way I did as a child when I drew multiple versions of my ideal house (and family) daily. It took connecting to others; a smart, creative, and deeply generous-of-spirit husband and exceptional friends who created enough of a holding environment for me to reconnect with my creativity. Perhaps also, the arrival of my children (the ultimate creative act) released me or at least gave me permission to pursue this journey.

Poetry is the place where language comes closest to expressing the truth. Unlike linear thought or expository writing, poetry can contain contradictions and multiple truths at once. It can be clear and unclear at the same time. It can know and not know in the same moment.

Only in poetry can you combine the physical, emotional, and intellectual in an image or metaphor, in a few words. We react to the immediacy of very specific imagery and the surprise of metaphor. When a poem works, it feels alive and makes us feel alive, the same feeling I look for in every conversation with each particular patient, the feeling that emerges in transformative moments during psychoanalytic sessions (or pieces of sessions).

In my sessions with my patients, I find that I pay particular attention to the flow, the rhythm, the stops, the gaps, the inconsistencies, the tone, the metaphors, the images. These are my compass, marking my way to the unformulated, the unconscious, the dissociated states.

But it is not just my patient's voice that I am listening to. I am listening to my voice, its pitch, its stumbling, its strain, its strangeness. When my voice is fluid, authentic, and familiar, I am less likely to notice it. When my voice is off or feels like somebody else's, I use the discomfort of that condition to make my way to the enactment, countertransference, or whatever we decide to name it and begin to make sense of what has happened in the session, to come closer to an emotional truth. I attend to what I am not saying, my daydreaming, my reveries.

I listen for the flow of the session between the two of us, its smoothness, its lapses, its disjointedness. Does it spiral, circle, zigzag, or circumvent?

The process of writing poetry feels very similar to the process of doing psychoanalysis. Poetry and psychoanalysis have both taught me how to listen, a skill that takes experience and practice. And listening deliberatively has made me a better analyst as well as poet. Of course, most sessions aren't transformative and most poems do not emerge whole and complete, and we often slog through (resistance, defense, dissociation, avoidance, repetition) looking for a way into what is not known and refuses to be known. In poetry, we call it writer's block. We are stuck and the process of unsticking is a complex one. But I feel most engaged when immersed in the process, both in psychoanalysis and in writing.

As a poet and a psychoanalyst, you need a tolerance for frustration, but mostly, for not knowing and being stuck for long periods of time, and at the same time you have to trust that you will land, at least temporarily. While engaged with both poetry and analysis, I would tell myself, *I am working on it in my head*. A good deal of the time that doesn't mean I am thinking directly about either the poem or the session. Yet it is with me, on my mind in some way. I let the unconscious to do its work. Often enough, an insight or idea pops up when I am least expecting it, seemingly out of nowhere. Now, trusting more in the creative process, I no longer need this ordinary phrase to quiet my demanding superego and allow me space for play, dreaming, reverie and unconscious processes.

Port in a storm

Google recently completed a 3-year, multi-million dollar study, Project Aristotle, to determine what makes some workplace teams successful and others not (Duhigg, 2016). They came to the very obvious conclusion that a feeling of psychological safety contributes to effective teamwork. My safety zone as a psychoanalyst was another seemingly accidental event, the formation of a study group in the 1980s with two peers, Eleanor Esposito and Steve Solow. It says it all that 30 years later, we still meet once a week for peer supervision. Maybe it helped that we all were immersed in the arts as well as psychoanalysis; Ellie in painting, Steve in music, and me in poetry, and we were able to share deeply on this level as well. But we developed a level of trust and intimacy rare in this field. We feel comfortable and even eager to share our so-called failures, our mistakes, our fears, our countertransferences, and enactments. The depth we can explore without fear of judgment, the respect with which we regard each other's work and thinking and the richness of our differences make this group the ideal learning environment, and I feel I owe most of my development as an analyst to the sharing that took place week in and week out in this group. We have changed and we have stayed the same. We have evolved in our respective voices and our beliefs, and we have weathered storms and losses together. Indebtedness and gratitude do not do justice to what I feel towards Ellie and Steve.

Google's description of psychological safety is what we aim to provide for our patients and in such an emotionally demanding profession, it is what we need in order to take personal or professional risks and develop our voice as analysts. Too often, our professional training spaces are rife with judgment and prohibitions and we are left to find these safe spaces on our own.

Parents, teachers, and mentors

My parents were children of Russian immigrants fleeing religious persecution who arrived here shortly after the turn of the century. They grew up in families desperate for survival, struggling with poverty, extreme dislocation, the Depression, and illnesses. They experienced early losses of their own parents including a suicide. My responses to my parents' traumatized selves were to suppress my own longings, fears, and especially anger to become the good girl, the girl hiding in plain sight. My goals, while I was not aware of them, were to regulate my mother's depression, my father's self-preoccupation and absence, and their progressively imploding marriage. "Bounded in a nutshell" (Shakespeare, 1997, p. 1696), I was reluctant to ask anyone for anything if at all possible, not a really effective method for learning and growth.

Growing up, I didn't feel that I "fit" in my family. Being someone who was so focused on the inner world, creative writing and culture made me different from my family members whose strengths and interests varied but included business, statistics, and real estate; more the world of money, mathematics, and the material. The role that fit my strengths and allowed me to be more connected was one of family therapist, sensing what everyone was feeling but couldn't express. But I also felt different (other) and wished that I was part of another family with members who were more like me and more likely to recognize and affirm me.

Despite my conscious disconnection from my family that increased as I approached adolescence, I now see ever more complexity in those relationships. My mother's considerable intelligence, her political, financial, and even visual artistic interests never stood a chance of expression given the intergenerational transmission of trauma and her paralyzing fears (her own mother afraid to leave the house) as well as the social constraints on women of her generation. My father loved the world of the mind and stopped just short of getting his PhD in economics. He was an idea person who wound up creating a group called "The Strategy Workshop" within a large advertising company in the 1960s when this was a radical move. He shared with me the ideas of futurists Marshall McLuhan and Buckminster Fuller. I always admired and appreciated his enterprising, creative spirit and leadership qualities. I like to believe that I identified with those parts of him that created collaborative groups and communities based on his passions. It partly accounts for something that has and continues to feel central to my adult life—creating, often with others, meaningful projects and organizations in my various communities like a Young Writers Workshop for children, a survey and advocacy project calling into question the "travel sports" culture for increasingly younger and younger children, and more recently, a Community Support Council focused on mental health issues and facilitating recovery in crises (from suicides, to societal violence to debilitating storms) in the community in which I live.

By the time I entered analytic training, I was a little more trusting, but still reticent to connect with mentors or supervisors. My analytic training case turned out to be with a very troubled young woman whose idealized father (the only one in the family she claimed to care about) had just died at a young age. We used to call someone like my patient a borderline and maybe now would see her as traumatized with poor affect regulation. This was not your classic neurotic training case, and she spent most of those years in treatment cursing at me, honing insults that hit too close to home as well as abusing herself in multiple ways. My supervisors tried to be helpful, but in retrospect, we were applying inadequate models of both diagnosis and treatment until I got to supervision with Marv Hurvich who understood my patient's profound annihilation anxiety and was comfortable with my hatred even though I was not.

A few years later in the early 1990s, I wound up in a supervision group with Larry Epstein. His paper, "The Therapeutic Function of Hate in the Countertransference" (1977) informed his supervision and turned out to be the perfect antidote to my good girl/ hiding style. Could I tolerate my own hateful feelings towards patients—the Kurtz inside of me—as well as theirs towards me?

Therapy: third time the charm

I left home for college in the fall of 1968. I graduated three years later, using my high school AP credits because I was eager to move on. But the three years stand out in saturated colors. Leaving home for the first time was an uneasy transition. I had from early childhood a deep shyness that made entering the dining hall on my own and finding a place to sit an extremely anxious proposition. But beyond the ordinary transition, these years were marked by some dramatic and traumatic developments. Leaving home was more difficult given the state of my parents' marriage, and it was during these three years that my father left my mother for the first time. He returned and left again several times before he left for good a few years after I finished college.

Also at play was a major cultural upheaval, which had begun my senior year in HS with the deaths of Martin Luther King and then Robert Kennedy. The seismic shifts of the late 1960s permeated my years at Brandeis, from student strikes to sit-ins to demonstrations. Normal college life was disrupted in wonderful and horrible ways. The assumptions I had grown up with— what and whom to trust and what was true—were being blown apart, which I loved, but I couldn't get through a semester without classes being disrupted, which I hated.

I challenged my parents, who were paying for my college education, about the shady connections of the Coca Cola Company, my father's major client, to the White Citizens' Council. My parents were beside themselves with my increasing radicalization but were at a loss to understand this social upheaval. In their confusion they reverted to the familiar—the Cold War and the Joe McCarthy Communist infiltration explanation. We students were being manipulated by the Soviet Union. For many of us, the normal separations of young adulthood and the coming of age took on more expansive proportions in the late 1960s as the cultural and political ground shifted beneath us.

Finally, a dramatic break-up of my first relationship, with its Romeo and Juliet themes concerning religious differences and family disapproval, put me over the edge. Desperate for grounding, I found my way to the university counseling center and my first therapist. I had already met one psychoanalyst, the father of the boy I had just broken up with who became an idealized object, a thread or stored object for my journey to becoming a psychoanalyst. Because of him, I already knew that it was possible to be really listened to by an adult. Nonetheless I was challenging this less-than-idealized new therapist in every way imaginable and like a jujitsu master, he took my blows and redirected them where they belonged, always recognizing and affirming my observations and feelings, holding me in his mind. Whether it was true or not, I felt he secretly knew I was on a path to becoming a psychologist and was teaching and guiding me as much as helping me regain my footing —which he did with grace and compassion.

My second therapy (which became analysis) began just before I started my PhD program and lasted over 20 years. I had gotten a list of names of therapists for my mother who was desperately struggling during the divorce proceedings. I wound up using one of the names on the list for myself—a perfect reversal of past dynamics. When I was a child and my mother and I shopped for my clothes, all I could think about was finding clothes for her, not for myself. This analysis was nurturing and emotionally corrective, and that support allowed me to get through the traumatic upheaval of my parents' divorce and actually move on with my life professionally, get married and create a family, despite pulls to stay connected to and identified with my bereft mother. I will always be grateful for that analysis, despite some very great limitations to the treatment and a disturbing ending as my analyst's health deteriorated.

However, it was when I began my third treatment (second analysis) in my late 50s that I was finally secure enough to face the unknowable and unacceptable thoughts and feelings and let go of some of my less than effective workarounds. My third analyst is relentless, gently dogged about not letting me masterfully (after many years of practice) weave and sidestep as if between linebackers. When I got to her office, I felt I had once again landed in the right spot, even a familiar spot. Here was someone who was interested in knowing the parts of myself I was terrified to know. Many of those parts are about aggression and maybe that's why I am using football metaphors. I was clearly more ready and able to work, but I was lucky to find in my analyst a wise, experienced, but fierce soul who loves art and literature and can hear my voice through my poetry as well my prose.

Parenting

There is this. Nothing has been more healing and transformative for me as a person and psychoanalyst than raising my children—from their early all-consuming needs to the jagged process of separation and the development of autonomy to tolerating the loss as they leave home as young adults. Nothing has been more emotionally challenging with a learning curve as steep and potentially dangerous as Everest. And how often do I have to laugh at my early commonplace and strident belief "I will be nothing like my own parents"?

I hit a wall on more than one occasion (still do on the newer challenges of letting go), meaning I reverted to a more critical, narcissistic stance—all too familiar from my own upbringing. They were times when my dreams for them did not coincide with their dreams for themselves or when my expectations were dashed—and hence, my moments of genuine failure of empathy for which I have great regret, a good understanding but only moderate self-forgiveness.

From this particular vantage point in time, I can see that their dreams are laced with aspects of my own unacknowledged longings and themes from my life and my husband's that they have incorporated. My son channels the boundless curiosity, creativity as well as the passion for problem solving and business of his father and my father, his grandfather. Family is feeling more like a symphony—movements, themes, and instruments interrelated—than four characters in search of an author.

At a young age my daughter, curious and perhaps jealous of who I was with when I was not with her, asked me about my patients as I was tucking her into bed. So I made up bedtime stories, embellished bits and pieces of my day so she would feel included. Less interested in the reality of it all, she jumped in and together we created Petunia and Peter as well as other characters and their elaborate life dilemmas—building stories together, co-creating narratives.

Now with a courage and determination that stops me in my tracks, she is telling stories as a theater director with her own company—jointly devising plays with the intent to challenge her audiences, to inspire them to think and feel something new, something potentially uncomfortable. Her plays are rooted in history, politics, and social issues with one of them focusing squarely on the period that coincided with the drama of my coming of age—the social and political upheaval of the late 1960s.

Fierce souls and love

A few years ago, I took a week-long summer writing seminar with the poet, Mary Ruefle. I have been in many poetry workshops and seminars over the years, but this one stood out. I was agonizing about the ending of a particular poem and said to her, "I know we can't use the word 'love.'" The tirade that followed from her about false prohibitions, about over intellectualization and the overvaluing of obscurity by those in the "poetry establishment" and about the ridiculousness of not using "love" in poems, shook us all up. But, to be fair, almost everything she said and did in this seminar shook us up. It was the first time I had encountered anything close to the power of the Alan Grossman voice. During that same week, I was presenting a series of poems I had written on "long marriage" and was a little uncomfortable since the vast majority of the students in the room were in their 20s, and I worried they would see these poems as too ambivalent or disenchanted. Mary opened the discussion of these poems entitling them "love poems," which knocked me over. She went on to tell her students that these are what real love poems are, this is what real love is like, not that idealized stuff of youth. In one short statement she affirmed real and long love, over time in all its complexity, its foibles, its delights, its disappointment and constant renewal. Here's the ending of one of those poems, possibly about the "marital third." It is entitled "Marriage."

> We are shrinking, but the thing
> that lives between us swells, extends
> tentacles which sometimes
> cradle us, sometimes flail about
> like the arms of a desperate survivor,
> stranded, at the scene of a crash.
>
> I half expect it to lend a helping hand,
> bring in the groceries, catch me
> if I stumble on the stoop—
> you know how I am prone
> to step off into midair.
> (Hillman Chayes, 2014)

I have let those close to me get closer as I have to them. I have painfully and painstakingly learned how to love without cutting myself off from hate. I have softened some pretty rigid boundaries that I always believed protected me but also left me lonely. My analytic self is intimately entwined with my personal self. In my work, my capacity for real empathy has grown, and my desire to protect myself has lessened. I feel much more present, authentic, and engaged with my patients, and with their transferences. The work on myself is far from over, but feels more integrated into my day-to day-life.

Freedom and constraint

Just as writing is a way of formulating what I am thinking, teaching and supervising also helps me discover and articulate what I think and believe about doing psychoanalysis. I have loved supervising doctoral level beginning therapists these 30 or so years; each one presenting unique challenges. They all enter the treatment room as therapists with uncertainty and insecurity.

They enter with different amounts of knowledge and experience. They enter with different personalities, with their own innate strengths and interests, and it is clear as the work evolves whose worldview is compatible with psychoanalysis and whose idiom takes them in other directions.

Many of the students I have supervised rush into the treatment room wanting to help, cure, or fix their patient. They are overly supportive and overly involved. Full of enthusiasm, spontaneity, and a wish to be proactive, they struggle to just sit with or tolerate the pain of another. I encourage them to be inquisitive, curious, hold back, listen, tolerate negative feelings, and let the transference evolve. Others start with the yoke of a version of classical psychoanalysis on their shoulders alongside their own fears that manifests as setting strict boundaries, withholding, and reluctance to show warmth or support. With these students I want to facilitate their being comfortable in their own skins, to depend less on imagined rules and to get them to acknowledge the ways the patient makes them feel, and again, to tolerate the transference.

I recognize them through all their disguises because I wore those disguises too. My early proclivity for boundaries and hiding made the "Freudian model" ideal for me as a young clinician because I could remain relatively anonymous and narcissistically safe in the treatment room. We all walk our own tightrope of constraint and freedom, inhibition and spontaneity, emotional support and insight—and the understanding of the impact of any extreme on the transference. There is no perfect map to becoming a psychoanalyst. Whether we identify with Freudian theory, relational theory, self psychology, or interpersonal theory—even when we carry these multiple models in our mind, we have to understand the implications of what we do and say, the unintended consequences. We just get more and more adept at balance.

Now that my goal is to allow love and hate to flourish in both the patient and myself, I walk the thin line between too much distance and silence and too much presence or involvement. I rely on my feeling state and reverie to check in with myself and explore that space between my own unconscious and that of my patient, our "unconscious intersubjective construction" (Odgen, 1997, p. 719) At the times I am feeling tortured, non-existent or unable to think, I turn to trusted colleagues for help. My patients and I unearth ghosts and muddle our way through the unacceptable, the forgotten and the unknowable. I point to contradictions and discrepancies, we reformulate narratives, I hold them in my mind as well as holding a vision of who they might be when they are free to be themselves. I learn and grow from each of them, for which I am grateful everyday.

I am at home in the relational model and yet deeply grounded and in my early Freudian training. I am never sure where to place myself in the psychoanalytic kingdom (I am thinking about the elaborate three-dimensional model that opens *Game of Thrones* with different schools of psychoanalysis standing in for different powerful families/kingdoms/edifices). I hover somewhere between Contemporary Freudian and Relational, holding models of the unconscious and inter-subjectivity in my mind at the same time, weaving in and out of metaphors. The latest work on trauma has deeply influenced my thinking with its concepts of witnessing, ghosts, and the unconscious transmission of trauma. It has expanded my thinking to include previous generations, the influence of groups and culture, and enlarged my repertoire of metaphors. Sometimes I am working to uncover, other times to integrate split off selves. Sometimes I am co-creating an increasingly complex and authentic narrative, other times living in the space we have created with the immediacy of love, hate, or loss—whatever seems most compelling in that moment. And of course, there is that word "love" again—"analytic love," which is its own blend of listening, recognition, sharing, restraint, and giving—very much alive in all its permutations in every one of my psychoanalytic relationships.

Ending

> Was I sleeping while the others suffered? Am I sleeping now? Tomorrow when I wake or think I do, what will I say of today?
> —Samuel Beckett (1954 [and my HS yearbook quote])[1]

My choice of yearbook quote tells me that in High School I was already thinking about memory and consciousness—how it is constantly changing and how each time it reconfigures, you finally feel awake. This narrative is also just a moment on a non-linear journey of awareness. At this particular place and time, even with hindsight, I have only these anecdotes and stories. And this.

Earlier I referred to Martha Graham's "blessed unrest." Here is how her exchange with Agnes De Mille begins:

> There is a vitality, a life-force, a quickening that is translated through you in to action and because there is only one of you in all of time, this expression is unique ... It is not your business to determine how good it is nor how valuable nor how it compares with other expressions. It is your business to keep it yours clearly and directly, to keep the channel open ... You have to keep open and aware directly to the urges that motivate you."
> (De Mille, 1991, p. 264)

Did I want to become a psychoanalyst because I wanted to have a deeper understanding about life and love? Did I choose this path to help heal my patients, my parents, or myself? All I really know is that I wake up every morning, choose this work, journey with my patients everyday because it is both enlivening and disturbing. Because I can't imagine not doing it. Because engaging with my patients so that they have a chance at their own vitality, life force, and quickening is exactly where I want to be.

Note

1 Excerpts from *Waiting for Godot* copyright © 1954 by Grove Press, Inc. Copyright renewed 1982 by Samuel Beckett. Used by permission of Grove/Atlantic, Inc. Any third party use of this material, outside of this publication, is prohibited. Also reprinted by permission of Faber & Faber, Ltd.

References

Beckett, S. (1954). *Waiting for Godot*. New York, NY: Grove Press.
Conrad, J. (1990). *Heart of darkness*. New York, NY: Dover.
De Mille, A. (1991). *Martha: The life and works of Martha Graham—A biography*. London: Hutchinson.
Duhigg, C. (2016). Group study. The New York Times Magazine. February 28, 20–26, 72–75.
Epstein, L. (1977). The therapeutic function of hate in the countertransference. *Contemporary Psychoanalysis, 13*, 442–460.
Hillman Chayes, L. (2014). *The lapse*. Georgetown, CT: Finishing Line Press.
Holland, N. (1968). *The dynamics of literary response*. New York, NY: Oxford University Press.
Ogden, T. (1997). Reverie and metaphor: Some thoughts on how I work as a psychoanalyst. *International Journal of Psychoanalysis, 78*, 719–732.
Shakespeare, W. (1997). *The Norton Shakespeare*. New York, NY: W.W. Norton & Company.
Sutton Smith, B. (2008). Play theory: A personal journey and new thoughts. American Journal of Play, 1(1), 80–123.
Winnicott, D. (1975). *Through pediatrics to psychoanalysis: Collected papers*. New York, NY: Basic Books.

Chapter 9

Curiosity didn't kill the cat
(or how I became a psychoanalyst)

Carolyn Ellman

My earliest memories are of being a very curious child. I seemed especially to want to know things that I wasn't supposed to know, such as searching all the drawers to find out what my parents were up to. I found all kinds of things I shouldn't have (but this was way before there was an internet). I also searched out books all the time from the library (five or six a week by the time I was 8 years old) and was drawn to trying to know about other people's experiences that didn't seem to be like mine (homosexual love, slavery, people in far off lands. As a child, I was particularly intrigued with Brazil and the big Christ figure on the hill). I longed to see the rest of the world and started saving at an early age to go to Europe (never realizing, until I was writing this, that my curiosity about the world probably had to do with the unspoken life my mother had left behind in 1917 when she was forced to leave during the Russian Revolution). The 4 years it took her to get to this country she buried somewhere so that I was never given access to in her memories and thoughts. My mother's experiences left me with a void that had a profound effect as I tried unconsciously for my whole life to understand other people's pain and suffering.

For example, I was also obsessed with the Brooklyn Dodgers and particularly any of the Dodgers, who were going through a slump. I was there when Jackie Robinson came to play in 1947, this always felt like one of the greatest and most moving moments of my life. I was very drawn to people who had to struggle to survive, and when any player had a slump I would write and tell them to keep up his spirits because I knew this would pass. When Ralph Branca threw that famous pitch to Bobby Thompson (1951) and the Dodgers lost, I cried my heart out, but then I stood outside the church where Branca was getting married because I was afraid everyone hated him and no one would come to his wedding. When I saw a lot of people there, I left. A number of players including Jackie Robinson later wrote to thank me for being a fan through thick and thin.

The need to make sure everyone was okay seemed to go underground in high school, when the only thing that was important was getting scholarships to college, but finding out why people did what they did was an obsession. I was particularly curious why people were religious since I couldn't find any of that in myself even if I identified with being Jewish. Later, in college I couldn't decide whether to major in biology, psychology, or philosophy. I knew I was searching for the most meaningful answer to the riddles of life. At this point, I was very far away from any thoughts about psychoanalysis or working with people. I was on the pursuit for a field that would encompass the most facts about human experience. Biology seemed incredible in the way one system seemed to interact with every other system. Philosophy was my other favorite subject since I was in awe of the Greek philosophers and the way they asked questions about the world and the self. They seemed to be asking the very same questions that I sought to answer. I was also drawn to Aristotle and the experimental method to try to find answers to everything. I guess I believed that the rational mind could somehow overcome the irrational (what a delusion!).

I had no idea at the time how afraid I was of my own feelings and unconscious fantasies. My world was totally a world of concepts. I actually went to a college that was quite anti-Freudian (NYU Liberal Arts School) with a strong emphasis on experimental psychology and behaviorism in its search for explanations of observable phenomenon. The other major influence on my life in college was reading Darwin because in my non-religious world when I read Darwin I felt I had the answer to my seeking the truth about how life developed. When I read Darwin I felt everything could be explained. I was still totally absorbed in what could be proven objectively.

I decided to major in psychology with a minor in philosophy and biology. It seemed to me that psychology could encompass all of these areas. But, when I graduated Phi Beta Kappa and was asked about the most important event that had shaped me, I said, "Reading Darwin." I'm sure they were looking for an answer that was more personal. I didn't realize until many years later, reading George Makari's book *Revolution in Mind* (2008) that Darwin was such a crucial factor in the intellectual world during the period that led up to Freud. I had a lot of catching up to do in order to realize how much of what I was thinking had been in the minds of many, many people before me. I was on the right path in terms of my wish to understand everything by choosing psychology, but at that time I was only interested in the experimental method. I completely rejected the idea of an unconscious, and believed I would spend the rest of my life in a laboratory.

Graduating with honors, I was given a full scholarship to Berkeley. The NYU clinical program had rejected me partly because I was so unaware of myself (and full of myself) that when I was asked why I was applying to the NYU Clinical program, I said, "I am very interested in psychology, but I don't believe in the unconscious." I had no idea that this was a program very committed to clinical work. I just thought anyone would want me with my grades and honors!

Once I was at Berkeley and away from home for the first time, I finally started to get in touch with more of my emotions. I had only a very brief contact with psychotherapy in my college years, and it became clear when I was far away from home that I had been too overwhelmed with my parent's problems to know what I was really experiencing internally. Perhaps I should have just moved out of my mother's apartment, but, in any case, the separation had a transformative effect on me. I decided the program in Berkeley was actually too experimental, and so I returned home to enter the NYU clinical program. Suddenly I was intent on a career in clinical psychology and not just the experimental part. It's not that I totally turned my back on the experimental world, but now I really needed to look inward. I entered treatment three times a week with someone from the Postdoctoral Program in Psychotherapy and Psychoanalysis (which had just begun in 1961). Bernie Kalinowitz (the Director of the Clinical Program) told me later that the faculty had decided I needed to leave home in order to "find myself." It was true. I came back a different person. How amazing that in one interview Dr. Irv Paul, had diagnosed a problem that needed a concrete answer "She needs to separate in some way from home." It was a major behavioral intervention, but it worked.

It was quite interesting to reflect on how I had blocked out everything that was happening in my home and withdrawn into a purely intellectual world. Apparently I was unable to deal with the pain my mother suffered all the time because of her early losses and in her unhappy marriage. I had blocked it all out and taken my mind off to very far off places and ideas that I could escape into. I am still amazed that Dr. Kalinkowitz and others saw something else in me even though I was so dissociated and blocked. I was then ready to live on my own in Greenwich Village, tackle graduate school, and be in treatment.

What an amazing difference it was to be in a real clinical program. I had a scholarship from NIH, which required that I work part-time at the NYU clinic for the first year. I was able to start immediately doing intakes and assigning patients to upper class students.

I had my first patient on November 22, 1963 at 1 p.m. The reason the date is so clear is that my very first patient came in and said, "I didn't want to cancel my first session, but I don't think I can think about myself right now because John Kennedy was just shot." How can one ever forget a moment like that? I first thought he might be delusional but after seeing tears in his eyes and hearing how he got this information, I said I think it is best we all go home today and deal with this tragedy, fighting back my own tears. (Shades of 9/11 when one had to think very quickly about not seeing one's patients that day and dealing with the real threat and pain of the day!)

The year at the clinic with Doris Heller and the courses with both Freudians and Interpersonalists at NYU was exciting and overwhelming, but I had no doubt that I was studying what I really wanted. When I got a chance then to do research at the Research Center for Mental Health, where Bob Holt, George Klein, Leo Goldberger and Donald Spence were teaching psychoanalytic theory I jumped at the chance, (especially when I heard that most of them had been trained at New York Psychoanalytic, which in those days was very prestigious). Everyone idealized the people at New York Psychoanalytic as the true "Freudians."

I was drawn to the Freudian model at the time. and, like the Postdoctoral Program at NYU later on, you had your choice of either studying a more interpersonal approach with teachers such as Bernie Kalinkowitz, Ben Avi, and George Kaufer (who had been trained at the William Allison White Institute) or studying with the Freudians (who were being trained at New York Psychoanalytic). But I was definitely drawn to the thinking at the Research Center and wound up working with Donald Spence and doing my thesis with Lloyd Silverman on Subliminal Perception.

It's only in retrospect that I realized that my questioning attitude about everything was fostered by this group. Even though they had trained at a rigidly Freudian Institute, they were *considered* outsiders there. They had to sign a waiver at that time that they wouldn't practice psychoanalysis because they weren't MDs. They were teaching us psychoanalytic thought with a questioning view rather than accepting everything as gospel. George Klein (1970, 1976) distrusted metapsychology and wanted people to stay close to the clinical phenomenon in describing their concepts. Many of the researchers at the Research Center were trying to prove ideas about the unconscious by doing work on subliminal perception and they were doing sleep research that was connected to understanding the meaning of REM sleep and dreams. Using tools they had learned as psychologists, they were testing out many of Freud's hypotheses.

I decided to try my luck at doing an experiment on a very controversial Freudian idea: penis envy. Using the words, "women menstruating" subliminally with women who had tested high on a scale for the Female Castration Complex, I found that these women did have a depressive reaction on TAT cards after subliminally "seeing" that stimulus. Women low on the complex did not have a reaction to those words. I had become a true convert and a dedicated Freudian.

I later completely rethought my dissertation (Ellman, 2000) and then rethought it even further in 2012 (Ellman, 2012) when I explored the topic of envy again and again. My journey on that topic alone is amazing to me given all the blind spots I had and how my ideas have evolved over the years as I grew emotionally and intellectually. I was becoming a dedicated Freudian but not a dedicated researcher because towards the end of my thesis I wondered what it would have been like to have interviewed all these women about their conflicts over their femininity. I was much more intrigued by that than my impersonal handling of my 80 subjects. I wondered if I had interviewed them all in great depth, whether I would have learned more in the 4 years it took to do my very complicated dissertation; I had measured defenses against envy in every possible conceivable way; but I won't bore you with that.

Besides the intellectual world of the Research Center, I also did my internship at Montefiore Hospital. When I went there in 1966 it was run by Drs. Mort Reisner and Herb Weiner and the people that came through and taught Grand Rounds and courses were some of the top Freudian psychoanalysts in New York: Bill Grossman, Bennett Simon, Frank Baudry, David Wermer, Bernie Herron, and Lester Schwartz. I also met Arnie Richards, Graciela Abelin, and Richard Marks, and studied with Edith Jacobson, Myron Hofer, and Phyllis Ackman. My fellow intern was Darlene Ehrenberg. It was exciting and challenging, but as with everything else in my career there was always a disconnect between what was being taught in the classroom and what was happening in the clinical setting.

One of the most powerful influences in my professional development at Montefiore and until this day was my supervisor, Sheldon Bach, who wasn't from New York Psychoanalytic but a graduate from the new NYU Postdoctoral Program. Shelly spoke to me in a language that seemed more connected to my work with patients. It seemed as if the people who claimed to understand Freud better than anyone else (or so they said) seemed to be working from theory, but were not really staying with the patient's feelings, and so the treatment was not taking place in the here and now. I read later that Ferenczi had made the same challenge to Freud (Falzeder, Brabant, & Giamiperi-Deutsch, 2000).

Psychoanalysts in those days seemed obsessed with neutrality, anonymity, and the use of parameters. Many patients couldn't handle the frustration that was imposed on them by this technique, and psychoanalysts at that time didn't understand how to treat patients with narcissistic problems assuming, like Freud that such patients weren't analyzable. There were exceptions to this way of thinking, such as Edith Jacobson (1964), Annie Reich (1973), Frieda Fromm-Reichmann (1950), and many British analysts such as Guntrip (1968), Balint (1968), Winnicott (1965, 1971), etc. But their impact in the United States was still very limited. Yet my supervisor didn't seem like these other people at Montefiore. He not only listened to the patient without telling me what theory I should be following, but asked me how I felt. When I told him I sometimes felt as if I didn't exist for the patient, he said, "Because she is so threatened by the other, she has to talk to you as if you don't exist." He was just starting to work on his ideas relating to the treatment of narcissistic patients for which he would become well known (Bach, 1977). This was actually the time when Kohut was writing his first papers on treating people with narcissistic vulnerability in a less classical way (1968, 1971).

Somehow, all of this resonated with me. Shelly also felt as I do, that if a patient needs you to open the window, pay late, call you on the phone (many actions that were then being called parameters by Eissler, 1953), you should think about why they need that and not get caught up in what is not "analytic." What Shelly was teaching me made sense to me as a clinician, but in those days you were afraid to say these things out loud because you felt that you would be told that if you did any of these things you weren't being an analyst. I felt I was already carving out my own way of doing things and Shelly was a tremendous help in supporting my search for ways to be with the patient that allowed them to feel alive.

After the internship, I found work at the Mental Health Consultation Center on 81st and Central Park West. Every Wednesday morning an amazing teacher named Martin Bergmann gave a seminar on Freud that was required if you wanted to work there. It wasn't that Martin was just teaching Freud—he really made you think. He took passages out of the text and asked you to think about what Freud must have meant, "What did Freud see? What was he trying to get at?" It was a much more profound way of thinking about the text. Shelly was asking about the patient's "meaning," and Martin was asking about Freud's "meaning." Both encouraged critical thinking. It was 1968 and Kohut had written two papers. Martin didn't bat an eyelash when someone suggested we study them, but said, "Of course, we have to know anything that broadens our views." These two teachers taught the way I wanted psychoanalysts to be taught. I loved the openness, the challenges, and the curiosity. I never understood what had happened to all of that in the history of psychoanalysis that led to so much rigidity in thinking. There was something about being an outsider that seemed to keep my mind active and alert. I wanted to read Klein, Kohut, Balint. When the Relational school started at the Postdoctoral Program (1988) I went back to read Greenberg and Mitchell (1983) since this came out just as I was graduating, and I wasn't fully aware of the movement that was starting to take place at NYU Postdoctoral Program.

I didn't realize then that my training at NYU Clinical and then my training from 1977–1983 at the NYU Postdoctoral Program trained me in a different way as a Freudian. All of these other influences seeped in and I thought that some of the criticisms the Relational school put forth were justified, such as emphasizing the importance of the role of the analyst in providing a certain environment and reducing the authoritarian position of the analyst.

I had many problems later with the extreme positions the Relational group took especially throwing out Drive theory, but I was willing to listen to what they had to say. My supervisors at the NYU Postdoctoral Program, Irving Steingart and Mark Grunes, reinforced a much more human relationship with the patient in which one tried to help the patient to feel that the therapist wasn't outside of the patient's experience. I felt the blank screen notion that the Relational school attacked as a Freudian model was not the type of work I had been taught. I liked reading the Freudians (Arlow & Brenner, 1964; Greenacre, 1954, etc.), but not as much as I loved reading Klein (1957), Winnicott (1965, 1971), and the Modern Kleinians (Schafer, 1997). As for the Freudians, I was particularly drawn to Loewald (1960). But why? As I read Makari (2008)I felt angry that the early Freudians, in order to establish themselves as a science had to reject Ferenczi, Jung, Adler, Reich, and Stekel. Later Anna Freud had to reject Melanie Klein and Kohut, etc. I think that because

I so loved philosophy and even the philosophy of religion, I have always wished to include everything in my vision of the world and have it make sense. I thought Klein was right about the primitive nature of envy and aggression, I thought Jung was right about basic archetypes. I thought Winnicott was right about the development of the self being so crucial in order to own one's impulses. Wasn't that what Shelly was trying to teach me about certain patients and their lack of awareness of the self? I identified strongly with Ferenczi's 1933/1955 writings before I really understood the profound nature of his clinical ideas about treating a person in a certain way so as to not re-traumatize them. My husband Steven, whom I had met in graduate school, was also drawn to teaching Balint, Guntrip, Winnicott, and Klein even though he ultimately became known as a Freud scholar (Ellman, 1991). We didn't know that not everyone was reading all these people the way we were. In 2010 he wrote a very comprehensive book called *When Theories Touch* (Ellman, 2010), which spoke to the type of integration that we both have been striving for.

I noticed when I started supervising City University doctoral students in psychology after I received my PhD (Ellman, 1970) that I couldn't practice the same neutrality that I had been taught. I seemed to follow a model very similar to Leo Stone's ideas in his 1961 book *The Psychoanalytic Situation* in which he describes a therapeutic situation in which if the patient asked where you were on vacation you could tell them since he felt these weren't issues related to deep unconscious conflicts, and, if they did touch some conflict, the issue could be analyzed. Students were surprised at this point of view, but they found it helped deepen the treatment not to remain so blank. I was able to write about this many years later in a chapter on anonymity in a book that was co-edited with Andrew Druck, Aaron Thaler, and Norbert Freedman (Ellman, 2011). I enjoyed supervising and helping students use their own thoughts and sensitivities and not just theory. I feel I learned this kind of supervision from Shelly and other supervisors at NYU. I still supervise at the City University Program more than 40 years later, and I am grateful that I was able to get this opportunity early in my career from my husband who was teaching there.

But none of this could have solidified without my going for psychoanalytic training at NYU and my seeing patients in intensive three or four times a week psychoanalysis and being in my own analysis. I was convinced that the greater the trust in the relationship the more regression would occur, and that my intensive work with patients made it clear that this was true. In fact, I learned that during the working-through process, patients will test you more and more to see if you really are like their original disappointing objects.

The way one handles these situations can make or break a very long treatment that looked as if it were going well!

In many ways being a psychoanalyst has been everything I could have hoped for. One is always learning, always being challenged by patients and new discoveries in neuroscience and other fields, and the challenges from different theories are also crucial. After graduating from the Postdoctoral Program in 1983, I realized more and more what I didn't know. I joined a study group, which continues today, before I even finished training. The group consists of colleagues from the NYU Postdoctoral Program and it has been invaluable. We not only have read contemporary literature as it comes out in journals, but have read books from many different orientations so that we could keep having new and fresh perspectives, especially with our most difficult patients. I also joined the Freudian Society, now called the Contemporary Freudian Society, in order to be with more colleagues who thought of themselves as Freudian. A few years later I joined the Institute for Psychoanalytic Training and Research (IPTAR), which seemed at the time to be a more questioning and open place. I still now divide my time teaching and supervising between NYU and IPTAR.

During this time I became somewhat of an expert on running conferences, initially with Dr. Anni Bergman at the Freudian Society and then at the NYU Postdoctoral Program and finally at IPTAR. This gave me a chance to meet with many people (including Ronald Britton, Betty Joseph, Edna O'Shaughnessy, Elizabeth Spillius, Antonio Ferro, Ed Tronick, Mary Target, and Peter Fonagy, and many more). The exposure to the Kleinians must have had a major impact on me because somewhere around 1998, while working at IPTAR on the Anxiety of Authorship Conference my views on envy seemed to change. I realized that it made much more sense to think of envy as something more fundamental to human existence than the concept of penis envy implied. I suddenly had the insight that Klein (1957) must have been right: that envy goes back to the mother–child relationship! In my work with patients it was clear that envy was a universal phenomenon. I told the group that I would like to do a workshop on envy at the Anxiety of Authorship conference in order to test my hypothesis about how universal envy really was. My workshop was sold out immediately. It seemed that everyone wanted to talk about how inhibited and terrified they were of people's envy. Many people felt it was a big factor in why they couldn't write anything, and if they had written something they hadn't spoken to people about it! For the first time I had a burning desire to write a paper. So with their encouragement, and, it felt, lack of envy, I wrote "The empty mother: Women's fear of their destructive envy." It was published in the *Psychoanalytic Quarterly* (Ellman, 2000) and then in 2002 this article was expanded into a piece called "Women's fear of being envied," which appeared in the *Round Robin* (a publication of Division 39 of the American Psychological Association).

It is hard to explain how one comes into one's own in this field. Some of it comes from being in analysis, teaching, supervising.

But it also seems to come from writing and having people know you. Until that paper, I think I was always so afraid of women's envy that I had to do everything in a quiet way that wasn't so noticeable. I had had a reasonable amount of success as a therapist and supervisor, but I did not talk about it too much—at least until now! The fact that the group and Donna Bassin really wanted me to publish the paper gave me some other opportunities to express myself. Donna gave me a book to review, Nancy Burke's book *Gender and Envy* (1998) and also selected me to give the Doris Bernstein Memorial Lecture at IPTAR. I am indebted to her for that encouragement. Nancy Burke's book was an inspiration for a course I then developed on Gender and Envy at NYU. All of these things were important and point to how one needs to encourage colleagues to express themselves in ways that may seem frightening to them. I took my new view of the importance of envy in development and was able in the last few years to go to a deeper place with this concept. I was invited to a conference in 2012 in Canada devoted to envy, and so I wrote a paper entitled "Desire beneath the elms: An evolutionary and developmental model of envy"(Ellman, 2012). This paper was particularly gratifying because I could bring in not only my clinical work but also some of the contemporary views of evolutionary biologists, and of course, Darwin.

I have jumped at every chance to do something new if I was offered the challenge. When Abby Adams asked me to help with the scientific programs at the Freudian Society in 1994 I said yes, and that launched a very long association with Anni Bergman. We ran programs first at the Freudian Society (where we wound up doing a book called *Omnipotent Fantasies and the Vulnerable Self* (Ellman & Reppen, 1997)), and then later at the NYU Postdoctoral Program when as part of the Faculty I volunteered to run a conference that also became a book called *The Modern Freudians* (Ellman, Grand, Silvan, & Ellman, 1998). I had never run a conference before these opportunities came. I ran conferences from 1996 to 2010 for one place or another, and still do that occasionally. Mostly that has been a wonderful experience because I have learned skills I didn't know I had, met people from many different countries and orientations and felt much more part of an international community.

I have also had opportunities by being on the training committees of various Institutes (especially IPTAR) to try and make my opinions known about not having a very judgmental role with students. In the same way that I don't believe in having an authoritarian structure in the analytic setting, I don't believe in that with students. I was happier supervising at the City University Doctoral Program when I didn't have to write any evaluations on the students. I never saw that as a detriment to getting very excellent work from the graduate students.

I have been at three different institutes: NYU Postdoctoral Program for my training, the Contemporary Freudian Society, and IPTAR. I feel that I have a good sense of what works and what doesn't work in different places. I have been trying hard to find what I think is the "perfect model" for training. It isn't easy. I love the atmosphere at NYU because everyone is treated respectfully as a professional and the requirements are also not that strict. The sequence of courses is not programmed. You can choose your own analyst from outside your Institute, and you can graduate without having to present a case to anyone as soon as you fill your requirements. You can join the faculty or become a supervisor 5 years after graduation if you write up a course outline and it is approved, or you present some material to a small group to become a supervisor. However, at NYU there is not enough oversight as to what type of case you are treating. You can change supervisors every year, and you can have supervisors from different orientations if you like. The problem with this from my point of view is that you don't necessarily learn something in depth. As much as I appreciate reading other points of view, I am glad that I stayed with the Freudian group, had intensive treatment, and then was able to reject or accept what I thought made sense as I had more experience.

Because everyone is treated as an adult, I am impressed, however, how many people really do seek out intensive treatment, study in groups when they finish their training, and continue their treatments. Choosing to do something for intellectual and clinical reasons seems to further curiosity, as far as I can see, rather than have it dictated. I have had many supervisees from NYU who continued supervision with me for many years after finishing their training because they wanted to continue to learn. This is true of candidates at all the institutes I have taught and supervised at but there is a danger when the institute requires that the treatment be with someone from your own institute that the treatment might not feel that it is truly one's own to be used for therapeutic purposes. This can also make for countertransference problems for the analyst during the treatment, for example, the teachers being talked about some of whom are one's friends, or the fellow candidates that the patient mentions who the analyst may have taught. It can be confusing when someone graduates and/or terminates treatment when they are still around their analyst at meetings, etc. It can sometimes be a reason not to get active at the institute because it may directly challenge one's previous analyst.

When I first went to the Freudian Society in 1983, after graduating from NYU, I was very unhappy with how many students were being monitored in an authoritarian way, and my experience on the Training Committee at that time was painful since many people were being failed for reasons that were very personal and irrational. There were a few voices that tried to change things at the time such as Dale Ryan, and fortunately it has changed greatly now. I am very happy to see that. I went to both the Contemporary Freudian Society and IPTAR because I was very curious to see how students did in a place that was truly Freudian and more rigorous in its requirements, where students had to take a sequence of courses, had to have three and then four times a week treatment (four times once these institutes joined the IPA in 1989). Students not only were evaluated every several years with a written evaluation based on their course work but also had an oral evaluation before seeing patients. They also had to write 6-month summaries on their cases and then had to present a 3-year case to a committee in order to graduate.

Of course this was totally different from what I had seen at NYU.

The more rigorous requirements seemed to promote a greater appreciation for doing analysis, but the open and challenging atmosphere of NYU wasn't there. When I first starting teaching at IPTAR, I was surprised at how many students didn't question things and speak up. I realized this was because they were being evaluated so often. I worked to have this changed by making the final presentation non-evaluative. I did accomplish that but recently I have realized that this didn't change the way students felt because they were still being evaluated in many other ways. Actually, I felt they were being evaluated in ways that didn't make sense to me. I recently asked a class whether taking a written exam on their first 2 years of classes was actually a good learning experience: for a few it was and for some others it was just something to get through. I didn't see that the exam predicted anything in the future, since I learned that some of the very good people at the institute who were writing, publishing and teaching, and were highly intelligent had originally failed this exam, whereas others, who seemed no longer to be involved, had done very well. How to have openness and rigor is my ideal. I think a personal tutorial with several of one's supervisors and some chosen teachers might be a good system. I keep looking for the right answer. My curiosity led me to ask my colleagues in France and Canada and other places, "How do you evaluate your students?" I have yet to find the right answer, but, in the meantime, reading and teaching and working with candidates gives me access to new ideas, and that's what makes this an amazing field. I realized while writing this that what bothered me about the way psychoanalysis was being taught in my early years of training was that it was discouraging curiosity rather than opening people up to ask what the meaning was of certain behaviors. In trying to teach Freud many of the senior analysts were trying to get someone to learn a doctrine, but they weren't teaching students to think like Freud. Freud was never finished learning, and he questioned over and over the very things he was saying. He was curious until the day he died.

One last comment about the importance of being in analysis and how life-changing it can be sometimes even with a different analyst at different times in your life. I don't think analysis is only about looking at one's countertransference (something that is crucial in terms of learning to understand oneself). It is also learning to trust another person and understand how the process works (in terms of transference). It is also amazing in terms of seeing the many ways that one's own unconscious conflicts play themselves out, the many ways that one's early identifications show themselves, despite every attempt to sometimes be the opposite of our parents, and the way different stresses in life can tap areas that one never knew were there just waiting to play themselves out in yet another way. There were many points in my life that without analysis I would have been unable to make the next important step I needed to make for a better life.

Also the question whether an analysis is satisfactorily finished after an apparently successful termination is also an interesting question. I think there are many challenges throughout our life—finishing training, marriage, children, parents dying, success, aging, etc.—and so we can't really predict how anyone will react to all or any of these things. I don't think it is a failure to have to go back into treatment to deal with life's challenges. Many of my colleagues have gone into once a week treatment many years later to deal with some of these issues.

The mind is an incredible thing, and different layers of conflicts and reactions and defenses can show themselves in many unusual ways especially under stress (even in the healthiest person). On the other hand, I have seen how conflicts over dependency, loss, and Oedipal guilt play themselves out and are transformed unconsciously over and over throughout the life cycle. They seem part of being human.

I have also been somewhat disappointed to find out some of the areas that had been overlooked by many of my psychoanalysts. While I was reading Joseph Berger's (2001) book *Displaced Persons*, I started to realize that his experience with his immigrant mother wasn't so different from mine and I began to realize that with all my years of treatment no one had picked up that my mother was an immigrant from Russia. Her driven personality and need for her children to succeed had never been tied to anything about her immigrant background. No one ever picked up how displaced she felt and how desperate she was to succeed and feel she belonged. That opened my eyes in so many ways to things I hadn't seen before and also to something the field often ignores (the importance of some crucial sociological issues as they impact the individual). Since I have recently read Emily A. Kuriloff's book *Contemporary Psychoanalysis and the Legacy of the Third Reich* (2014), I have been getting some insights into why the area of immigration might have been neglected. Many of the analysts that were the leaders at New York Psychoanalytic had their own trauma that they may have wished to hide behind a blank screen.

If I were looking for a field in which I could forever discover something new, delving into the human mind feels as if one is on an amazing journey. I will forever be grateful to Freud's genius for starting the field of psychoanalysis and setting a model for constant exploration into the human psyche. I have been studying all of Freud's works with a group of colleagues for the last 17 years, and no matter how much we read we find more and more fascinating and brilliant insights that are still there to be discovered. I know there are things I will never have time to study, however, and I am sorry about that. For example, I wish I had time to do a course in infant observation or group dynamics. I feel these areas are crucial to the way we see things, and I hope that these will become requirements of every institute over time. I do hope that with the tools this profession has provided me, and the patients and supervisees and wonderful professional friends I have, that I will continue to be open and curious forever and not be afraid of what's next.

References

Arlow, J. A., & Brenner, C. (1964). *Psychoanalytic concepts and the structural theory.* New York, NY: International Universities Press.

Bach, S. (1977). On the narcissistic state of consciousness. *International Journal of Psychoanalysis, 58,* 209–233.

Balint, M. (1968). *Schizoid phenomenon, object relations, and the self.* New York, NY: International Universities Press.

Berger, J. (2001). *Displaced persons: Growing up American after the Holocaust.* New York, NY: Washington Square Press.

Burke, N. (Ed.) (1998). *Gender and envy.* New York, NY: Routledge.

Eissler, K. R. (1953). The effect of the structure of the ego on psychoanalytic technique. *Journal American Psychoanalytic Association, 1,* 104–143.

Ellman, C. (1970). *An experimental study of the female castration complex.* PhD dissertation. New York: New York University.

Ellman, C. (2000). Women's fear of their destructive envy, *Psychoanalytic Quarterly, 69,* 633–665.

Ellman, C. (2002). Women's fear of being envied. Round Robin. Division 39 American Psychological Association Publication.

Ellman, C. (2011). Anonymity: Blank screen or black hole. In A. B. Druck, C. Ellman, N. Freedman, & A. Thaler (Eds.) *A new Freudian synthesis: Clinical process in the next generation* (pp. 157–172). London: Karnac.

Ellman, C. (2012). Desire beneath the elms: An evolutionary and developmental model of envy. *Canadian Journal of Psychoanalysis, 20,* 229–245.

Ellman, C., Grand, S., Silvan, M., & Ellman. S. (Eds.) (1998). *The modern Freudians.* Northvale, NJ: Jason Aronson.

Ellman, C., & Reppen, J. (1997). *Omnipotent fantasies and the vulnerable self.* Northvale, NJ: Jason Aronson.

Ellman, S. J. (1991). *Freud's technique papers: A contemporary perspective.* Northvale, NJ: Jason Aronson.

Ellman, S. J. (2010). *When theories touch: A historical and theoretical integration of psychoanalytic thought.* London: Karnac.

Falzeder, E., Brabant, E., & Giampieri-Deutsch, P. (Eds.) (2000). *Correspondence of Sigmund Freud and Sandor Ferenczi. Volume 3: 1920–1933.* Cambridge, MA: Belknap Press.

Ferenczi, S. (1955). Confusion of tongues between adults and the child. In S. Ferenczi, *Final contributions to the problems and methods of psychoanalysis* (pp. 156–167). London: Hogarth. (Original work published 1933)

Fromm-Reichmann, F. (1950). *Principles of intensive psychotherapy.* Chicago, IL: University of Chicago Press.

Greenacre, P. (1954). The role of transference-practical considerations in relation to psychoanalytic therapy. *Journal of the American Psychoanalytic Association, 2,* 671–684.

Greenberg, J., & Mitchell, S. (1983). *Object relations in psychoanalytic theory.* Cambridge, MA: Harvard University Press.

Guntrip, H. (1968). *Schizoid phenomena, object relations and the self.* New York, NY: International Universities Press.

Jacobson, E. (1964). *The self and the object world.* New York, NY: International Universities Press.

Klein, G. S. (1970). *Perception, motives and personality.* New York, NY: Alfred A. Knopf.

Klein, G. S. (1976). *Psychoanalytic theory: An exploration of essentials.* New York, NY: International Universities Press.

Klein, M. (1957). Envy and gratitude. In M. Klein, *Envy and gratitude and other works, 1946–1963* (pp. 176–246). New York, NY: Free Press.

Kohut, H. (1968). The Psychoanalytic treatment of narcissistic personality disorders-outline of a systematic approach. *Psychoanalytic Study of the Child, 23,* 86–113.

Kohut, H. (1971). *The analysis of the self.* New York, NY: International Universities Press.

Kuriloff, E. A. (2014). *Contemporary psychoanalysis and the legacy of the Third Reich.* New York, NY: Routledge.

Loewald, H. (1960). On the therapeutic action of psychoanalysis. *International Journal of Psychoanalysis, 43,* 16–33.

Makari, G. (2008). *Revolution in mind: The creation of psychoanalysis.* New York, NY: Harper Collins.

Reich, A. (1973). *Annie Reich: Psychoanalytic contributions.* New York, NY: International Universities Press.

Schafer, R. (Ed.) (1997). *The contemporary Kleinians of London.* Madison, CT: International University Press.

Stone, L. (1961). *The psychoanalytic situation: An examination of its development and essential nature.* New York, NY: International Universities Press.

Winnicott, D. W. (1965). *The maturational process and the facilitating environment.* New York, NY: International Universities Press.

Winnicott, D. W. (1971). *Playing and reality.* New York, NY: Basic Books.

Chapter 10

Developmental struggles in psychoanalytic training
Developing a psychoanalytic identity

Jonathan Eger

I distinctly remember overhearing my mother, on a family vacation, saying to a friend of hers, "You need to destroy an object to love it." I was 8 years old. You might *destroy* something that you love? Or, you have to destroy something *in order* to love it? What an intriguing and confusing idea: love and destruction are connected?! As the child of an analyst and a psychologist, these kinds of comments were not unusual, but this one stands out as one of my earliest memories of this kind.

One place to start thinking about what it is like growing up as the child of psychologists is at the dinner table. For many children this is where they start to hear about their parents' days and professional activities, and it can be a time of great intrigue and mystery. It can also be a place where they start to hear vague snippets about their parents' interactions behind closed doors with their patients. Of course, what parents do and talk about behind closed doors is already a topic of great curiosity. This inevitably creates fertile ground for sexual and competitive fantasies (sometimes conscious but more often, unconscious) that then extend to the parents' interactions with these *other* children and adults, their "patients"—and that then also become mixed up with the terms their parents are using about them, like "narcissism," "transference," and "borderline psychic structures." For me, this engendered a mild confusion between the boundaries differentiating children and "patients," and even between "patients" and "normal people." As one contributor writes, "4-year-olds have some notion of what a baker, lawyer, and salesman are, but most of these toddlers are not well acquainted with the world of a psychoanalyst" (Strean, 1987, p. 39). Or, as a prominent psychoanalyst with a home office remembered about his then 4-year-old child who had always heard about "daddy's patients": after passing one in the hallway for the first time and the mother saying, "Shh … that's one of daddy's patients," the child expressed astonishment, "You mean a patient is a person!" What these contributors do not go on to elaborate is that the 4-year-old is fully competent to weave the patient that he hears about at the dinner table into intimate infantile fantasy versions of his personal family romance. Personally, I imagine that it was not only my identification with my parents, but also my desire from an early age to be in the consulting room with them that contributed to my entering the field of psychology; the fantasy is related to the wish.

There is also the difficulty of how to explain your parents' profession to friends and how to respond when people find out that your parents are psychologists. "Wow. You seem pretty normal," usually said with a bit of surprise, is one of the more common initial reactions that I would get growing up. As the daughter of Franz Alexander writes,

> I do remember that if I told my school friends that my father was a psychoanalyst they would often express puzzlement. "What's that?" It was hard to explain, and when I did I often felt that being a doctor who cured crazy people didn't really gain their admiration ... I learned to answer ... with the simple response, "He's a doctor."
>
> (Strean, 1987, p. 5)

For me, my father was the school psychologist at my elementary school (while also maintaining a private practice), which forced me to balance my own feelings of pride that he helped other students and held an important and respected position within the school, with knowing that for other children (and some teachers) meeting with him was often something to be avoided because it meant there was some unrest or difficulty they were experiencing. That is, my inner feelings about him did not always align with those of others when they "needed to go see the psychologist."

While the emphasis is often on whether or not the *questioner* will understand, these exchanges are more of a problem for the child of the analyst than for the questioning friend (or stranger). The child of the analyst is already trying to understand his parent's profession, and since he feels expected to share his thoughts and feelings, it becomes easy for him to transfer onto friends what is becoming an over-cathected struggle for the child of the analyst. For instance, I remember feeling mildly uncomfortable that my friends would not understand or might judge me for my parents' profession. I think these concerns were, to some degree, a defensive position guarding against my own feelings of discomfort at not fully understanding my parents' profession and concern that it somehow made me different from children whose parents had what I considered to be more "normal" day jobs.

Despite such struggles, I am not suggesting that being the child of an analyst is a predominantly negative experience. Understanding what it means for your parent to be a psychologist/analyst may be confusing, but as Strean's son writes, "There are some definite advantages to having a therapist at your dinner table every night" (Strean, 1987, p. 39). In Strean's book, most of the contributors express their appreciation at their parents' ability to understand and speak openly about their own and others' feelings and experiences. For instance, Strean's son goes on to say,

> Having grown up with a psychoanalyst as a father, I have been fortunate to develop the skills of both a good patient and a good therapist; I have learned to speak openly about my feelings and I have learned to analyze.
>
> (Strean, 1987, p. 39)

Echoing this sentiment, a woman writes, "So thanks to what may have seemed at the time an overdose of psychoanalysis, I was able to mature into a perceptive, empathic, reflective person with the ability to make healthy choices" (Strean, 1987, p. 56). Personally, I grew up appreciating the sense that my parents knew what my friends and I were going through, leading to the important feeling of being understood by them. However, respondents also reported the less desirable consequences as parents would sometimes slip in to "psychoanalese" (p. 1) or, worse yet, offer interpretations without reacting with enough emotional spontaneity.

The experience of growing up an analyst's child

That shift begins to capture the ambivalent feelings of frustration expressed by many of the contributors that their parents' ability to understand their and others' experiences tended to cut two ways. While many authors did appreciate the ability to openly discuss and understand their and others' feelings, which was considered to be relatively unusual compared with other families, there was also the distinct sense that these analyst parents could err towards making interpretations to them about themselves—interpretations that were experience-distant. For instance, one woman described feeling as though her mother interpreted reality in a "confusing" way that did not make "sense" of her world (Strean, 1987, p. 34). In a slightly different cause of discontent, a daughter complained to her mother,

> Every time I tell you that one of my friends is being obnoxious, you always say, "so and so is that way because she is unhappy at home ... or doesn't feel good about herself." You never just think that when my friends are obnoxious, it's because they *are* obnoxious!
>
> (Strean, 1987, p. 67; emphasis in original).

This concern was validated by this girl's analyst mother, who described her own contribution to this interaction:

> First, I was certainly being the analyst (though not a very good one). Second, I was trying to understand rather than just react—not necessarily a good procedure when it comes to personal relationships. Third, I was also trying to make my child into the perfect analyst (as I couldn't be), teaching her to be always empathic, understanding and dynamically oriented in her thinking. Fourth, I was denying my own angry

feelings that I had during the day and, concomitantly, was denying my daughter's anger as well. Finally, I was not letting her feel her feelings, but instead I was rationalizing, intellectualizing, and interpreting her feelings away.

(Strean, 1987, p. 68)

Even this mother's answer, well-intended as it was, is so long-winded and comprehensively complex that all the immediacy and affect are completely drained from it—perhaps duplicating for the reader what she did with her child.

One problem is that interactions such as these can leave the child feeling as though his or her parent is an "omniscient scholar of behavior" (Strean, 1987, p. 61). An additional, and especially serious problem is the lack of "emotional privacy" (p. 55). One woman wrote that this empathic understanding led her to think "that [my mother] could read my mind because she would often tell me what I was thinking, feeling and even contemplating and, what made it worse, was that she was usually right" (p. 55). In addition to its intrusiveness it often has uncomfortably regressive qualities and the potential to foster dependence on the "all-knowing" parent.

Experience and response

A number of the contributors to Strean's (1987) volume described such conflicts rekindled by returning to this "familial" environment. For instance, much of the ambivalence children of analysts expressed revolved around feeling appreciative that one's analyst parent understood one and welcomed open conversations about thoughts and feelings, while at the same time resenting that this understanding could, at times, feel experience-distant and rob them of knowing their *own* thoughts and feelings for *themselves*. Perhaps this is a form of the process that Bollas (1989), with his special feel for language, calls "extractive introjection."

A related phenomenon is described by Kohut (1977), in writing about his work with children of psychoanalysts (who consulted him for second analyses). He writes,

> They were afflicted by a vague sense of not being real (often in the form of their inability to experience emotions), and they experienced an intense (yet conflictual) need to attach themselves to powerful figures in their surroundings in order to feel that their life had meaning, indeed, in order to feel alive.
>
> (p. 146)

Kohut states that in their initial analyses, these patients were reluctant to reveal themselves and had difficulty engaging in free association. They rarely questioned their analysts, taking the analysts' pressures and interventions for granted, as they had their parents' intrusiveness; it was the way of life they knew growing up.

I would like to suggest that some children's responses to the intrusive experience of these interactions can be grouped under the mantel of inhibiting defenses. For example, one woman, in describing her response to having her behavior interpreted—in this case, that she spilled things because she was angry at her mother—wrote, "That made me feel I was bad and anger itself was bad ... I got the impression that I was supposed to be without intensity or passion, and that strong feelings themselves were undesirable" (Strean, 1987, p. 33). Indeed, the need to hide and to say the right thing was an experience shared by several of the writers, contributing to their struggle with confronting the "expert's" opinion—whether the expert was an analyst parent or a non-parent psychologist they were sent to for treatment.

This sentiment is supported by a small study on psychotherapy with children of analysts, in which Strean (1987) found the children to exhibit difficulty with "expressions of assertiveness, separation, and autonomy" (p. 89). He found, additionally, that "the parents unwillingly squelched the child's maturational movement and induced guilt and depression" (p. 89). An interesting implication of this study was that some patients who left treatment with a negative transference nevertheless had a good prognosis on the grounds that it was considered a developmental achievement to be able to express anger and other negative feelings (Strean, 1987) rather than turn aggression against the self by developing an array of inhibiting defenses. In describing his work with children of psychoanalysts, Kohut (1977) supports this point of view:

> [T]he patient's resistance against being analytically penetrated is a healthy force, preserving the existence of a rudiment of a nuclear self that had been established despite the parents' distorted empathy; it also leads to the recognition that this nuclear self is becoming increasingly reactivated ... and, finally, it leads to the recognition that a working-through process is being mobilized which concerns the claims of the reactivated nuclear self in one (or several) of the varieties of a self-object transference.
>
> (p. 149)

Given my own experience of feeling burdened by my psychologist-parents' desire to engage in introspective conversations and my own move, at times, towards greater silence and introspection, I believe that Kohut's (1977) theoretical stance is quite valuable. A patient's silence may not reflect more traditional conceptualizations of resistance, but may be an adaptive response to unwanted intrusions or to overly intrusive parents (at least as experienced by the patient)—a healthy privacy. Along the lines of Winnicott's (1958) concept of the "capacity to be alone," the patient's silence may reflect a developmental achievement. Yet, as the psychologist, this can leave me uncertain about how best to address a patient's need for privacy and whether I will be identifying with an intrusive parent: Is enquiring about the patient's experience repeating an unwanted intrusion into the child's, now patient's, inner world? Is tolerating silence and/or vague replies respecting the patient's need for privacy? Or, is it colluding with a defensive stance that could be understood?

Of course, the best-known instance of a parent analyst and a child patient who follows in the parent's footsteps are Sigmund and Anna Freud. The analysis was conducted between 1918 and 1922 and resumed in 1924; they met with a frequency of 6 days per week, at 10 o'clock in the evening after Sigmund Freud's full schedule (Young-Bruehl, 2008). Although it is not fully determinable to what extent, it is widely believed that Anna Freud was one of the patients discussed in Sigmund Freud's 1919 paper, "A Child is Being Beaten," and that Anna Freud's 1923 paper (which she presented in 1922), "The Relation of Beating-Phantasies to a Day-Dream," was based on her own reconstructed history in her analysis with her father (Young-Bruehl, 2008). It is easy to imagine that in addition to the papers' content (see A. Freud, 1923; S. Freud, 1919), the titles themselves reflect some aspect of both Sigmund and Anna Freud's respective experiences during this analysis. While there is more that can be said about this complicated father–daughter relationship, it will have to suffice to say that they both considered the analysis a success (Young-Bruehl, 2008). In particular, for the child of the analyst parent, Anna Freud, it met her own goals of allowing "her to transform fantasy activity and daydreaming into the social activity of writing" (Young-Bruehl, 2008, p. 107). Young-Breuhl goes on to write, "Anna Freud's paper is both a study of sublimation and an act of sublimation" (p. 107).

Joining the psychoanalytic subculture

The psychic challenges experienced by children of analyst parents often parallel those faced by psychoanalytic candidates during training. Joshua Ehrlich (2003), a graduate of the Michigan Psychoanalytic Institute, cites a joke in the newsletter from the Philadelphia Psychoanalytic Society, "What is [the] proper technique for a candidate conducting an analysis? The answer: evenly hovering hypervigilance" (p. 177). This may be particularly true for candidates whose parents are psychoanalysts.

In discussing the dynamics of joining the psychoanalytic culture, Sandra Buechler (1988) has written, "In this paper I would like to treat the profession of psychoanalysis as though it were a culture. We are not born into this community, but choose to enter it" (p. 462). But, what if you *are* born into this culture? Born into a family culture of dinner conversations about the unconscious and dreams, where words like "interpretation," "conflict," and "internal objects" are used. Then, entering psychoanalytic training may be experienced as a return to an old, familial culture, and not a process of discovering a new culture with its associated language and code of conduct. During my own psychoanalytic training, I have experienced this familiarity as simultaneously comforting, and, at times, stifling in the struggle to develop my own differentiated voice out of it.

There is an ongoing interplay between the external pressures of psychoanalytic training that are shared by many if not all candidates, and those that are internally stimulated and particular to each candidate's own history, like joining one's parents' profession. Ehrlich (2003), whose father is a senior analyst, describes the reverberations that joining his father's profession had in relation to his clinical work and supervisory experiences. For instance, he relates his worries about being found out by his patients as being inadequate, to being discovered as still a student, and this in turn to his developmental struggles with regard to "[entering] a domain that belonged to [his] father" (p. 193) and whether he would live up to his (perception of) father's capabilities as a psychoanalyst. This led Ehrlich to momentary collapses of the as if quality of the transference–countertransference relationship as he "[assumed] the idealized role that [his patient] wished for [him]" (p. 195). Alternatively, Ehrlich describes being affected by his competitive strivings vis-à-vis his father and how they led him, at times, to wish that his patient not progress—if his patient was stuck, then he could be too—and "to deprive others (supervisors, [his] analyst) of the pleasures of [his] engaging the training energetically and successfully" (p. 197). Ultimately of course, he wanted his patient to progress and he appreciated the work with his supervisor, but success in these domains ran into conflicted Oedipal strivings with regard to entering his father's profession.

The conflicts experienced during the process of individuation and the regressive pulls experienced during adolescence parallel many experiences during psychoanalytic training. While education parallels a return to adolescence in many ways for everyone, the children of analysts face an additional problem—a double whammy, one might say—in that the identificatory objects of training are both symbolically and concretely reminiscent of the original parental objects. Thus, when the candidate is the child of analyst parents, the parallel with adolescent struggles around separation and individuation (Mahler, Pine, & Bergman, 1975) become exacerbated and, concurrently, the earlier developmental processes of the candidate are re-evoked and become even more complicated than they already were, before the educational process began. Again, the new analyst finds himself not going only somewhere new, but in addition, somewhere also old and familiar.

One similarity between the experience of growing up with psychoanalyst parents and entering psychoanalytic training is that both involve a great amount of introspection. As is well known, psychoanalytic candidates are asked to be self-reflective during their own personal analysis, supervision, coursework, and as developing psychoanalysts in their private offices. Introspection can be challenging on its own, but there is often an implicitly communicated additional pressure from one's training analyst, supervisors, and teachers that the candidate should be *comfortably* self-revealing (Buechler, 2008). Buechler states,

> [T]he candidate is expected to open himself to an unusual degree of personal scrutiny, and still maintain enough equanimity to function in his new professional roles. Since he often incorporates these expectations, he also expects himself to be comfortably self-revealing. At the same time, he is involved in a personal treatment process that facilitates less reliance on accustomed defenses, and therefore he is confronting anxiety his defenses previously kept at bay. He is learning a new, highly ambiguous task, absorbing complicated theoretical material, making new friendships, and attempting to integrate this new life with his previous responsibilities and relationships. And, often, any discomfort with this process is seen as problematic by the candidate himself, as well as others. (p. 363)

The candidate, like the child of psychoanalysts during adolescence, is faced with both the normative process of upheaval and restructuring of one's identity and defenses (A. Freud, 1958), and with the extra burden of being expected to maintain a non-defensive stance about reflecting on these challenging experiences while they are occurring.

This can leave the psychoanalytic candidate vulnerable to experiencing feelings of shame and other experiences of narcissistic vulnerability.[1] Many of the reasons for this parallel the experience of the child of psychoanalysts vis-à-vis his parents, for example:

1. During supervision, the candidate's defenses may be an important source of exploration in understanding his countertransference, but the genetic reasons for these defenses are often not explored, potentially leaving the candidate feeling self-conscious and ashamed that he needs these defenses, un-modulated by the understanding and compassion he may feel in his own treatment (Buechler, 2008).
2. It is infrequent that the supervisor's countertransference to the patient or the candidate is explored (Buechler, 2008).
3. When a candidate is assigned a patient who may not be well suited for analysis, the candidate may feel both inadequate to help the patient and ashamed during supervision that he his not conducting a proper analysis (Buechler, 2008).
4. When a candidate imitates his supervisor, rather than developing his own, unique style, especially when the supervisor fosters the idea that his/her approach is optimal, then the candidate "'learns' from this dehumanizing experience ... that the best he can be is a fairly accurate imitation of someone else" (Buechler, 2008, p. 366).
5. When a supervisor points out how the content of the session is being enacted during the session, the candidate may then feel like one does "when ... [her] slip was showing, and someone comments on it" (Buechler, 2008, p. 367), as when an analyst parent shines an unwanted light on an uncomfortable interaction.

While these may be unavoidable, and at times, necessary components of the supervisory relationship, even when supervision is going well, it is important to note how they may contribute to candidates' feelings of shame. This may be particularly so given the parallel between the child's experience of smallness relative to his analyst parents and the candidate's experience vis-à-vis his supervisors and teachers.

Over and above any one of these particular causes for shame in the psychoanalytic candidate, the candidate's shame *about* his shame can have the most lasting and deleterious effects (Buechler, 2008). Children of psychoanalysts may grow up in a family culture where self-revelation is not only expected, but is considered normative. This may leave the child vulnerable to feeling ashamed at violating this standard by maintaining an inward stance in his family of origin or later during psychoanalytic training, such as if one is reluctant to reveal oneself during one's personal analysis or supervision.

A related challenge for the psychoanalytic candidate who is the child of psychoanalysts is posed by having his training analyst affiliated with his institute. While this has been discussed and rectified with regard to the stultifying environment that reporting analyses created, there is another aspect of this that has not been as thoroughly written about. Like the developmental challenge posed to all children (and likewise their parents) with regard to their evolving view of their parents and the shifts in roll vis-à-vis their parents as children grow into adolescence and adulthood, candidates are faced with a similar challenge (Michael Singer, personal communication). This may not be particular to the children of psychoanalysts, but I believe it poses an extra wrinkle in the ability of the dyad that is the candidate and training analyst to analyze the transference when there is such a strong parallel with reality—a reality that may include evolving roles between the candidate and the training analyst as the candidate progresses through training and becomes increasingly involved in the functions of the institute where the training analyst may already be active, and eventually when the candidate graduates and feels more like a colleague with his training analyst than during the regressive period of candidacy.

Like the children's experience in Strean's (1987) volume, while the upside for candidates may be that they find the apparent familiarity of this analytic community comforting, the downside is the challenge of consolidating their psychoanalytic identity, which necessarily will become exacerbated if one's supervisors, teachers, and training analyst are experienced like the omniscient parent analyst of their childhood.

Dynamic organizers

For children of psychoanalysts, the powerful combination of the following dynamics[2] has the potential to make the process of consolidating one's psychoanalytic identity more difficult than it already is: a) feeling that one's inner world is exposed and as a result a part of the self needs to be walled off; b) the related feelings of being less than the all knowing parent (and later teachers, supervisors, and analyst); c) experiencing, through a process such as extractive introjection (Bollas, 1989) that the *other* has appropriated from you vital functions related to processing thought and affect; and d) feelings of shame at not living up to an internalized ideal of who and what a psychoanalyst is.

Based on several second analyses he conducted, Kohut (1977) begins to address the dynamics involved in the development of the self in the children of psychoanalysts. He writes,

> The pathogenic effect of the parental behavior lay in the fact that the parent's participation in their children's life, their claim (often correctly made) that they knew more about what their children were thinking, wishing, feeling than the children themselves, tended to interfere with the consolidation of the self of these children, with the further result that the [children became secretive and walled themselves off from being] penetrated by parental insights.
>
> (Kohut, 1977, pp. 146–147)

In the case of Kohut's patients this intrusion came in the form of comments about particular ideational or emotional contents of the children's minds (Kohut), and continued to occur long after such a degree of in-tuneness was developmentally needed, that is, after the pre-verbal stage when near perfect attunement with the infant's inner world is required for the formation of a cohesive sense of self (Winnicott, 1963/1965). These comments made by parent analysts, while intended to be empathic, had the unintended effect of being experienced as fragmenting as they were often focused on a particular aspect of the child's inner world, rather than as recognizing the total self and thereby fostering a greater sense of self cohesion (Kohut, 1977).

The child's sense that his analyst parents are able to read his mind, often reinforced by a parent's correct "interpretation," can leave a child narcissistically vulnerable (Kohut, 1977) to feeling less than the all-knowing parent and as though the parent knows more about the inner world of the child than the child does of himself. Thus leading the child to "wall off" parts of himself to protect them from being exposed to the parent and in an attempt to maintain a "coherent sector of his self" (Kohut, 1977, p. 151). One consequence of this, however, is that the child's sense of "archaic greatness and his wish for merger with the omnipotent objects" remain un-transformed and un-integrated (p. 150). This can manifest during psychoanalytic training and lead to countertransferential difficulties, or to over-identification with authoritarian institutional policies, figures of power, or superego representatives as overcompensation.

There are many possible responses to feeling that one's inner world is observed, by either one's analyst parents or by one's teachers, supervisors, and training analyst. Interestingly, 18th-century writers Edgworth and Edgworth caution against intrusive observation of children:

> Nothing hurts young people more than to be watched continually about their feelings, to have their countenances scrutinized, and the degrees of their sensibility measured by the surveying eye of the unmerciful spectator. Under the constraint of such examinations they can think of nothing but that they are looked at, and feel nothing but shame and apprehension.
>
> (as cited in Hultberg, 1988, p. 121)

In response to such observation, Hultberg (1988), like Kohut (1977), theorizes that children of psychologists use shame to defensively guard against this "invasion into the self ... However, by so doing the child also bars its own way to the self, and this is then experienced as a basic depressive state ... " (p. 121). Such a candidate may also risk becoming, as Kernberg (1986) writes, "attuned to all of [his] training analyst's interventions and to his thought processes ... [but] miss, by the same token, the opportunities of learning about psychoanalysis from [his] own unconscious" (p. 800).

Kohut's theorizing resonates with some of my own childhood experiences, aspects of which manifest now during psychoanalytic training. Like with the patients described by Kohut, I would, at times, turn inwards attempting to guard my inner world from what I experienced as my parents' intrusions into it (but were, of course, empathic attempts at connection). I think this felt particularly threatening given my fantasy that as psychologist parents they must already know my thoughts and feelings, as well as all of the reasons for them. In response, I simultaneously developed a somewhat walled-off (at least to my parents) inner world, while more outwardly trying to identify and join with their (adult) reflective capacities. While this was a comfortable enough compromise, it led to a certain false sense, or pressure, about being more adult than I was, and concomitant feelings of anxiety about not living up to my all-knowing parents. There can be a parallel experience during psychoanalytic training at times when I feel overly identified with my teachers and supervisors in a defensive maneuver to avoid exposing my thinking as being less than theirs. This repetition has the undesirable consequence of hindering the development of my own psychoanalytic thinking and trust in my own clinical interventions, as separate from those of my teachers and supervisors.

Bollas' (1989) idea of *extractive introjection* has clear implications for one's narcissistic equilibrium, and can be easily placed within Kohut's (1977) theorizing about the self, and in particular about the children of psychoanalysts. Bollas (1989) uses the term *extractive introjection*—in contrast with projective identification, which is a process in which someone rids a part of himself by putting it into someone else—to describe a process

> in which one person invades another person's mind and appropriates certain elements of mental life. The victim of extractive introjection will feel denuded of parts of the self. When this process occurs in childhood, the victim will not have a clear idea of why certain elements of mental life seem not to be his right.
>
> (p. 163)

For example, when a parent asks about his child's inner world but then goes on to organize for the child his (the child's) "private concerns into a false coherence. The more [the parent] organizes [the child's] state of mind into 'meaning' the less [the child] feels in contact with himself ... " (Bollas, 1989, p. 160). Or, when a teacher does not allow a student to fully represent his own views, but rather attempts to organize them for him (the student). As with the parent and his child, "gradually [the teacher] assumes the total function of critical thought, as [the student] simply provides the material for [the teacher's] superior thinking" (p. 160). Bollas (1989) calls this form of extractive introjection theft of mental content and identifies three additional forms: theft of the affective process, theft of mental structure, and the theft of the self. In each form, one person has appropriated from another an important aspect of the latter's ability to experience his own thoughts and feelings, to draw on his own structural functions (such as ego and superego elements) for self-regulation, and to know vital aspects of the self through the loss of a personal narrative.

The theft involved in the above processes can last from several seconds, to several minutes, to a lifetime (Bollas, 1989), and becomes increasingly pernicious when repeatedly experienced. The mother–daughter interaction cited above, in which the analyst mother interpreted away her daughter's reaction to being bullied, is an example of theft of the affective process. While presumably trying to help her daughter feel better by providing an explanation for the bully's behavior, the analyst mother's response runs the risk of leaving the daughter feeling stripped not only of her immediate anger at the bully, but more vitally of the ability to experience her own affective process in response to the bully; potentially leaving the daughter with the sense that the *how* of how one responds resides in her mother. The child who "has consistently had important elements and functions of his psyche extracted ... will experience a certain kind of loss. He will feel that a primary injustice has occurred, [and] that he has been harmed by something" (Bollas, 1989, p. 166). As a result, the child will try to recover what has been lost (Bollas, 1989). He may attempt to regain these parts through intrusion into the other, mirroring his own experience, and/or by staying close to the other who has appropriated, the now missing parts, in an effort to remain in contact with them to eventually "repatriate" them (Bollas, 1989). If there is a repetition of the experience that took place in childhood, now in training, where the *other* person's (e.g., supervisors, teachers, training analyst) experiences and reactions are felt as more important than the *candidate's* experiences, the candidate's struggle, sometimes impossible struggle, to trust his own inner processes will be accentuated.

Returning now, to that 8-year-old boy on family vacation and the "need to destroy the object to love it": In the course of writing this I have become more mindful of how mystifying and profound (not to mention challenging) the concept of *needing to destroy an object* is. Although the concept of destroying the object (and the parents' need to survive) is famously from Winnicott (1969, 1971), I am drawing on Loewald's psychoanalytic vision of individuation and personal responsibility. In "On Internalization" (1973), Loewald writes,

> By internalization, then, the libidinal–aggressive relations between subject and object, as well as identity of subject and object, are given up, *destroyed*, and separate "identities" are formed or reconstituted. The identity of the individual as well as the identity of his objects becomes defined or redefined.
>
> (p. 16, emphasis added)

And in the "Waning of the Oedipus Complex" (1979) he writes,

> [I]t is no exaggeration to say that the assumption of responsibility for one's own life and its conduct is in psychic reality tantamount to the murder of the parents, to the crime of parricide, and involves dealing with the guilt incurred thereby. Not only parental authority is *destroyed* by wresting authority from the parents and taking it over, but the parents, if the process were thoroughly carried out, are being *destroyed* as libidinal objects as well … Responsibility to oneself … is the essence of superego as internal agency … It involves appropriating or owning up to one's needs and impulses as one's own, impulses and desires we appear to have been born with or that seem to have taken shape in interaction with parents during infancy.
>
> (pp. 757–758, emphasis added)

"In this view," Chodorow (2003) writes, "individuation, autonomy and agency are more forms of responsibility for self and less a rejection of dependence on or involvement with others" (p. 909).

The related developmental tasks of needing to destroy the object (Loewald, 1973) and gradually experiencing and interacting with the object as a separate other (Winnicott, 1969) are essential components of forming one's identity as an autonomous self in the world (Mahler et al., 1975). In parallel, the psychoanalytic candidate is faced with the task of gradually developing and taking responsibility for his own way of working and thinking about the clinical data. This developing sense of professional separation-individuation (Mahler et al., 1975) requires the ability to muster a sufficient amount of aggression in order to loosen the libidinal ties to one's parents, and later teachers and supervisors (Loewald, 1973); the ability to tolerate Oedipal conflict and resultant guilt and anxiety at actually gaining one's "individuation, autonomy and agency" (Chodorow, 2003, p. 909); and the security in knowing that the other will ultimately survive this destructive process (Winnicott, 1969). There is an interesting paradox in all of this, in which the parents really have to be destroyed and yet survive and be preserved (through the transformation and internalization of our relationship to them).

This destructive, albeit necessary, process for developing one's identity as a psychoanalyst is potentially more challenging for candidates who are the children of psychoanalysts. There are (obviously) strong identificatory processes at play for candidates who enter their parents' profession. The ego ideal, as discussed by Schafer (1960) in his nuanced paper, "The Loving and Beloved Superego in Freud's Structural Theory," has the two related goals of relinquishing the Oedipal position and striving to be like the admired parents (cf. S. Freud, 1921 and 1923). Indeed, "it is *admiration*, along with hate, that motivates superego identification" (Schafer, 1960, p. 178, emphasis added; cf. S. Freud, 1928). When these ego ideals are met, the superego, as representative of "parents who provide love ... guidance ... and [who] transmit certain ideals and moral structures," can be a source of love and pride for the individual (Schafer, 1960, p. 186; cf. S. Freud, 1938). Failing to reach these goals, however, can leave the ego feeling inferior and in danger of losing the superego's (or parents') love (Schafer, 1960). Candidates entering their parents' profession are faced with the challenge of needing to relinquish certain early parental identifications while others are simultaneously enlivened. During psychoanalytic training then, candidates may be in conflict between feeling the need to live up to the standards of their teachers, supervisors, and analysts in order to maintain their love, and at the same time, recognizing the need to take responsibility (Loewald, 1979) for their own work, yet this may feel like it risks losing the love of their faculty.

Fear of losing the love of the object may lead psychoanalytic candidates to over identify with their teachers, supervisors, and analysts. Being drawn to, and depending on one's teachers, supervisors, and analyst may provide temporary relief from this fear, but also potentially exacerbates feelings of shame that candidates are liable to experience (Buechler, 2008). In particular, for the candidate who is the child of analysts, childhood feelings may be rekindled with supervisors and teachers related to feeling less-than (Kohut, 1977) with regard to one's ability to provide the "correct" interpretation or capacity to conduct an analysis on one's own. Candidates may thus feel ashamed about feeling as though they are not living up to their own internalized ideals (S. Freud, 1921) and for relying on their supervisors, teachers, and analysts in the first place. This may perpetuate a cycle in which it is difficult to more fully develop one's psychoanalytic voice for fear of being seen as not measuring up to one's ideals, now embodied in one's teachers, supervisors, and analyst, leading to even greater dependence on them.

In addition, children of psychoanalysts may grow up with a complicated mix of feeling like their analyst parents know more about their inner worlds than they do themselves (Kohut, 1977), and potentially as though their analyst parents have extracted and now contain vital mental processes that once resided in the child himself (Bollas, 1989). It may thus feel acutely dangerous for the psychoanalytic candidate to "destroy" or more fully separate from his teachers, supervisors, or analyst given the rekindled sense that these parental figures contain vital processes; to attempt (and fail) to wrest control of them back into one's own hands may thus leave the candidate feeling bereft of these processes and the needed other.

Alternatively, developing one's autonomous voice as a psychoanalytic candidate may be difficult as a result of worrying that one's teachers, supervisors, and analyst will not survive the candidate's destructive impulses (Winnicott, 1969). This is especially true if the supervisor or teacher is defensive (then you have a triple whammy!). Through the interpretations given by one's analyst parents, the child may have received the message that the parents are defending against their own narcissistic vulnerabilities by using experience distant and intellectualized "interpretations;" like for the woman in Strean's (1987) volume who felt that her mother's interpretations about her anger conveyed the message that intense affect could not be tolerated. That is, not only might the child wall off aspects of himself to guard against parental intrusions (Kohut, 1977), but the child may also identify with analyst-parents' superegos (S. Freud, 1933, pp. 65–67) that have led the parents to wall off parts of themselves from expression. These "interpretations," while intended to help understand the child's inner world, may paradoxically convey to the child that one's analyst parents—and later, one's teachers, supervisors, and analyst—cannot tolerate certain thoughts and feelings. In this case then, the candidate's inhibited expression of his own autonomous theoretical and clinical formulations may be the result of accommodating to a fantasy that one's teachers, supervisors, and analysts will also be unable to tolerate fuller self-expression.

These considerations lead to several suggestions for how analyst parents, as well as for how the teachers, supervisors, and analysts of candidates who grew up with these family dynamics can facilitate the child's or candidate's comfort with destroying the object and developing an autonomous voice. Following Kohut's (1977) thinking, analyst parents should work to reduce, what might be inevitable to some degree, the perception by the child that they know their child's inner world better than the child does. One possible way to mitigate this is to remain mindful of the child's maturational need for greater psychic privacy and less "in-tuneness" (Kohut, 1977). "Interpretive" comments, when made, should reflect the parents' awareness of the child's or candidate's need for "cohesion-enhancing responses to his total self" (Kohut, 1977, p. 151).

Parents' sensitive attunement is meant to minimize the child's defensive need to wall off particular thoughts or feelings (Kohut, 1977), and reduce the perception that the parent, supervisor, or teacher, rather than the child or candidate, is the holder of vital mental functions (Bollas, 1989). To further this end, it may be helpful for analyst parents, teachers, and supervisors to think with the child, and later psychoanalytic candidate, about their own experiences and countertransferential reactions in order to reduce these perceived "power differentials" (Buechler, 2008, p. 366). These acts of mentalization (Fonagy, Gyorgy, Elliot, & Target, 2004) would thus help reduce feelings of shame (Buechler, 2008) at not living up to his own inner standards, and those perceived to be held by his supervisors and teachers. The goal here is to facilitate the child's and, later, the candidate's emergence from behind the "shadow of the object" (Bollas, 1989; S. Freud, 1917).

In conclusion, it now seems, all of these years later, that the destruction is not just to love the object, but to internalize it as a loved object. Old objects then become internal resources contributing to the formation of higher levels of structural organization, involving greater capacities for neutralization and sublimation, and above all symbolizing capacities. Thus, learning the trade, entering psychology, is not simply a form of loving the object, but a result of internalizing a sublimated and neutralized version of it. While this is a difficult, life-long process that repeats at different times and at different structural levels for everyone, "destroying," or re-destroying the parent-as-analyst imago becomes a specific problem for the child of analyst parents during psychoanalytic training as current "parental" figures—teachers, supervisors, training analysts—are experienced and related to as the old objects from childhood. That is, the parent–child dynamics discussed in this paper—omniscience of parents, idealization, sense of transparency—are rekindled, making the "oedipal emancipation necessary [for] individuation" (Chodorow, 2003, p. 908) and the developmental task of consolidating one's psychoanalytic identity more difficult. However, these "parental" figures also present an in vivo opportunity for experiencing the "new discovery of 'objects' ... leading to a new way of relating to objects as well as of being and relating to oneself" (Loewald, 1960, p. 18), thus allowing for a fuller internalization and appreciation of what has been there all along.

Notes

I would like to express my gratitude to Richard Lasky, PhD, for his support and editorial and conceptual feedback with the writing and presenting of this paper; my deep appreciation to Fred Pine, PhD, Stephen Solow, PhD, and to all of my teachers and supervisors for their enduring insight and wisdom; my thankfulness to Alex Van Clief for being a needed sounding board; and a special recognition to David and Jane Eger, the best psychologist parents a developing psychoanalyst could want.

1 While there are many experiences of narcissistic vulnerability a candidate may experience, this section emphasizes shame because it is the affect most discussed in the literature in the context of the candidate feeling exposed with his teachers, supervisors, and analyst.
2 This is not intended to be an exhaustive list of potential dynamics faced by analytic candidates, whether or not the children of psychoanalysts. Other dynamics may be relevant but are outside of the scope of this chapter.

References

Bollas, C. (1989). *The shadow of the object: Psychoanalysis of the unknown thought.* New York, NY: Columbia University Press.

Buechler, S. (1988). Joining the psychoanalytic culture. *Contemporary Psychoanalysis, 24*, 462–469.

Buechler, S. (2008). Shaming psychoanalytic candidates. *Psychoanalytic Inquiry, 28*, 361–372.

Chodorow, N. J. (2003). The psychoanalytic vision of Hans Loewald. *The International Journal of Psychoanalysis, 84*, 897–913.

Ehrlich, J. (2003). Being a candidate: Its impact on analytic process. *Journal of the American Psychoanalytic Association, 51*, 177–200.

Fonagy, P., Gyorgy, G., Elliot, J., & Target, M. (2004). *Affect regulation, mentalization, and the development of the self.* London: Karnac Books.

Freud, A. (1923). The relation of beating-phantasies to a day-dream. *The International Journal of Psychoanalysis, 4*, 89–102.

Freud, A. (1958). Adolescence. *Psychoanalytic Study of the Child, 13*, 255–278.

Freud, S. (1917). Mourning and melencholia. In J. Strachey (Ed. & Trans.), *The standard edition of the complete works of Sigmund Freud* (Vol. 14, pp. 237–258). London: Hogarth Press.

Freud, S. (1919). "A child is being beaten": A contribution to the study of the origin of sexual perversions. In J. Strachey (Ed. & Trans.), *The standard edition of the complete works of Sigmund Freud* (Vol. 17, pp. 175–204). London: Hogarth Press.

Freud, S. (1921). Group psychology and the analysis of the ego. In J. Strachey (Ed. & Trans.), *The standard edition of the complete works of Sigmund Freud* (Vol. 18, pp. 65–144). London: Hogarth Press.

Freud, S. (1923). The ego and the id. In J. Strachey (Ed. & Trans.), *The standard edition of the complete works of Sigmund Freud* (Vol. 19, pp. 1–66). London: Hogarth Press.

Freud, S. (1928). Dostoevsky and parricide. In J. Strachey (Ed. & Trans.), *The standard edition of the complete works of Sigmund Freud* (Vol. 21, pp. 173–194). London: Hogarth Press.

Freud, S. (1933). New introductory lectures on psycho-analysis. In J. Strachey (Ed. & Trans.), *The standard edition of the complete works of Sigmund Freud* (Vol. 22, pp. 1–182). London: Hogarth Press.

Freud, S. (1938). An outline of psycho-analysis. In J. Strachey (Ed. & Trans.), *The standard edition of the complete works of Sigmund Freud* (Vol. 23, pp. 139–208). London: Hogarth Press.

Hultberg, P. (1988). Shame: A hidden emotion. *The Journal of Analytical Psychology, 33*, 109–126.

Kernberg, O. F. (1986). Institutional problems of psychoanalytic technique. *Journal of the American Psychoanalytic Association, 34*, 799–834.
Kohut, H. (1977). *The restoration of the self*. New York, NY: International Universities Press.
Loewald, H. W. (1960). On the therapeutic action of psycho-analysis. *The International Journal of Psychoanalysis, 41*, 16–33.
Loewald, H. W. (1973). On internalization. *The International Journal of Psychoanalysis, 54*, 9–17.
Loewald, H. W. (1979). The waning of the Oedipus complex. *Journal of the American Psychoanalytic Association, 27*, 751–775.
Mahler, M. S., Pine F., & Bergman, A. (1975). *The psychological birth of the human infant*. New York, NY: Basic Books.
Schafer, R. (1960). The loving and beloved superego in Freud's structural theory. *The Psychoanalytic Study of the Child, 15*, 163–188.
Strean, H. S. (Ed.) (1987). *Growing up observed: Tales from analysts' children*. New York, NY: The Haworth Press.
Winnicott, D. W. (1958). The capacity to be alone. *The International Journal of Psychoanalysis, 39*, 416–420.
Winnicott, D. W. (1965). From dependence towards independence in the development of the individual. In D. W. Winnicot, *The maturational processes and the facilitating environment: Studies in the theory of emotional development* (pp. 83–92). New York, NY: International Universities Press. (Original work published 1963)
Winnicott, D. W. (1969). The use of an object. *The International Journal of Psychoanalysis, 50*, 711–716.
Winnicott, D. W. (1971). *Playing and reality*. London: Tavistock.
Young-Breuhl, E. (2008). *Anna Freud: A biography* (2nd ed.). Ann Arbor, MI: Sheridan Books.

Chapter 11

The dice popper: how we describe what we remember

Rachel Altstein

In a dice popper, a pair of dice sits on a small, flexible metal floor. The dice are enclosed in a clear, plastic dome; the whole thing is about the size and shape of half a tennis ball. Perhaps you remember this gadget from the board game "Trouble"? You push down the dome, the metal floor bends downward, you let go of the dome, the floor springs upwards, the dice go flying, the dice hit the top of the plastic dome, and the dice descend, landing in a different configuration. You have just rolled the dice.

Sometimes when I think back to the moment I saw United Airlines Flight 175 from Boston fly intentionally into the south tower of the World Trade Center, my eyes, along with all the other eyes around me glued to the precise swatch of sky that was suddenly filled up by that roaring plane, our gaze adhesively fixed exactly there because we were already watching the north tower burn, our faces frozen into gape-mouthed, silent incredulity, our minds beginning to process that what was one second ago looking like an accident is now one second later looking quite clearly like an intentional attack, as we began frantically looking around for the third plane (as people were beginning to scream about), as we were ducking and wincing, trying to decide whether to run or whether to stay put, as we were trying to peel our eyes away from the now *two* buildings burning, but as we are now looking again to the southernmost part of the sky for the next plane, and now as we are returning our eyes back to the smoldering holes, when these memories come back to me, I picture the sky as a plastic dome that got pushed down by a giant, menacing thumb.

All of us on that street corner that Tuesday morning two blocks southeast of the towers—me, my infant daughter, my 4-year-old girl, the hundreds of people around us with our coffees and our newspapers and our work bags full of work (my own full of legal papers; at the time I was a public defender)—our floor sunk, felt metallic, bent downwards concavely, and snapped back to levelness, flinging us upwards until we slammed into the bright blue interior of a translucent half-orb and got plastered against the underneath of that globe, stunned and wrecked. And then, after we unpeeled ourselves, there we all were, descending back to earth in a free fall, only now unzipped with all of our parts disassembled, and when we landed—some of us hard and at high volume and some of us numbly and mutely—all of our parts were violently reshuffled, and we were other than who we were before.

There were so many free falls that day. My own elapsed over approximately 12 years and, somewhat to my surprise, when I landed, there I was, reassembled into who I am today: a psychoanalyst.

Among the many facets of psychoanalytic work that I treasure, what captivates me the most are the unpredictable, inexact, and imagistic ways in which we describe what we remember. Not how we *relay* what we remember, not how we *produce* what we remember, but how we *describe* what we remember, describe being a verb that demands that we come up with language of our own. In life, and especially in analysis when analysis is a part of our lives, we wait to see what words will emerge as we endeavor to describe our pasts, a time frame that includes everything from decades-old events to something that happened an hour ago. For me, this experience of listening for a person's eventual depiction of what has happened to them and how they feel about it is what generates the suspense that builds the momentum that carries an analysis along.

Aside from cherishing this aspect of analytic work, which might be a feeling well enough unto itself, I believe that this is the heart of the psychoanalytic process. It is certainly the core of my identity as a working analyst, this way of discovering which pieces of our patients' lived experiences stick to their memory, and listening deeply to how those sticky pieces get articulated. Because one's description of past experience requires imagination and creativity, imagery is a paramount part of what I listen for when I listen. Looking into the creases of imagery and gleaning meaning from what we discover is a staple of what my patients and I do together. Sometimes we find something valuable that we didn't set out to encounter, which makes serendipity a part of what I think about, too. In these cases, taking serendipity seriously and not just marveling at the uncanny but thinking about it and drawing from it is a most powerful and illuminating facet of the work.

Throughout all of my listening, the suspension of the expectation for factual accuracy in description and memory is fundamental, since it is not so much the content of what rises to mind, but the creative ways in which expression is given to this content that tell us the most. This idea rests on something quite anomalous to concrete "knowing"; it relies on a faith in our psychoanalytic theory even when we don't quite understand how it works. I am not the first person to observe and relish the idea that truth and accuracy are not interchangeable, not in psychoanalysis (Greenberg, 1986; Spence, 1982; Stern, 2003), not in psychoanalytic writing, (Levenson, 1983; Ogden, 2005; Plaut, 1999) and not in literature (Nabokov, 1951; O'Brien, 1990; Salter, 1993; Wolff, 2003). I'm not the first to muse on metaphor and the meaning inherent in the imagery that emerges in our language as we try to say what it feels like to be in our minds (Lakoff & Johnson, 1980, 1999; Modell, 2005, 2009; Stern, 2010; Vivona, 2003). But I am the first one to layer these ideas onto one particular story: my own.

This is a chapter in a book about how one finds their way into becoming a psychoanalyst, and, once in the field, how one finds their voice in the work. The description of remembered experience, as plain as that might sound, and in all of the complex ways elaborated above, is my answer to both of these questions.

Listening to memory

I have a plan. The fort that rings the tip of southern Manhattan—the West Battery, an important defense of New York Harbor during the War of 1812—I'm going to run to it and crouch. It's a very strong wall and I feel I can take good cover there. Also, there are a series of square windows in that stone wall that were used for cannons; I'll be able to peek out of them to see what's coming in from the south while keeping the girls safely low to the ground. I feel lucky that I am wearing pants, not a skirt, because I also dimly remember that if I tie knots in the ankles of my pants, take hold of the waist, and snap the legs through the air, I can make a flotation device. Since it's been at least 25 years since I learned how to do this at summer camp, I really hope it doesn't come to that, but I tuck the idea away anyway, and start to run towards the water.

As I run, people are screaming. Cops are screaming. When I hear cops screaming, I remember in a very crystalline way thinking the words "all bets are off" and feeling cool-minded about this observation. I remember stopping for a moment with my girls in the marble alcove of a big financial building on Broadway to catch my breath and marveling to myself how unremarkable it feels that we might die. I remember thinking to myself, and again this thought feels sparkling clear: "thousands of people die everyday, and today we are among them, and there's nothing more or less to it than that," and I remember being genuinely surprised at how ordinary my surroundings looked as this occurred to me. I remember feeling just like Maurice Sendak's Little Bear when he pretends to fly to the moon from his home on earth (Minarik & Sendak, 1957). He climbs a tall tree, closes his eyes, and lands with a plop only to open his eyes, look around, and think to himself, "My, my, here I am on the moon. The moon looks just like the earth ... the trees here look just like our trees ... the birds look just like our birds" (pp. 42–43). At that moment in the marble alcove, I knew exactly how Little Bear felt. How could everything look so much the same if things were really so very different? There was something almost marvelous about this. The Little Bear story was a warm favorite of mine as a child and it bolted back to me as I looked around feeling astonished by how regular everything looked, how impossibly regular: the buildings looked just like the buildings always looked, regal and stone; the letters in the Starbucks sign were still that immutable, annoying green; and the birds, unfathomably, they still looked like birds! All of this remained so—everything both sublime and irritating remained just so—even though I was about to die. As an immediate second thought, I remember thinking to myself, well, what did I expect? Cherubs and trumpets and a Velvet Underground soundtrack? I looked at my girls, my soft little cubs, and they were looking up at me, and I decide to keep going. I leave the alcove.

Further south on Broadway, just as the street forks, I see the Charging Bull, fierce and rather handsome. He is bronze, weighs over 7,000 pounds, is 11 feet tall and 16 feet long, a symbol of aggressive financial Wall Street muscle. He is low to the ground and kind of careens to his left, leaning back on his haunches, ready to charge. He's been a pal of mine all the many years I've worked in the cobblestone Wall Street area. All of my work in New York, both the lawyering jobs and all the clerical, temp-agency ones before that, have been in this neighborhood. Throughout them all I have felt a kinship with this snarly bull, and I've spent more than a few lunch hours communing with him. In a magical realism kind of a way, I feel our eyes lock for a long, slow second, me and the bull, and I know what to do. I abort the West Battery Fort plan and make a beeline for the Bowling Green Subway station, which is one block away. People begin screaming at me. They're screaming: "Lady! LADY! Don't go down! The subways aren't safe!" Someone tries to pull me away from the mouth of the stairs as I begin to run down with the girls. I shrug him off, look at my daughters, think about the bull, and say, quite simply, "Let's go home."

We descend the stairs and breeze onto the platform; no need for a metrocard swipe today. The 4 train is there—doors open. I feel it is my lucky day, and we glide in. The subway car is half full. We sit down, my big girl and I in seats next to one another, my little one facing me with her characteristic open gaze from the stroller nestled and braced between my knees. Bowling Green is the last stop in Manhattan and the next stop is Brooklyn; within seconds I am underwater, pushed off from one Island and barreling through a tunnel towards another landmass, surrounded by people who have no idea what just happened. I look around and decide to test my reality. I say, aloud, who just saw that. I say, aloud, who was there. I say, aloud and now louder, did anyone see what I just saw. My big girl squeezes me; she realizes before I do that I have become that person on the train who people inch away from.

We make it home to our apartment after getting off at our stop, this motley gang of three—me, a 4-year-old, and a 20-month-old—their lunches still packed just as they were at 8:30 a.m. when the world was different, in retrospect a kind of Wizard of Oz collection of unlikelies. It had been 90 minutes since we set out for the day.

At home, I immediately do the smartest (and the only) thing I can think of to do, which is to get them both a drink of water, check that they have all their parts, hug them, tell them that they were very brave and must have been so very scared, and park them in front of a videotape loop of optimistic PBS children's cartoons before walking zombie-style into the kitchen. There, I sit down with my hand-held landline—the mobile lines are out—to try to contact my husband, who is trapped in Manhattan, and my parents, who live out of state. Nobody is reachable.

I remember my hands were folded together on the table. I'm just sitting there, staring. I'm not sure if what I think just happened really did just happen. I turn on the radio and learn it really did happen. Then I hear someone on the radio say "the towers are gone" and I think to myself, yes, yes, that's *just* how I feel, they are gone, gone the way I've always known them to be, all vertically grooved and endlessly, bluntly rectangular, they have been gruesomely marred, and will never look the same. Seconds later, narrowing in on what the man on the radio is saying, it dawns on me that this is not a figure of speech. The towers are actually gone. They have fallen down. I kind of cock my head so that my ear stretches in the direction of the radio as if to say—to nobody—"*really?*"

Just then I hear the door open, and there is my brother. He lives near me in Brooklyn and has raced over. He and I are close, as it's just the two of us kids in our family. He is a doctor, and good thing, that. He checks the girls out head to toe, and says something reassuring and normal to them that I don't remember. Then he comes into the kitchen and makes sure I have a pulse. When it is determined that I am alive and still his sister, he gets me an icy shot of vodka from the freezer, and sits down with me.

And then something happens that wakes me up. He does something real. He does something subtle and off-the-cuff that lodges in my memory. One thing you need to know about my brother before I tell you this is that as a kid, he was nuts for those Time-Life books about disasters, with reproductions of actual *New York Times* front pages documenting catastrophes the world over. These are the gigantic books of your brother's that take up most of the kitchen table when you're trying to eat your cereal. The Hindenburg, the Titanic, tidal waves, earthquakes, sunken ship liners, mid-air plane collisions: he pored over them all. My brother looks at me from across the kitchen and melts into his 10-year-old self; I know exactly what he is going to say to me before he says it. He slowly leans in my direction, starts to smile and look fuzzy and says, very quietly, "What did it look like? What did you see?" I realize he is wistful, excited, even envious at my eyewitnessing. I remember feeling "there's my brother." And then, impossibly, I chuckled, and told him all about it.

The necessity of relationship

Recovery from trauma "can take place only within the context of relationships; it cannot occur in isolation" (Herman, 1992, p. 133). This simple idea that trauma cannot be approached and articulated cathartically in solitude is a constant, even within the vast diversity of philosophies undergirding contemporary psychoanalytic trauma theory. For example, and to name but a few, Boulanger, 2007 (adult-onset trauma); Brown, 2005 (drawing on analyst's alpha function); Ornstein, 2010 (resilience); Richman, 2014 (dissociation and creativity); and Van der kolk, 2014 (bodily and neurological underpinnings). We all need someone to refract what we are feeling into language by asking us to talk about it. This—the state of being in relationship—is the only way we begin to recognize ourselves as distinct from what has happened to us. Without it, the experience of what happened to ourselves and our experience of ourselves become synonymous. I learned this for the first time only a few hours after the attacks, sitting at that kitchen table with my brother as I encountered the immense relief and unmistakable lightening in being asked to describe what happened. The fact that his question sprung from such an authentic, familiar, and endeared part of his imagination was essential. It woke me up to the realization that despite the catastrophe of the day, he was still my brother, still so very much himself, and that had to mean that on some level, even if it wasn't apparent to me at the time, I was still myself.

I learned this foundational lesson again in analysis, which I like to say began on September 12. This is almost true. However, it was more like the end of that week when I lifted my head up and heard a distant and muted alarm bell go off, like when the phone rings from under a couch cushion, and realized I needed help. My husband heard it, too. We were both deeply worried about our girls, who were reverberating with trauma in their own ways, and about me. I had been in the midst of a phase that toggled between catatonic staring and hyper-focused efforts to see the towers hit; indeed, I was actively identified with Richard Dreyfus from *Close Encounters of the Third Kind* (Phillips & Spielberg, 1977), a character so obsessed with seeing and seeing again the image of a mountain that he carves it into his mashed potatoes at the dinner table as his wife and kids stare at him in worry and disbelief. That is as close as I can come to describing myself in the immediate days after September 11, driven to see the second plane again, waiting for footage to appear on the news, scouring the internet for glimpses (remember, this was a pre-YouTube world). I called one therapist I knew whose roster was full. I called a second who had time for me. I made an appointment.

If September 11 felt like being in a dice popper, to retain the contours of that metaphor, analysis was like being in a snow globe. In it, I felt surrounded by the sediment of memory that littered the floor like plastic chips of fake snow and not unlike, as it occurs to me in this very moment of writing, the white blanket of papers that littered the pavements of lower Manhattan after the towers collapsed. To the snow globe imagery, I associate not to a sealed up, airless feeling of being enclosed or a destructive feeling of being shaken up, but to the way two people can, in one very particular atmosphere—a manufactured one—agitate the shards of memory that surround us, swirl them up and then let them descend in slow motion in such a way that you can actually think about them as they float past you on their way back down. I now know to call the outlines of such an oxymoronic place where pieces can both fly apart and be held together "the frame" (Bass, 2007) and what goes on within its boundaries "holding" (Slochower, 2014; Winnicott, 1965).

In the first weeks, we plunged directly into the acute, minute-to-minute experience, working in the acrid, acidic air that filled lower Manhattan and, seemingly, all of the offices in it. I talked about seeing more parking tickets than I could count piling up on cars around my home and how each time I saw them stuffed under windshield wipers it took me a long, blinking moment to realize that the drivers had failed to move their vehicles in accordance with city parking rules because they were dead. I talked about the grit that covered everything in my path on the way to session—car hoods, shrubs, newspaper stands—feeling sure that it was comprised of bones and skin. The air, after all, was still practically sandy with the human dust of the incinerated in those early weeks. Using the language available to me at the time, I talked about what it felt like to be stuck on the ceiling of the dice popper and how the ground looked to me from up there. I talked about my girls, how sore and brave they both were, how angry and frightened, and was guided expertly through helping them to integrate their trauma. These were the initial, raw months that stretched into the initial, raw year. Soon, the mashed potato feeling ebbed, the need for such frenetic, insatiable, wordless re-living at an end.

And then, something else happened. Undetectably, trauma-focused analytic therapy turned into psychoanalysis proper. Imperceptibly and without knowing it, the sting left the wound and trauma stopped dominating the airtime of my sessions. I started talking about other things: subtler, deeper, more enduring things, things that predated September 11, the sore spots of childhood, the edges of dreams. I talked about these things for a long time. I talked about them for years.

In the middle of this period of feeling clearer and better, something serendipitous happened. A book fell into my hands—literally—that caused my life to dogleg even more. I was leaving the assisted living facility where my grandmother was living. I adored Sadie and even though she had stopped talking, I would come often to be near her, make abundant eye contact, and talk to her as if nothing was different. I had to dash quickly after this particular visit and had a long subway ride ahead of me. Waiting for the elevator, I kicked myself for forgetting the newspaper at home. I glanced around and saw something that I had never noticed: a rickety circular book rack familiar to anyone who hung out in school libraries before the digital age. The single book in it had no cover and was so old I could barely read the spine, but it was definitely a book, so I grabbed it. The elevator came and I walked in. I exited the building and walked to the train. I got on the train and opened the book. And once immersed, I felt its contents soak into me. It was filled with ideas that felt deeply familiar even though I had never encountered them before. It was about the delicate process of uncleaving that happens over time, and from the moment of birth, between babies and mothers. I read sentences like I had never read before, sentences describing "the earliest dialogues with the world," referring to the way parents and babies talk to each other, dialogues that "continue to be prominent in our dialogues with the world—not abstractly, but in the familiar and commonplace and in the illusions that hold us together" (Kaplan, 1978, p. 36) I began to feel I had found something I hadn't known I was looking for.

The book turned out to be something of a relic: *Oneness and Separateness*, an overview of the ideas of Margaret Mahler (Kaplan, 1978). I was 34, and this was my first brush with traditional psychoanalytic thinking, one of life's rarely felt epiphanies. Hardly in vogue today, I still (and will always) have a soft spot for Mahler, as her name instantaneously calls up that crucial, serendipitous gateway moment for me. Brimming with curiosity, I asked my therapist about the theory I had encountered and began to learn, bit by bit, about this new discipline. I was steered to Beatrice Beebe—the pioneering mother-infant researcher—and, ironically, poignantly, uncannily, became a research assistant on her project helping the mothers and children of September 11 (Beebe, 2012). This experience provided not only someone who would become an important mentor, but also a precious opportunity for repair, the kind that comes from helping other people who have been damaged by the same toxin as you. I read more, and more still. I took a class. I kept reading.

Slowly, I began to allow myself to consider a career change. As timing would have it, New York State law had recently changed to allow people with postgraduate degrees in non-mental health disciplines to enter psychoanalytic training for licensure (N.Y. Edn. Law § 8405: NY Code—Section 8405). My Juris Doctor counted, and I began to contemplate training. My analyst likened this idea to a young, tender thing, and suggested that I treat it with a hushed, guarded reverence and a drumming patience, like kids in science classes do when they wrap seeds in damp paper towels and set them on quiet, sunny window sills to germinate. Probably without knowing it, she hit an uncanny bull's eye with her imagery and I drew hope and strength from this analogy. It nestled right into the place where I was living: one of hope, nascency, fragility, and the possibility of sprouting.

In training, I felt myself unfurl. It was clear to me that I had been thinking psychoanalytically about myself and the minds of others for a very long time without knowing there was an academic discipline to house and nourish this way of understanding the world. I began to link lifelong feelings I thought nobody else talked about to actual terms that appeared in actual books, learning to call my childhood state of mind looking quietly out of a car's backseat window at the back porches of houses blurring by "reverie" (Ogden, 1997), matching the surprising feeling of having a perfect phrase ripen and emerge into awareness at just the moment when I'm not trying to reach for it "unbidden" (Stern, 1990), and defining the warm feeling of being seen and understood by a middle school teacher when I overheard her talking admiringly about my thinking as "mentalizing" (Fonagy & Target, 1998). I came to cherish these words as I had these concepts before I knew there were words for them, and in doing so learned something about another idea: "the unthought known" (Bollas, 1987). I came to know these ideas, as I think so many of us do, if we're lucky, from the inside out. I kept learning.

My first analysis at its natural end and presenting thorny issues of termination, I began analytic work with a much different person who coaxed out a new array of issues, and it was in this new alchemy that I really began to think and to dream. Concurrent with the classroom learning and a fresh analysis, I began seeing patients, initially a tight and self-conscious experience that became looser and more natural over time. My instinct developed, and I began to understand the need to let go of theory and simply be. I began to write, and writing became a vital way for me to discover aspects of the very treatments I was writing about, especially the dimensions of analyses that were not available to be noticed but were pressing for expression (Altstein, 2016a, 2016b).

Slowly, clinical writing reignited major parts of my pre-analytic identity, an identity of a lawyer who relied exclusively upon writing as a mode of advocacy. I began to feel that September 11 had made me into the person I had always been, only different, rather than a different person altogether.

The reassembling function of trauma

To say that trauma changes a person is absurdly broad and abundantly obvious. But to ask how trauma changes us does not feel as apparent to me. My own experience is not so much of being changed as it is of being rearranged. Remember the dice popper? In addition to resonating with the feeling of a bottom falling out from under me and of crashing into the dome of the sky, I also identify with this imagery because of the reshuffling element of a dice roll. Like that reshuffling, change catalyzed by trauma for me was comprised of the deep jostling and reassembly of pre-existing internal component parts that resulted in someone who is not so much different, but differently organized.

Up until now I have emphasized the process of change that followed a violent unspooling. I want to end on a note of sameness, which hopefully will be illuminated in the following anecdote. When I meet someone new and am asked about my work, I say that I am a psychoanalyst. If I'm met with an expression of curiosity or friendliness rather than aversion or blankness, I might add that this is a second career, and, if my new friend is hanging in there with me, I might add that I used to be a public defender. Public defenders are the lawyers assigned to represent indigent men and women who are accused of committing crimes, whereas psychoanalysts are people who listen deeply, sometimes interpret, and collaborate with their patients to find language for conveying what it is like to be themselves. Given these two nutshell definitions, it might not sound surprising that, unanimously, I'm met with a remark noting the vast difference between the fields. How ever did you get from that to this? People seem to expect me to say how much I hated being a lawyer, how unhappy I was working with an often feared and despised element of the community, and they seem especially keen on hearing about how different it must feel being an analyst rather than a criminal defense attorney.

But the thing is, I didn't hate being a lawyer, I wasn't unhappy advocating for an unpopular social tier, and I don't experience my first and second careers as feeling all that different. In fact, both jobs pull on the very same parts of myself that make me feel so very much like me: the part that itches to spring people from their traps and the part that pays careful attention to the language used to tell a life story that feels real, rings true, and can make a difference. Crucially, the goal of each vocation is to unshackle a person, in the first quite literally from concrete prisons, in the second quite figuratively from internal confinements. This is the thread of sameness that crossed through my domains of change, and emerges with regularity in my analytic voice. Sitting with my patients who are locked up in one feeling of stuckness or another, I frequently have the same stirrings I used to have fighting to get my incarcerated clients out of prison. And often, when I am with analytic patients who are particularly glued into a painfully narrow and negative definition of themselves, a memory from my lawyering days resurfaces that reinforces the idea that I'm still the same person, with the same stirrings, doing, on a very deep and abstracted level, the same thing as I did as a young attorney. The memory is this:

One summer in law school, I worked for a man named Bryan Stevenson. Stevenson works in Montgomery, Alabama on behalf of death row inmates, where fair fights are few and far between in the criminal courts.[1] Living and working in Montgomery sealed my idea to become a public defender, and provided me with a life changing moment, the morning I sat in Bryan's office looking for guidance on how to craft a particular section of a motion I was writing on behalf of a client appealing his death sentence. Bryan reminded me of something he thought I knew anyway, but perhaps had never put into words. "We're all worth more than the worst thing we've ever done," he said, coaching me on how to frame an argument in the penalty phase of a trial, the time when defense lawyers endeavor to paint a picture of their client's entire life in its fullest and most contextualized extent. This is a conviction that dares anyone to judge—to presume to understand—the entirety of a person's life by only one moment: one's worst. It is a statement full of forgiveness and the vital notion of context, bandwidth, and flexibility. It is part of an antidote to shame and self-hatred, and can loosen a rigid act of shaming and hating others. It was the sentiment that guided me most of all as a lawyer and that guides me today as an analyst.

As an appellate defender, my clients had been through their trials, had already been found guilty, and were already in prison (N.Y.C.P.L. § 450.10). Mine was a very particular brand of defense, entailing not the live action of a criminal trial courtroom, but a quieter kind of advocacy made up largely of combing through the trial transcript, finding an error to raise on appeal, and submitting these arguments to court in a written brief. In those briefs, I would argue that my client's moment of transgression came from somewhere, out of somewhere, because of somewhere, and in order to understand the moment, one must understand the somewhere. As I wrote, I tried to create this environment of "somewhere." Culled from the trial record, a bound document resembling something between the yellow pages and a screenplay, I would piece together the story of my client's life, and although strictly speaking the job was to lay out for the Court a picture of what happened in the trial proceedings and include the biographical detail of the accused's life, internally I was framing a much more delicate and powerful question: how did *this* person get to the point of committing *this* crime? How did he get to the point of doing anything transgressive for that matter? In my mind, I would reframe: how did this baby, this 10-fingered, 10-toed, soft, warm thing, become a different thing: an adult who stole, assaulted, burned to the ground, even killed?

These are the questions that carry over very directly into my analytic voice. Sitting with my patients, I am frequently filled with a feeling of wonderment about how the person across from me got to be the person she is, someone who doesn't believe she can thrive, or is trapped in an identity that can do nothing but thrive, someone who feels she is unlovable, or is too invested in loving attention, someone who bruises easily, or doesn't bruise at all.

This story, like every story we hear from our patients, is laden with imagery, data, and clues. And, as with any other story we encounter in analysis, it invites us to reach under the words and in between the letters and mine the language we encounter for meaning. In this case, since this is a chapter in a book not only about how one gets to be a psychoanalyst but how one works psychoanalytically, I want to explore how so many of the images and themes I've conjured explain not only how I got to be where I am but how I work now that I'm here.

First, it's not only that I have told you about my experience of being shaken up. It's that I believe every patient has a dice popper moment of their own to one degree or another, be it a shattering exposure to violence, a withering look from a second-grade teacher, or the tenor of a D-minor chord. These, the moments when we come undone for reasons we either understand or do not, are often the ones that lodge into us, fragment us, halt our contentment, and lead us into analysis. Our job is in the reassembly, which requires helping our patients land in new, more explored and more whole configurations. Likewise, I didn't include my memory of learning from Bryan Stevenson only to make the point that I'm the same person I was before 9/11, with the same ideology that revolves around justice and second chances. I included the story about Bryan because I believe that every patient suffers in one way or another from feeling defined not by iterations of their best selves, but by identities calcified during their worst and most shaming moments of life: off the top of my head and thinking about my own patients, may I present the B-minus student, the boy who wet his bed, the klutz, the flirt, the smarty-pants. Who among us cannot relate to the experience of getting trapped into a reputation simply by doing one dumb or mean thing. These reputations, whether reiterated in mythological terms around the family dinner table or the playground, advance into nothing short of non-negotiable expectations, and so often we are so good at fulfilling those expectations. Our job in these cases is to zoom outward from these narrow moments into something more contextualized and whole, and coax our patients into the idea that they, too, are better and more than the worst thing they have ever felt or done.

And it's not just that I'm a writer who generates a tangle of images, among them mashed potatoes, a brother, a seed on a damp paper towel, a board game called Trouble, the roll of the dice, the sound of a phone ringing from under a couch cushion, a disaster book, birds, snow globes, human dust, icy vodka and the death penalty. It's that in my office every day, dominantly, I listen to the idiosyncratic imagery that studs my patients' expressions of memory, and I love waiting to see the threads that pull together seemingly different images, an anticipation that can be breathtaking.

The suspension of the expectation for accuracy in historical narrative, so very important in this, and all stories. How else to participate in listening, for example, to my relationship with the Charging Bull? Bronze statues don't wink or make eye contact, but that's not important, not at all. The important thing is that I made him into who I needed him to be in a moment of thought-stopping pandemonium, someone who could help me focus and strategize, and do so with ironclad muscle. This is something our patients do all the time as they make their analysts into the people they need us to be. Whether we are made into figures heroic, indifferent, or abusive, this, too, is part of the job, and not just to be understood in terms of transference, but of memory, and memory of trauma in particular. In conversation with Philip Roth, Aharon Appelfeld (1994) says that he is not able to write nonfiction about the Holocaust simply because nobody would believe it if it was presented as true. The authenticity in expression for Appelfeld lies in the way the things that have happened to him have been formed in his mind: "time has kneaded them and given them shape" (p. 68). He says that to integrate the creative element in narrative memory means to "order, sort out, and choose the words and the pace that fit," which ultimately results in a product that is "an independent creature" from historical truth. This is a sentiment that pulses through my listening to patients as they share in creative terms what they might consider to be unbelievable if conveyed in a literal way.

Lastly, and I confess, my favorite part of listening, there is serendipity. The serendipitous moments of my story, the Mahler book, for example, are the moments I treasure most of all. The reason is twofold. On the one hand, there is the mystery of it. Indeed, sometimes it feels wise to not try to understand what feels inexplicable, as if understanding would demystify something importantly magical. On the other hand, there is something to be said for considering the state of preparedness, the ripeness of mind one has to be in for something serendipitous to occur. That circular book rack, it wasn't just that I *thought* it was there by the elevator all along, it *was* there all along. Theoretically speaking, I needed a way to connect my potential and newly opened self to concrete, symbolic thinking. This, I believe, is what Bion (1962) elucidated when speaking of the moment when a preconception, which has yet to find shape through articulation, meets experience in the real world.

And serendipity doesn't end when I get my license to practice psychoanalysis. How to understand, for example, that on the very day when I am almost ready to give up on 9/11 as the anchor of this chapter, feeling that it has become an empty meme, I find myself standing next to my oldest daughter on her college campus at a memorial for the victims of the recent terror attacks in Paris, her face lit up by the candle she is holding, an image that washes away any feelings of vacancy or doubt, and restores solemnity to the phrase "September 11." How to explain that in the midst of my writing this chapter, a new patient notices the dog-eared, barely-held-together Mahler book that now lives in an inglorious ziplock bag on my bookshelf and asks me to tell her about it. And finally, how to understand that just as I am struggling with how to locate myself within the voices that have already written about memoir, memory, and psychoanalysis, my daughter—the baby in the stroller with the open gaze—shows me the book she is reading. It is Rilke's *Letters to a Young Poet* (1875–1926/1984), and as I look at the page her thumb is open to, page 4, I hear him tell me to try, "as if no one had ever tried before, try to say what you see and feel."

Notes

I would like to thank Andy Bachman, Donnel Stern, Susan Obrecht, and Philip Gardner for their continual encouragement during this writing.
1 Bryan Stevenson's tireless and inspiring work on behalf of the poor and condemned is based in Alabama's Equal Justice Initiative. http://eji.org. The sentiment I recall here can be found, among other deeply important lessons, in his recent book *Just Mercy* (2014).

References

Altstein, R. (2016a). Finding words: How the process and products of psychoanalytic writing can channel the therapeutic action of the very treatment it sets out to describe. *Psychoanalytic Perspectives*, *13*(1), 51–70.

Altstein, R. (2016b). Ghosts and growth: Reply to commentaries by Anthony Bass and Steven Kuchuck. *Psychoanalytic Perspectives*, *13*(1), 89–95.

Appelfeld, A. (1994). *Beyond despair: Three lectures and a conversation with Philip Roth*. New York, NY: Schocken Books.

Bass, A. (2007). When the frame doesn't fit the picture. *Psychoanalytic Dialogues*, *17*, 1–27.

Beebe, B. (2012). *Mothers, infants and young children of September 11*. New York, NY: Routledge.
Bion, W. (1962). *Learning from experience*. London: Karnac.
Bollas, C. (1987). *The shadow of the object: Psychoanalysis of the unthought known*. New York, NY: Columbia University Press.
Boulanger, G. (2007). *Wounded by reality*. Hillsdale, NJ: The Analytic Press.
Brown, L. J. (2005). The cognitive effects of trauma. *Psychoanalytic Quarterly*, 74, 397–420.
Fonagy, P., & Target, M. (1998). Mentalization and the changing aims of child psychoanalysis. *Psychoanalytic Dialogues*, 8, 87–114.
Greenberg, J. R. (1986). The problem of analytic neutrality. *Contemporary Psychoanalysis*, 22, 76–86.
Herman, J. (1992). *Trauma and recovery*. New York, NY: Basic Books.
Kaplan, L. J. (1978). *Oneness and separateness*. New York, NY: Simon & Schuster.
Lakoff, M., & Johnson, M. (1980). *Metaphors we live by*. Chicago, IL: University of Chicago Press.
Lakoff, M., & Johnson, M. (1999). *Philosophy in the flesh*. New York, NY: Basic Books.
Levenson, E. (1983). *The ambiguity of change*. New York, NY: The Analytic Press.
Minarik, E., & Sendak, M. (1957). *Little bear*. New York, NY: Harper Collins.
Modell, A. (2005). Emotional memory, metaphor, and meaning. *Psychoanalytic Inquiry*, 25, 555–568.
Modell, A. (2009). Metaphor: The bridge between feelings and knowledge. *Psychoanalytic Inquiry*, 29, 6–17.
Nabokov, V. (1951). *Speak, memory*. New York, NY: Harper & Bros.
New York Criminal Procedure Law § 450.10.
New York Education Law § 8405: NY Code, Section 8405.
O'Brien, T. (1990). *The things they carried*. New York, NY: Houghton Mifflin.
Ogden, T. H. (1997). Reverie and metaphor. *International Journal of Psychoanalysis*, 78, 719–732.
Ogden, T. H. (2005). On psychoanalytic writing. *International Journal of Psychoanalysis*, 86, 15–29.
Ornstein, A. (2010). The missing tombstone: Reflections on mourning and creativity. *Journal of the American Psychoanalytic Association*, 58, 631–648.
Phillips, J. (Producer), & Spielberg, S. (Director) (1977). *Close encounters of the third kind* [Motion picture]. Los Angeles, CA: Columbia Pictures.
Plaut, F. (1999). The writing of clinical papers: The analyst as illusionist. *Journal of Analytical Psychology*, 44, 375–393.
Richman, S. (2014). *Mended by the muse*. New York, NY: Routledge.
Rilke, R. M. (1984). *Letters to a young poet* (S. Mitchell, Trans.). New York, NY: Vintage Books. (Original work published 1875–1926)
Salter, J. (1993). James Salter: *The Art of Fiction No. 133* [Interview with Edward Hirsch]. *The Paris Review*, 35(127), 55–100.
Slochower, J. (2014). *Holding and psychoanalysis, second edition: A relational perspective*. New York, NY: Routledge.
Spence, D. (1982). *Narrative truth and historical truth*. New York, NY: W. W. Norton & Co.
Stern, D. B. (1990). Courting surprise: Unbidden perceptions in clinical practice. *Contemporary Psychoanalysis*, 26, 452–478.
Stern, D. B. (2003). *Unformulated experience*. New York, NY: Routledge.

Stern, D. B. (2010). *Partners in thought*. New York, NY: Routledge.
Stevenson, B. (2014). *Just mercy*. New York, NY: Random House.
Van der kolk, B. (2014). *The body keeps the score: Brain, mind and body in the healing of trauma*. New York, NY: Viking.
Vivona, J. M. (2003). Embracing figures of speech. *Psychoanalytic Psychology, 20*, 52–66.
Winnicott, D. W. (1965). *The maturational processes and the facilitating environment*. London: Hogarth.
Wolff, T. (2003). *Old school*. New York, NY: Knopf.

Chapter 12

My psychoanalytic self
Discovery, embrace, and ongoing formation

Dorothy Evans Holmes

Psychoanalytic precursors in early family life

The roots of my psychoanalytic self were established in the vibrancy and texture of my family of origin and the culture that surrounded us as I grew up in my home city of Chicago. Those early influences, unbeknown to me as particularly formative for my identity as a psychoanalyst until my mid-20s, included abiding intellectual curiosity, pursuit of academic excellence in college and beyond (my mother's side of the family) and/or dedication to skilled crafts (my father's side of the family). Those highly motivated and focused folks pursued their professions and trades with vigor, purpose, and joy. In addition, there was lots of singing, piano and saxophone playing, and poetry recitations, often in Latin by my maternal grandmother. My identical twin sister and I, and our many first cousins in our large extended family, were clearly expected to follow suit, particularly in the academic track, and all of us did so! There were many encouragements along the way—the good example provided by our elders and their particular and persevering interest in the development of our minds, shown by a great readiness to engage us in discussions of family life and history, community and world issues. We were expected to be interested in such matters, to have answers to their questions and to have some questions of our own. There was a great emphasis placed on thinking, and deeply. Feelings and their importance were also recognized, but more as context and backdrop, not so much spoken or elaborated.

Painful feelings in particular (for example, those associated with my uncle's death in the Pacific Theatre of World War II when I was 2 years old; my parents' divorce a few years later) were expected to be "worked through." The kind of working through that was most valued in my family was using one's life work, or preparation for same, as salvation through mastery of what could be mastered in the face of that which could not. Working through community and personal challenges by talking about them was not pooh-poohed, but also was not emphasized (e.g., challenges like a strictly enforced segregated city, or like being told to skip college and become an operator for the local telephone company, even though I was Salutatorian of my high school class in a college preparatory high school). My maternal grandmother was given more to uninterrupted engagement of her routines (she cooked superbly and presented her meals elegantly; she would instructively recite her favorite poem, *Invictus*, at troubled times, showing one can persevere against the odds).

At times of sorrow and loss, my mother would sing and play Spirituals and ballads on the piano, which was cathartic for her. Her father—my maternal grandfather and a prominent Protestant minister—when hardship struck, was prone to concentrate more on his sermon preparation and on a hopeful theme that he would then deliver in a lively, sometimes fiery way enhanced by breaking into song in his mellifluous baritone voice. His most well-known recorded song was *Fifty Miles of Elbow Room*. The lyrics promise justice, liberation, redemption, and vindication. It was a perfect song for a segregated city with lyrics such as "When the gates swing wide on the other side."[1] My grandfather's richness and complexity were inherent in his love of that song and those words. It was clear to me as a Black child that he was not referring just to what was promised in heaven, but to what was possible here on earth, on the other side of racial and class prejudice and their imposed limitations. The lack of emphasis on direct experiencing and expressing of one's feelings was an unconscious hedge my family placed against the possibilities of being overwhelmed by them, especially anger and disappointment associated with social injustice. In retrospect, I realize that my eventual turn towards psychoanalysis was motivated in part to give me additional tools to open the gate wide to the feeling aspects of myself, including my racial self.

Stirring the pot: the impact of early exposure to psychoanalytic thinking

I first became consciously aware of the rich possibilities of psychoanalysis for my own life, first and foremost for my personal development, when I was in my early 20s while a Clinical Psychology Intern in the Department of Psychiatry at Case Western Reserve University (1966–1967). The Department was known then as "Hanna Pavilion"; it was a bastion of psychoanalytic thinkers, scholars, and practitioners. It was chock full of towering psychoanalytic figures including Brian Bird, Douglas Bond, Robert Tyson, Anny and Mauritis Katan, and in the Child Division, Robert and Erna Furman. Also, keenly interested in psychoanalysis and partially trained in it was the famed pediatrician, Benjamin Spock. The Department stood out for me, too, for one of its most gifted psychoanalytic supervisors, Charles DeLeon, MD. Striking in its singularity at Case, and rare anywhere, this gifted supervisor was a Black psychiatrist and psychoanalyst.

Consciously, I did not go to Cleveland to study with the psychoanalytic giants just named; rather, I chose Hanna Pavilion in order to reunite for a year with my identical twin sister, Doris, who was then a third-year medical student at Case. In the rich complexity of re-engaging my twin sister, I became aware of further work I needed to do regarding my own identity formation, and became frustrated that the tools I had based on my graduate study to that point were not binding considerable anxiety I was beginning to experience. Yet, it was a stretch and a strain for me to embrace psychoanalysis for two reasons:

1. I had chosen a graduate school (Southern Illinois University, Carbondale) that emphasized behaviorism (ala Hull, Spence, and Skinner) and social learning theory (e.g., Julian Rotter and Janet Rafferty). Those points of view adhere to a black box notion of the mind, which assumes that you cannot see into it, and that one does not need to, but rather one need only work with observable behaviors. In some senses, that kind of thinking is parallel in psychoanalysis to working only with manifest content. Coming to Case Western Reserve created cognitive dissonance in me, or in our psychoanalytic language, conflict. In some ways I felt like I was abandoning my graduate school. I had felt secure in what I was learning at SIU and proud of its traditions and its luminaries (e.g., Hull, Spence, Skinner, and Harlow). Learning about the power of reinforcements, and how to objectively manipulate them to create desired effects was important to me, and until my internship felt sufficient and intellectually satisfying. I thought I had all the tools I needed to, in the words of my grandfather's favorite song, "swing the gates wide" open to understand and relieve suffering.
2. To some extent I also felt like I was betraying my family of origin who were not really "black box" folks, but neither did they look into the feeling aspect of the box very often or very directly, for reasons already stated. They used, and offered me, other tools to solve intellectual and emotional problems—for example, hard and successful work, close family connection, music, and "music therapy" (my mom's piano playing at times she was in pain). Of the many musically gifted folks in my family, I am not one, though I am a music lover. Perhaps if I had the gift of music making, I would not have begun to feel so keenly during my internship year that something needed to be added.

What made it possible for me to begin to embrace psychoanalysis during that formative internship year, despite the just identified conflicts? In the main teaching conference for psychology interns, what I had to say about behaviorism was engaged with as much curiosity and respect as was asked of me in listening to psychoanalytic perspectives. Believe me, I worked hard at presenting behavioral and social learning conceptualizations and treatment recommendations. Like in my family of origin, more value was placed by my first psychoanalytic mentors, teachers, and supervisors on the fact that I was thinking, that I loved to think, that I strove to be a worthy representative of my ideas, and that I would listen to others in turn. When my mid-year internship evaluation was presented to my graduate school program director, it was reported that I was wonderfully enthusiastic, and that I was a clear and convincing thinker and writer. Confidence was expressed that I would resolve my dilemma about how to frame my work. That evaluation initiated a transformative process for me. I felt affirmed in the same ways I had felt in my childhood—in being invited to think, in receiving the gleam in the eye of those I esteemed for my efforts, and in ultimately being affirmed for whatever my choices would be. I came to realize that the choices available to me were wide open (again as my grandfather would preach and sing) and that I did not need to reject options. I still retain a love for and faithfulness to the behavioral and social learning traditions that honored objectivity and parsimony in focusing on direct observation. In addition, I have dared to open the mind's black box in psychoanalytic pursuit of understanding and relief of suffering. Both traditions course through me and inform what I do. The behavioral and social learning approaches keep me faithful to meticulous observation and help curb any tendency I may have for "wild analysis." Psychoanalytic approaches make it possible for me to include all that needs to be included.

So, how did I make my newly forming embrace of psychoanalytic tools a reality in my life? During my internship at Case, I entered my first psychoanalytic psychotherapy. It held me steady as I began to change my identity—from a behaviorist only to one who came to know the importance of looking inside the mind, and one who would learn to do so without disavowal of previous perspectives. That therapy helped me understand that my family of origin's most important preparation of me was for me to become whoever I was becoming, and not to be a strict adherent to their methods. Particular internship experiences were also helpful to me in feeling emboldened to take on the breadth and depth of human functioning. Charles DeLeon was my first psychoanalytic supervisor. He supervised me in my treatment of a self-loathing Black woman who angrily projected her self-hatred into me—demanding to know why the Clinic had assigned her to me. When I somewhat timidly suggested to Dr. DeLeon that my prospective patient seemed very angry as evidenced by clear observables such as arms locked across her chest, scowling facial expressions, exasperated sighs whenever I spoke). He laughed and said, "There is no 'seemed' about it; tell her you notice her anger and that you are interested to know what's making her angry." I tried the recommended intervention, and wow! The patient said, "They gave me you." I said, "What is there about me that angers you so?" The patient said, "You're a Negro; you're a woman, and you are a psychologist." In all three aspects, I was, in her eyes, and in her projected self, worthless. And so, a year of very productive work began by first allowing my patient to use me to empty herself of what she could not abide about herself, to have me contain it and with Dr. DeLeon's superb supervision, help her eventually own her feelings and become more self-accepting. I am forever grateful to Dr. DeLeon and also to my first psychoanalyst therapist and my first internship patient for helping me open the gates wide to a rich and rewarding embrace of psychoanalysis.

My psychologist supervisors on my internship also had a deep understanding and love of psychoanalytic theories and techniques. Each had been analyzed, and each supervised me using psychoanalytic perspectives, as in my learning of Rorschach interpretation based on Roy Schafer's approach, the interpretive tools of which were steeped in psychoanalytic understandings. Of equal to greater importance were those supervisors' subtle influence on my thinking about obtaining my own analysis one day. The supervisor most influential in that regard was Dr. Richard Wortman. He made clear that personal psychoanalysis had been indispensably important for his development. It vitalized his life in many ways, including helping him find his true and differentiated self (he, too, was a twin, like me!), and in providing the clarity and scaffolding necessary for him to leave an earlier successful but insufficiently vitalizing career to become a psychologist. He encouraged me to stay attuned to who I really wanted to become, and to trust myself that I could make it happen. At nearly 90 years old today, he still sees a few patients in psychoanalytic psychotherapy. His thinking in general, and psychoanalytically, is as sharp and deep as ever!

In returning to SIU-Carbondale after my internship to complete my dissertation, my psychoanalytic identity was emergent but not crystalized and not dominant. As such, I formulated my dissertation with social learning theory concepts. It was a study of the value of setting and rewarding positive expectations in learning tasks among underachieving socio-economically disadvantaged and African-American inner city elementary school boys. The manipulated variables were positive expectancy and rewards for performance in the positive expectancy groups. At first I was surprised and disappointed that the learning tasks were mastered as well by control subjects as by the experimental subjects. In the control group, the learning tasks were administered neutrally, that is, without introduction of positive expectancy with rewards for performance. The control group subjects had formed a very positive attachment to their test administrator who, though neutral with respect to the study's experimental variables, was a very kind, warm, and patient middle-aged African-American man. Aha! What I had already learned about psychoanalytic thinking began to affect how I interpreted my dissertation data: Relational factors were as influential as the experimental variables I manipulated to improve learning. I inferred that the test administrator in the control condition was in fact received as the welcome father figure who was a missing link in the lives and spirits of the subjects in my study. In the positive connection he made with them, he helped them learn just as much as subjects exposed to specifically manipulated experimental variables. Most of the boys were from single family homes headed by mothers. Thus, I left graduate school with some recognition and appreciation of the mutative effects of working alliance and positive transference.

My first full embrace of psychoanalytic perspectives

In focusing on next steps in my last year of graduate school, I knew that I wanted to select a postdoctoral setting that was psychoanalytically oriented. I was accepted into the two year postdoctoral program in the Department of Psychiatry at the University of Rochester. I was fortunate to join that program when it was still in its heyday (1968–1970). Led by the charismatic and brilliant John Romano, MD, and with luminaries such as George Engel (in psychiatry and medicine) and Irving Weiner (psychology chief in the Department of Psychiatry), the Department was chock full of wisdom, high energy, and an open receptivity to psychoanalytic thinking and practice, accompanied by healthy skepticism and integration of multiple points of view within psychoanalysis and beyond it. It was in that context that George Engel's biopsychosocial model flourished and became a national standard for assessment of patients. On the quieter side of fame there were many at Rochester who were also highly influential for their deep knowledge and love of psychoanalytic thinking. In particular, I fondly remember Otto Thaler, a psychiatrist and psychoanalyst who had fled the Nazis in Vienna. He gave reverent attention to his ongoing study of psychoanalysis. He studied and reflected on psychoanalytic works as one might study scripture. He showed a degree of mastery of psychoanalytic thinking that I had not seen before, nor have I since. His interest in all things psychoanalytic was lively, supple, and inquiring, not dogmatic or closed. He was a great mentor and supervisor.

It was also at Rochester that I had the great privilege of being supervised by Irving Weiner. He is the most effective psychology chief I have ever worked with. He was masterly beyond compare in applying psychoanalytic points of view to psychodynamic therapy and to psychological testing, including forensic evaluations, which I learned to do under his supervision. He and Otto taught me to make clear and parsimonious psychoanalytic formulations, and to do so with efficiency. They taught me that psychoanalysis is able to be understood and expressed with clarity, and that mystification of psychoanalysis is the result of incomplete understanding based on poor preparation, doctrinaire attitudes, and/or unbehooving personal characteristics such as pompousness. So, I learned that while psychoanalysis indeed opens the "black box" of the mind, its tools permit inclusion of complex, not always directly observable variables that can be formulated clearly and parsimoniously. A particular and challenging test of this learning came to me in a Grand Rounds in which the distinguished Chair, Dr. Romano, formulated a case of a white protestant minister who suffered a recurrence of his schizoaffective illness. As was true in past episodes, the most obvious stressor was a relapse in his wife's serious physical illness that was chronic and progressive, and the most obvious, though misguided coping mechanism used by the minister was that he had an affair. What was unique in the episode being formulated in Grand Rounds was that the woman with whom he had the affair was, in the language of the day, a Negro. Dr. Romano, usually brilliant, circumspect, and parsimonious in his formulations, stated that the cause of the minister's illness was that he had had an affair with a "Negress." I was deeply disturbed by his assertions—both in what to me, and others, seemed like uncharacteristic "wild analysis" in elevating the affair to causal when clearly affairs had always been an expression of the manic aspect of his illness, and in the pejorative, dare I say, racist put down of the man's paramour by designating her a "Negress."

In my progression towards a psychoanalytic identity, and emboldened by all of the good lessons in judicious and informed uses of psychoanalysis already taught me by Dr. Romano and the other giants at Rochester, I made an appointment to speak with Dr. Romano. We had a respectful exchange about the matter. I did not persuade him to desist from using the term "Negress," nor did he change his formulation. I felt the loss of collaboration to think together about what role the paramour's race may have played. What did her Blackness mean to the minister? While Dr. Romano did not offer us those opportunities, he did offer me a position in the Department. While I chose to leave Rochester to pursue my career in a larger, more culturally diverse city, I recognize and honor my Rochester years as *the most formative ones in setting me on my path to becoming a psychoanalyst.* I learned to love psychoanalysis at Rochester, not because it or its proponents were perfect. They were not, but even the imperfections were so informative and could be understood in psychoanalytic terms. Also, both at Rochester, and at Case Western Reserve before it, psychoanalysis was offered as a set of tools preeminent for their powers to understand and to effect change, but needing to be used according to the patient's need, and not for hegemonic purposes to be imposed on departmental politics or individual patients. The Grand Rounds experience just described, and the experience of my internship with the Black patient who despised herself in gender, career, and racial terms, all of which she projected into me, galvanized what has become a career-long clinical and research focus on the psychodynamics of race and class and how they are pivotal in the formation of symptoms and character (ours and our patients), and how to work with them in psychoanalytic treatments.

Psychoanalysis proper, here I come

In leaving Rochester, having completed my formal education and training, I began a 41-year career based in Washington, DC (1970–2011) where I maintained a career focus divided between part-time clinical practice and full-time academic life, the latter expressed in three institutions: briefly in the Department of Psychology at the University of Maryland (1970–1973), then lengthily in the Department of Psychiatry at Howard University (1976–1998), and for the last 13 years of my academic career (1998–2011), in the Center for Professional Psychology at The George Washington University where I directed the Professional (PsyD) Program. (Before joining the Howard

Faculty (1973–1976), I served as Chief Psychologist in the Alexandria, VA Community Mental Health Center to give myself clinical and administrative immersion while I determined which academic post I would next pursue). In each of these settings, I sought to bring psychodynamic thinking to bear, as I continued to deepen and consolidate my own psychoanalytic bona fides. The latter included two psychoanalyses, one before psychoanalytic training and one during. Each analysis was immensely helpful to me. My analysis before training played a decisive role in freeing me from embedded "father issues." To make that progression required intensive work with my Black male analyst through the vicissitudes of my paternal transference manifestations, which were in some ways very gratifying, but in very important ways liberated me from anxiety about the father I had lost through divorce in my early childhood.

My first analyst made clear that how well, or not, he sustained himself was his responsibility, not mine, and he remained faithful to the work we needed to do to set me free of the strictures that resided in me as a function of my father hunger and father rescue fantasies and motivations. I continued that work and much more with my training analyst, a Southern white man. The sweep of the many ways he helped me grow is beyond the scope of this narrative. There is one point I do want to emphasize, that is, the way he worked with me on race, including its great importance to me personally as a Black woman, and as a focus of my career. He was open, respectfully curious, hopeful, and fully able to receive my multiple, intense racial transferences with rich but not disruptive countertransference manifestations. It is impossible to overstate the value of that dimension of my training analysis in making me whole, particularly racially, in terms of becoming proudly and unselfconsciously identified as a Black woman.

The value and vicissitude of psychoanalytic training

As to which psychoanalytic institute I "chose," there was not really much room for choice. As a psychologist, I was determined to be trained "on the record," meaning I respected but could not follow the example of brave psychologists and brave psychoanalysts who fashioned training programs behind the scenes with teaching, training, and supervising analysts who were willing to defy the limitations imposed at that time (the late 1970s) by the American Psychoanalytic Association (APsaA). From all I have said about my journey so far, I hope it is clear that from my early childhood years, I was taught that my voice and my dreams are valid, and always to be expressed by my choice (versus the recommendation of my high school counselor who advised me to become a telephone operator). There were many people who helped me strengthen the view of myself that I should nurture and pursue my ambitions, many of whom I have named in this narrative. I also had learned not to yield to prejudice, and to recognize it and challenge it, even when it was disguised (for example, the Rochester Grand Rounds experience). Thus, I decided to enter the one APsaA Institute in the Washington, DC area that would receive applications from doctoral-level mental health professionals other than physicians, namely, the Baltimore Washington Institute. That meant undergoing the "waiver" application process for waiving of medical qualifications. As part of that process, one was expected to state that in becoming a psychoanalyst one would not become a practitioner, but would use the full training to enhance research or strategic placement (for example, as a program head). I declined to write my application that way. Rather, I argued that any of my research, teaching, or administration would necessarily and irreducibly need to be informed by practice. My institute allowed me to submit the application as I wrote it, and APsaA accepted me, though (because?) I challenged them.

While I personally found the waiver process insulting and as representing thinly veiled prejudice, I decided to become one who would try to fight that prejudice from within. By the late 1980s, the old waiver system was dismantled as a result of a restraint of trade lawsuit brought to bear by four brave psychologists. As I said, there was not really a choice available to me as to the Institute in which I would train. However, training in the Baltimore Washington Institute proved to be most fortuitous. It was a perfect fit for me, given my total history. The Institute was largely, though not dogmatically, an ego psychologically-oriented institute. Emphasis was placed on what could be directly observed, especially on manifestations of defense that impeded expression of drive derivatives. The approach proffered that by analyzing defenses, the ego would be strengthened in its many capacities, including making the person strong enough to experience and voluntarily express drive derivatives. This orientation was very welcome by me. Its emphasis on direct observation of defense honored my early behavioral training. Its emphasis on the importance of the ego and its capacities honored the family I grew up in, as well as the great appreciation for the mind and its capacities I learned in the great institutions in which I was privileged to study, including Case Western Reserve and the University of Rochester. The allowance for affects made by ego psychology fit my family of origin, too, and especially my grandfather's hopes for the exuberant celebration of life when the gates are open wide. I learned ego psychology from its most famous proponent of that era (the 1970s and 1980s), Dr. Paul Gray. While he was passionate, clear, and unswerving in his faithfulness to his approach, he, like those from whom I learned at Case and Rochester, showed creativity and flexibility in applying theory and technique to patients, in accord with their need.

Becoming a psychoanalyst has been an indispensably important mainstay of my life and my career. Without its requirements for disciplined learning about every level and every realm of human functioning, without its call to be respectfully curious, without its radical tools to explore, to upset the status quo, and to make wellness where there was disabling sickness, I could not have thrived in my profession or personally. It has been the third leg of the stool on which I have built my life, along with the rich resources of my family and my formal education and training preceding psychoanalytic training. The three together have made it possible for me to love, to be resilient in the face of heartache and setback, and to come to my sunset years with profound gratitude for the riches of my life.

Psychoanalysis sustains me still as I look at, participate in, and continue to try to help those hurt by our broken world—a world still and perhaps always to be subject to brokenness by the "isms" that I have made the focus of my entire career. Psychoanalysis has the tools to understand and help remediate the "isms." My current focus as a psychoanalyst is to study and publish on institutional as well as individual manifestations of the "isms," including their manifestations in psychoanalytic institutes and institutions. As Dr. Romano, a decent and honorable man, taught me in the Grand Rounds he chaired at Rochester many years ago, none of us are immune from using our individual or institutional powers to express an "ism." In that era of entrenched racism, he was not prepared to change his racist views, or to recognize the distortions they caused in his usually impeccably astute thinking. I have had the experience many times since, in the consultation room and in institutions, that people are willing to treat these issues in themselves and in their institutions, if only in little steps at a time. I say "treat" these issues because my realism/pessimism tells me that the human propensity to prejudice and the broad and ever expanding range of "isms" are intrinsic and perhaps incurable. However, as I have said in many a classroom, in supervisions, and in the consulting room, that which cannot be cured, like hypertension, can and must be treated ... daily.

Ongoing formation: continuing to grow my psychoanalytic self

Writing this narrative has in itself been therapeutic for me. I have chuckled along the way, and I have wept. It is sweet and it has been fun to remember those people and experiences that have so substantially helped me form my psychoanalytic self. Some of the tears have been tears of joy and deep appreciation. Some have expressed the sadness I can still feel for those who have influenced me so much to my benefit, but who are now in their final resting place. Such a rich array of people and experiences! Even those who were once ghostly in their impact, are now transformed, as Freud would say, into ancestors. I do not idealize psychoanalysis or its representatives, as I once did. I know that we as psychoanalysts are flawed. My own flawed tendency is to be too exacting in my expectations of myself and others. I keep treating that tendency each day. In that sense I will always be in the process of becoming a psychoanalyst, and I am enjoying the process! Since 2011, I am maintaining a private practice of psychotherapy and psychoanalysis in Bluffton, SC, and I continue my scholarly activities.

A final appeal for analysts to make more use of our radical discipline to heal the "isms"

In having had the good fortune in my career to advance to Teaching, Training, and Supervising Analyst, I had the privilege to be able to teach and supervise psychoanalysis in my institute and to be able to analyze those in training to become analysts as well as others outside our field. I also was able to teach applied psychoanalysis in three universities and a community mental health center. I am happy that I had those opportunities and influences. I have also valued becoming a psychoanalytic scholar whose focus has been to help myself and others to understand the multiple negative impacts of racism and sexism. My particular interest has been to demonstrate the necessity of addressing these and other cultural influences and their histories in psychoanalytic teaching, supervision, and practice. It is my very committed position that psychoanalysts can and need to do more with this particular application of psychoanalysis. In doing so, we will more fully realize the radical possibilities of our discipline. We live in our cultures and they live in us. It is my view that whatever resides in us, in our personal psychologies, including our cultural experiences and histories, is the proper focus of psychoanalysis.

While I love psychoanalysis for all that it has given me—including the full articulation and strengthening of my voice to speak psychoanalytically about race and class—I recognize that we can do more. I appeal to all of us do so. If we, as psychoanalysts, continue to give puny attention in our self-understanding, our conceptualizations, teaching and clinical work to forces such as racism, we risk discrediting ourselves as worthy heirs of psychoanalysis, a truly radical discipline. I ask that we at least make a better showing than we have, first by recognizing that as psychoanalysts we are as prone as any citizen to expressing any "ism." At the same time, as trained psychoanalysts we have tools beyond those available to any citizen to combat the "isms" as they seek to gain ground within us. With respect to the "isms," I suggest that all of us are still becoming the best (not perfect) analysts we can become. I wish for us all that we will make the effort—in our own ongoing analyses, whether formal or self-analysis, in our teaching and supervision, and in our clinical work.

Note

1 *Fifty Miles of Elbow Room* by A. P. Carter. Used by Permission of Peer International Corporation.

Chapter 13

Untranslatables

Spyros D. Orfanos

> In memory of my sister Eleni D. Orfanos,
> and to my ancestors, all of them, all the way back.

Where the blue really begins

It was a Tuesday, June 30, in the summer of 2015 on the Greek island of Ereikousa. In that tumultuous political summer, the European Union was imposing devastating economic austerity measures on Greece while she was receiving close to a million refugees fleeing the Syrian Civil War. I was travelling from a Toronto relational psychoanalytic conference. I was one of the co-chairs of the conference and it had gone well. My body was tired and my heart was full of energized pessimism. Greeks view Tuesdays as unlucky because the city of Constantinople fell to the Turkish invaders five and a half centuries ago on Tuesday, May 29, 1453. This would, however, be a joyous Tuesday despite Greece's free falling into financial and social ruin.

The island was having a celebration. Ereikousa is a tiny island, rarely found on maps, floating where the Ionian Sea meets the Adriatic Sea, where the blue of the "wine dark sea" of Greece really begins. Oceanographers measure the island at 39 degrees latitude north and 19 degrees longitude east. Ereikousa is as unsophisticated as Toronto is cosmopolitan. In the 18th century, pirates inhabited the island. Today, the population numbers under 240 people though in the mid-20th century Ereikousa had over 500 inhabitants. My parents were born on Ereikousa.

As the ceremony began close to a hundred people gathered on the small plaza, facing the sea. There was no breeze. The heat was almost unbearable. People had traveled from the United States and Israel to mark the island's heroism during World War II. Broadcast and print journalists from different countries were there. Organizers spoke, the grandchildren spoke, and I spoke about the events that had taken place on Ereikousa over 70 years ago. My daughter Lina sang her signature aria, Theodorakis' "Song of Songs" in

Greek and in Hebrew. This was an experience of collective mourning and an act of revenge for a time of enormous suffering.

On style, clinical and otherwise

In this chapter, I trace a few influential elements in the development of my psychoanalytic style or *aesthetic*.[1] My narrative may reveal how my journey in psychoanalysis is really a return. There is a significant link between my aesthetics, my cultural *ethos*, and my personal history. When Aristotle writes about the subject of style in Book III of his *Rhetoric*, he does so apologetically.

He holds that writers are influenced by emotions and tricks of eloquence. You don't need style to teach geometry he argues. Being neither a writer nor a mathematician, this essay is discursive. It proceeds informally. The reader may not find any Aristotelian logic here. I am acutely aware of my time and place context. The time is shortly after my younger sister's death and the grave illness of a great friend, a brother-in-life. The place is one of deep grieving and fear. Fortunately, I contain multitudes as the poet says. My dissociations can be weakness but they also allow me to carry on.

A Greek island custom declares, "Don't tell me what you ate. Tell me who you ate with." I have shared bread and wine with countless personalities. There are no metrics for their impact in my pursuit to become a psychoanalyst and have a "voice." Mythological figures have also stirred my conscious and unconscious mind since childhood (Orfanos, 2006). So have my two analysts and numerous teachers (doctoral and postdoctoral). They have been present like Muses whispering into my ear. My first analyst helped me liberate my "self" and my second helps me with the arduous task of knowing how to be free. At times, these two activities are not the same. That's why I need two analysts and a cargo ship of teachers and friends.

I do feel some self-conscious anxiety in writing about my psychoanalytic style. For one thing, I write with an accent. The enormously talented detective novelist Dashiell Hammett had something to say about style that I appreciate. In his latter life, he said that he stopped publishing because he felt he was repeating himself: "It is the beginning of the end when you discover that you have a style." He tried to alter his style. He wanted to go mainstream, leave the detective novel behind. He wrote and wrote, but he never accomplished anything that satisfied him (Acocella, 2007). Like Hammett, having a style worries me. Still, I do think I have one in both my personal life and my psychoanalytic life and that it is quite often situation and clinically specific. When asked, W. B. Yeats said about style, "How do you separate the dancer from the dance?"

My clinical style is conversational, dialectical, existential, and contemporary relational. It cannot really be separated from my deepest personal convictions and feelings. I have a lifelong attachment to the particular and concrete and an enduring suspicion of the general and abstract. Conceptually, I tend towards clinical theory versus metapsychology. I believe my authentic qualities are likely to be the most important factors in any therapeutic effectiveness I court. Psychoanalysis examines subjective liberty and spontaneous assertion. It explores conditions of free, independent, and creative subjectivity in the context of self and others. I recognize the sheer power of what goes on unconsciously between two people. The psychoanalytic approach is about aliveness, imagination, witnessing both suffering and resilience and the ways in which we can alter our agency in the context of mutual vulnerabilities. I am committed to taking the limits of my self-awareness seriously.

One of the elements of style that I knew I possessed but simultaneously did not know was highlighted a decade ago during a short-term analysis. The analysand was a Greek psychiatrist, let's name her Athena. She was on a temporary work visa in the United States. Speaking in Greek, we were navigating some complex coping mechanisms of hers and likely mine. In contemporary language we were in an enactment. I remember feeling challenged by the cunning unconscious of this woman with despairing eyes. Most of the time, I fielded her aggression with ease, like Willie Mays playing center field. But during one session, I was apparently frustrating her with my efforts to unpack our mutual vulnerabilities (Aron, 2016). I was acknowledging my own permeability and vulnerability and also the erotic elements of our tensions. To my surprise, she called me a *polymechanos*. Athena's tone was admiring. She saw me as skilled and clever and having her best interests in mind. A *polymechanos* is a complex person, full of inventiveness and resources. The ancient word appeared first in Homer and it was used to describe Odysseus. It fit an unformulated sense of style for me rather well. I felt deeply recognized. The desire for recognition went back to my childhood. Being a *polymechanos* was not just personal idiom it is my *Weltanschauung* (Orfanos, 2003).

I possess a transcendent, sensual identification with the sea. Odysseus was my imaginary playmate and muse. I grew up both consciously and unconsciously identifying with him. Unlike the other great Homeric hero Achilles who was an aristocrat warrior full of pride and wrath, Odysseus was a master "trickster" who wanted to get the Trojan War over with in order to journey back home to Ithaca. Most importantly, Odysseus at his core was in possession of a highly valued gift: a plentitude of strategies. He was creative in thought and action. The multiple sides to him could switch depending on the situation. Most of all he endured. Only later as I matured did I abandon my idealization of Odysseus, who had returned to Ithaca to reunite with his son and wife, while his crew apparently lost their lives due to his adventures.

When Athena called me a *polymechanos* she could not have known about my childhood desires. Still, she did know me unconsciously. Once I was leading a small expedition of relational analysts and children (including my wife Sophia and daughter Lina) during a dangerous crossing from the island of Kerkyra to Ereikousa. Poseidon must have been annoyed and unleashed a storm with swells 5 meters high and winds at seven Beauforts.[2] The regular ferry boat refused to undertake the crossing. We waited a day but the storm would not die down. I hired a small fishing vessel of 12 meters length. The fishing boat was unseaworthy and did not have enough life jackets for all 15 of the passengers. I recall being in a state of *kentrosis*—fully focused, alive, and present. I was planning our survival as the storm hit us with its full fury. I imaged I was a better adventurer than Odysseus. We would all return home safe. Of this I was certain or so I believed. And we did.

Quantum entanglements: language and memory

No matter how carefully I pin my words to paper they slip off. I try to communicate their intent but the translation process seems to fail. Greek was the language they gave me. It inspired my imagination. Then at age 8 they gave me English. It is common for me to defensively explain a mispronounced word, a mangled adage, or a slip of the tongue with, "Remember my dear, English was not my first language." Most in my circle are on to my intended deflection by now. Interestingly, it took close to 10 years for my wife to help me correctly pronounce the word "compromise." I use to pronounce it "come promise." The reader can interpret what she or he wishes.

Those that gave me the Greek language also gave me other things, now core to my individual and collective anxieties and strengths. Like many children of immigrants I was the translator for the family and the social worker. This placed a heavy burden on me while at the same time making me sensitive to what is lost in translation. I learned early on to be a caretaker for my immigrant parents. Like many children of immigrants, I translated formal letters and documents for my parents. At times, the sentences and paragraphs were too complicated for my reading levels. I would read haltingly and my father would often smack me behind the head and yell with contempt, "Why am I sending you to school?" I felt shattering shame and a pain in the neck.

Language bewitches me because even precise words are in motion. Language is enigmatic. Language plays games rather than housing truth. Clinically, I believe that much of the time we are dealing with untranslatable experiences. To complicate further, I know there is a link between the words "transference" and "translation." I believe that emotions are central to language. "I felt before I thought," recounted Rousseau in the opening of his *Confessions*. I am sure that in the womb I heard many things but certainly I heard muffled voices speaking Greek, some anxious, some boisterous, some despairing, and always nostalgic. That is my hypotheses, not my memory. Besides language there is another quantum entanglement: memory.

Being human I often abandon myself to the sorcery of memory. In a clever opening to a personal and professional essay on how he has changed as a clinician over the years, the distinguished psychologist and psychoanalyst Paul Wachtel (2001) warns that his own memory is likely based on fragmentary impressions and strongly influenced by the present: "If there's anything at all valid in my fundamental views of how the mind works, then my account of how I have come to those fundamental views must be powerfully biased and flawed" (p. 83).

Who's Freud?

I started my psychoanalytic career a mere 23 years ago. Thus, I consider myself a very young and promising psychoanalyst. I am a work in progress. My aim is to achieve enough mastery in my chosen professional specialty so that I can go about my enterprise with confidence and creativity. Deep down, however, I believe there are no master psychoanalysts. We're all sophomores. That's the nature of the enterprise.

I first heard the name Freud in September 1967. I remember it well. It was during my senior year in English class at Charles Evans Hughes High School in Manhattan's Chelsea neighborhood. The school was considered "inner city," which meant back then it mostly enrolled poor, black kids. Fortunately for me, my teacher Henry Katz (now known as the novelist and music critic Henry Edwards) was interested in teaching students more than in teaching subject matter. During a class on a suffering Danish prince, Katz was writing something on the chalkboard and made a puzzling verbal slip of the tongue concerning his mother. "I wonder what Freud would think of that?" he asked himself out loud.

This moment startled me because I made similar slips myself. I was curious about what was going on with my mental processes but never thought others experienced anything similar. I asked, "Who's Freud?" Katz explained his slip and the comment that followed and to this day, almost half a century later, I am grateful to him. Reading *Hamlet* was another serendipitous event that led me to theorize about the unconscious and form a deep love of the humanities.

Who's Marx?

In August 1835, a young German-Jewish boy, a student at the Friedrich-Wielhelm Gymnasium at Trier on the Moselle River in Germany, wrote his final examination. It was called *Reflections of a Young Man on Choosing a Profession*, and it was sparkling with ideals. In choosing a profession, said Karl Marx at 17, one must not act merely as a servile tool of others. One must obtain independence; and everyone must have a field to serve humanity. We shall never be able to fulfill ourselves truly unless we are working for the welfare of our fellows: then only shall our burdens not break us, then only shall our satisfactions not be confined to poor egoistic joys (Wilson, 1940).

If I was his examiner, armed with my Greek ideals (back then the Germans loved Greek ideals) and my contemporary psychoanalytic knowledge (which didn't exist in 1835 even if I had existed), I might point out to the young Marx that his aspirations contained two elements that would serve him well: (1) personal independence and non-conformity in relation to self-states; and (2) serving humanity, i.e. the Other. These relational acts make us human (Slochower, 2014).

My concern about self and the larger social order has its roots in my family and community. Work alienation also played a role. The underlying economic world of the immigrant and working classes were a painful reality for me. I understood them inside out. You could not grow up in Greek restaurants, diners, and coffee shops in New York City like I did in the late 1950s and early 1960s and not be influenced by Marxists. When my friend Nick, a short-order cook, first suggested I read *The Communist Manifesto*, I thought he said *The Communist Pesto*. I did, however, ask, "Who's Marx?"

On seductions and thrills

In August 1968, I was living with my parents in the Robert Jay Fulton Projects on Ninth Avenue in New York's Chelsea neighborhood and preparing for my first day at college. It was never a given that I would attend college. In fact, what was only a given was that I would become an electrician—a Local 3 union electrician if I didn't run my own restaurant with wall paintings of the Acropolis. When the school's college advisor (she was also my history teacher and knew first hand about my interests) maneuvered a Yale University summer school scholarship that would lead to admission to their college, I was eager to go to New Haven, but my immigrant parents feared that I would separate from them and their values. Pathetically, I did not have the strength to go against my family's wishes. I was too anxiously attached. The compromise was that I would attend an engineering school in Brooklyn. At least that would allow me to build badly needed roads on Ereikousa.

A 4-year scholarship to a major engineering school proved I was a diligent student with a good mind. The week before starting college, my beloved cousin Giorgi, had taken me shopping for two suits. He paid for them. Giorgi is 20 years older and possesses one of the most sparkling minds I have ever known. He also owned a few successful restaurants on the Upper West Side. Giorgi wanted me to look good for college. On the first day of student orientation at Polytechnic Institute of Brooklyn (Polytech) I wore my new suit. I was horrified to find myself the only person not wearing a T-shirt and jeans. My higher education had an ominous beginning

My good fate was to be thrown out of Polytech. Perhaps this happened because I was culturally unprepared for college life. I was also bored and uninspired. In high school, I had wonderful mathematics and science courses and enthusiastic teachers even if Charles Evan Hughes High School was an inner city setting. I did very well in my classes, especially in the study of physics. But there was something deadening about how I was being educated at Polytech and my reaction was withdrawal. These days, good engineering schools have a social consciousness built into the curriculum and they recruit women, but back then it was slide rulers, big-bellied corporate mentalities, and no women. It was not a world I enjoyed. There was little humanity and passion. It was all about building rockets to get to the moon. It was not about the beauty and mystery of the moon.

Booted out, I felt ashamed. I was squandering an opportunity to raise my family's fortunes and social status. I kept the expulsion from college a secret. I worked hard in Giorgi's restaurant on weekends—about 36 hours in total—and made enough cash from tips to enjoy myself the rest of the week. I was also ashamed of having secrets but that did not keep me from a life of debauchery on the Upper West Side. I was intoxicated with audacious erotic desires and acts. I was seduced by dangerous thoughts. I abandoned my inherited Byzantine Orthodoxy. My life became filled as the Ancients might say with decadent *Eros* and supreme *Eros*. The former was sexual and the later intellectual. Life was exhilarating.

Intellectually I was growing rapidly. I spent countless hours sprawled over the long oak tables lit by elegant bronze lamps in the Main Reading Room on the third floor of the New York City Public Library. My mind was ablaze learning from books written by great scholars. This was my Yale and Harvard. I had wandered into the library after some adventures in seedy Times Square. After a 3-year *moratorium*, as Erik Erikson might put it, I entered Fordham University. This was the start of a career in psychology that led to a career in psychoanalysis (Orfanos, 2011). In turn, this led to less debauchery in life. That's the way it goes sometimes.

During my moratorium, I learned the art of talking to single, attractive women. Many women would come into the restaurant and I was upset with myself for being intimidated by their beauty. So, I devised a plan in which I would practice having a conversation with them when they were seated alone. I told myself I should concentrate on learning to speak with them and not try to take them to bed. I would ask about their lives and experiences. It was easier than I thought. I learned that talking created certain kinds of feelings in them. They enjoyed my attention. And it was great for tips. They would light up when I asked with a heavy accent, "Do you like *mademoiselle* the Greece?" and as they smiled at the fantasy I would then add with a sly grin, "Let's go. I'll take you there." But more than such flirtations, they especially loved my listening to their stories. Listening deeply seemed to create an erotic spark. When my fellow workers asked me how I was able to seduce so many, I would say that, "I don't seduce, I thrill." Incidentally, this is exactly how I met my future wife. Without that great fortune, who knows how I might have ended up had I continued with my womanizing.

Divine Eros was the major thrill of my young adulthood. I met Sophia (not *sophia* as in wisdom but a woman named Sophia). Actually, it was not the first time we met. I ignored her the first time because she was with another man. But the second time we met she was alone and I was her waiter. The rest, as they say, is history. I will make a 44-year relationship story short. At first glance, lust dominated but she would have none of me. I think Sophia thought I would be fun but not a keeper. Shortly after, a chance rendezvous in mid-Manhattan led to a phone call that I shall always remember. It was the first time we were speaking on the phone. I don't remember what we spoke about but I do remember her speaking voice. It was her slightly accented, lyrical, and soft speaking voice that I fell in love with first. I was under her spell. Then we married and lived happily ever after. Well, we had our good days and our not so good days.

Sophia, already a psychologist and studying to be a psychoanalyst, played a huge role in my career choice. Her influence led me to do graduate study in psychology. I knew I was always interested in psychology. In fact, Sophia helped me understand some of the psychological games I would create for myself at the restaurant. I played games in order to keep my mind from going numb from all the alienating, repetitive work. If I recited a depressed description of "split pea soup" and then an excited description of "Manhattan clam chowder," I discovered a significant number of customers ordered the chowder. When I reversed my expressive descriptions of the soups, the customers would go for the enthusiastically presented soup. Sophia helped put into words the social psychology influence model I was using. This was amazing to me.

Sophia's influence on my psychoanalytic aesthetic is subtle but profound. This does not mean that our aesthetics are identical. She has her originalities. Over the decades we have had thousands of clinical and theoretical conversations. We both love to talk about each other's cases and offer consultative advice. She is non-impinging to a fault. Sophia's intimate knowledge of my countertransference comes in handy during knotty problems even if sometimes I can't stand her special access into my *psyche*. Her authenticity and values keep me from straying into pretentious theoretical acrobatics. Her work as a painter and her scholarly work on trauma and creativity (Richman, 2014) have deepened my own interests in creativity. My impact on her clinical aesthetic is also present. For instance, my playfulness, spontaneity, and risk-taking has loosened up her more reflective, cautious manner. During imaginative flights, I can be Henry Miller to her Anaïs Nin.

Immigrants and Priests

Working in restaurants on the Upper West Side was a huge education for me. I cannot overestimate it. It taught me about personal style and identity. I learned that the person is the voice. I started working in family restaurants at the age of 10 and continued through my first year of graduate school. I learned how to be a responsible employee, make money, and to practice *phronesis*. *Phronesis* means practical wisdom. Giorgi always emphasized practical wisdom but he couched it in wit. He was and continues to be a raconteur.[3] I worshipped him and to this day in my own clinical work with all types of people I wonder how he would handle a tricky clinical moment. For example, I was in a session with a troubled and troubling adolescent boy. He was a darker than usual Goth hipster and told me he was going to partake of a few drops of his girlfriend's blood. I said, "Why don't you have a rare steak?" We both laughed hysterically and to my relief, he never drank her blood (Orfanos, 2006b). I was channeling Giorgi.

I remember as a young boy, however, my mother and father repeatedly instructed me to be *phronemos*. But my parents and sometimes my teachers did not mean the word to be anything like the Greco-Romans and Giorgi meant it. They meant I should stay seated and quiet. They thought I behaved like a "wild animal" so I was always yelled at to sit with *phronesis*. I was indeed too active for my immigrant parents. Our tight fifth-floor walkup with the bathroom outside in the hallway was not a place to raise a child.

As I climbed up the restaurant career ladder from the basement where I peeled potatoes and onions to the kitchen grill and subsequently became waiting staff, I was exposed to a rich array of comrades. Besides Giorgi the Boss, there was Nectarios the Voice, Tommy the Lover, Stavros the Professor, Nick the Communist, Stelios the Fat One, Yannis the Cypriot, Maria the Widow, Socrates the Young, Socrates the Old, and Jimmy the Mute. I was Spyros the Americanaki (the little American). Often, I was called Spyros the Sensitive. I loved most of my co-workers. I knew their wishes and desires, and how their bodies would hurt from the hard labor. It was a harsh life for many of the unskilled workers. The skilled chefs in the kitchen did better than the dishwashers, the countermen, the waiters and waitresses because they would come in at 4:30 a.m. and leave by 2:30 p.m. The work shift for everyone else was a 10- and/or 12-hour day. Sometimes the workers would develop serious medical problems. Giorgi was better than most restaurant owners in taking care of his workers. I learned how to rely on my co-workers—we depended on each other. This lesson was familiar to me from early childhood, but now I was growing into more mature dependencies. The relationships I cultivated were what made me a successful waiter. I understood interdependence.

Jimmy the Mute got on my nerves. He would hardly ever talk and when he did he was monosyllabic. He seemed misanthropic. One day I decided to go all out and engage him in conversation when he was away from his burning hot water sink and on a coffee break. To my surprise, Jimmy not only knew how to speak, but he was also a man of great substance. He had fought for Greece on the Albanian Front against the invading Italians and Germans during World War II. His wife and child had been murdered during the Civil War that followed. He had traveled the high seas as a merchant mariner and had even met the great poet Nikos Kavadias. This wounded man just needed someone to show some genuine interest in him. For the next 6 months I spent hours listening to Jimmy's stories late at night when business was slow. I learned that some people just need simple and genuine interest to tell their stories. I also learned that my impatience and quick judgments were negative traits.

In the 1960s and 1970s laboring as I did in adolescence, I was acutely aware of the wishes and fears of the many undocumented immigrant workers, mostly

Greek but a few Mexicans too. Every few months, immigration officers would conduct massive sweeps. Giorgi, who himself had been deported five times, could recognize the immigration police immediately as they entered the restaurant. They looked like they were from the Midwest. They wore black suits, white shirts, and thin, unfashionable ties and had darting eyes. Giorgi would yell "Priests!" in Greek and all the undocumented would drop whatever they were doing and run for an escape. Were it not for the terror they struck, these raids would seem like a bad circus clown act. I remember small-framed Socrates the Young hiding from the officers in a garbage can. By the time it was over the restaurant would lose half its staff. I lost many important attachments.

My sweet uncle Plutarchos was captured at a Bronx coffee shop. Instead of being placed in the usual immigration detention center, as was the custom, he was sent to Rikers Island. There he was beaten badly by other prisoners and correction officers. We think it was because they mistakenly believed he spoke English. Plutarchos could not confess even if he wanted to. Plutarchos never returned to America and decades later, like Coleridge's ancient mariner he would recount his traumas of violence and humiliation at every Ereikousa gathering to me.

Others who were captured accepted their fate and sometimes we might see them a few years after they returned to this country, still undocumented, older and worn. Deportation is a horrible external reality and it is also a brutal drama in the internal world of the deportee. It injures. I grew increasingly sensitive to their suffering, uncertainty, and apprehension. A dishwasher once explained, "Each of us has two nightmares. One is that he will die here in America. The other is that he will be caught by the immigration police and sent home to die in Greece."

Besides learning from my co-workers, I was also learning a great deal from customers. The restaurants on the Upper West Side I worked in were near Lincoln Center and were frequented by actors, analysts, ballerinas, garbage men, Holocaust survivors, intellectuals, Mafioso, pimps, priests, prostitutes, undertakers, and writers. I learned how to learn from them, always asking them what, how, and why questions. Many of them took a liking to me, some ignored me, and others used me as a translator so that they could get some food cooked by the Greek in the kitchen the way their mother use to cook it. It was fascinating to learn how people dealt with their hunger needs and to observe thousands of people eat. I learned that most did not feel loved enough by their mothers. Finally, I learned, despite Melina Mercouri's reasoning, to always work on Sunday.

Sundays

Doing psychoanalysis can be wonderfully rewarding in every sense. From my vantage point, psychoanalysis is supreme to any behavioral or social science in capturing the complexities of the human condition. Most of all, it is about a certain engagement, at times moral, with the lives of others and thus my own. Socrates took this relational stance when he said that, "If the soul is to know itself, it must look into a soul." But if there's nothing else in your life besides psychoanalysis, watch out. I have always felt deeply engaged in the study and practice of psychology and psychoanalysis but I have known that I needed to be doing something for my personal *psyche* even if it involved an internal Other.

For decades I practiced long-distance running (marathons, 100- and 500-mile races, 10ks, etc.) and this permitted my mind, especially after a few miles of warm up, to reflect about life. What I loved most, however, was the way my mind would freely associate. Maybe it was the adrenalin kicking in, but I would have exhilarating flights of imagination. But one day my Achilles knee screamed: this is too much and you have to stop. To my surprise and the astonishment of my family and friends, I started practicing yoga. I experimented with it and I enjoyed the calm. I was fortunate to locate a mature teacher with brilliant somatic intelligence. Her name was Joyti. She taught me the ways of a yogi. At times, I taught her the ways of Yogi Berra, the great Yankee catcher. She really enjoyed his "You can't think and hit at the same time," and especially his explanation about how he could see bad pitches "good" because the ball "looks like it saw me, too." I spent a decade with her doing twice a week individual yoga. I had the capacity to switch from a pounding, repetitive physical activity to one that required physical calm and the pursuit of inner peace. Despite many differences between running and yoga, the common factor for me may have been the deep breathing. When, Joyti died, I abandoned yoga. When dealing with the clinical, I am mindful not lose my breath, but I forgive myself if I do.

During her early growth and development our daughter Lina studied voice. In childhood, she performed in numerous operas at the Metropolitan Opera of New York. In adolescence, her vocal interests were interrupted because she was ambushed by a deadly brain tumor. We were all ambushed. To my gratitude, Sophia has eloquently chronicled this traumatic time in our lives (Richman, 2002) so I will not write about it here. I will say only that during her great trial Lina possessed an inner strength and courage that would rival any hero I have ever known or read about. Some 21 years later, my wife Sophia and I still marvel at her ability to face death and utter the great "No!"

Fast forward: Now in her college years, Lina was about to have a senior voice recital. The performance requirement was classical songs in Italian, French, German, and a language of her choice. To my obvious delight she chose Greek (Who knew? I think this counts as a gratuitous denial). It was a voice and piano recital, but after wrestling approval from her school authorities Lina phoned and asked that I find a *bouzouki* player for her Greek songs. "You're kidding me," I said to Lina. "How am I supposed to get a bouzouki player to come to Princeton?" "You know how to get things done, dad." she replied. "Figure it out. And please remember we have to rehearse and you can choose the songs if you want to." It was *polymechanos* time once again.

Lina's assertiveness with the university administrators coupled with the beauty and force of her musicality, and her attunement to some of my unacknowledged desires created an ocean of new possibilities for me. Thus in 2002, I began my career as a music producer. Not bad for someone who cannot carry a tune. Since the dawn of this century, I have produced countless national and international musical concerts and six albums for Lina.

My friends know that my greatest fantasy is to run, for one day and one day only, the Metropolitan Opera of New York. I want to start the day early advising stagehands and electricians, listening to the orchestra rehearse, and making tempo suggestions. At lunchtime, I meet with a potential donor who makes millions selling Twinkies, followed in the afternoon by persuading a *mezzo soprano* diva to abandon her retirement for the sake of art. In the evening, I attend a brilliant performance of *Tales of Hoffman*. Close to midnight I sip cognac with my friend the maestro-tenor Placido Domingo. Then I go back to the Met with my Sophia and make sure the stage is ready for the next day's performance. That's my fantasy. In reality, I only get offers to manage Athenian artists and composers. Still, this is flattering.

Over the years, I have learned to express aspects of my own artistic aesthetics through Lina's career. This type of father–daughter relationship can be problematic. We have had our artistic differences. But my pleasure in organizing and coordinating musicians and artistic productions is enormous. I have a feel for words and music and Lina knows this and trusts me.

In the course of producing I have learned a few things. First, I think in terms of developing the "voice" of the artist. It may not be that different from helping an analyst "find" his or her analyst voice in psychoanalysis (Greenspun, 2011). If you have patience and knowledge and if you are aware of most things that are happening around you, you will court something unexpected. You will facilitate the creation of voice. Second, when asked, "How do you write your novels?" Umberto Eco replied, "From left to right." I realize that "inspiration" is a bad word that tricky musicians use in order to seem artistically respectable. As the old adage goes, genius is 10% inspiration and 90% perspiration.

A psychoanalytic style is like a vocal style. Both are convention bound. The simple classical delivery of a jazz song by a "trained" voice may sound uptight to an audience used to listening to Ella Fitzgerald. In turn, *Lady Ella* singing German lieder may sound wrong. While crossing boundaries is perilous, the mysterious constraints of style do crucial work for much vocal music (Bostridge, 2015). Fluidity across the boundaries (classical, opera, "art songs," Wagner, Puccini, Theodorakis, hip-hop, country, pop) and respectful borrowings, and even thefts do essential work in keeping any art alive.

Mikis and me

One of the most enduring set of aesthetics in my psychoanalytic thinking and practice comes from an unlikely non-psychoanalytic source: the Greek composer and activist Mikis Theodorakis. Back in the 1960s as I was developing my identity, I received unexpected inspiration from the songs of Theodorakis. He created beautiful melodies and set them to magnificent poetry. He created "art for the masses." He erased the barriers between high art and low art by combining folk instruments like the *bouzouki*, of the lower and working classes, with more typical classical instruments like the cello and oboe. He wedded the music of the concert halls with the music of the *tavernas*.

Theodorakis' musical themes and motifs have great psychological depth. They are meaningful and memorializing. For example in 1965, he set to music the poems of a survivor of the Austrian concentration camp of World War II named Iakovos Kambanellis. The song cycle is titled *Mauthausen* and contains four arias. The first is "Song of Songs." This song about a girl murdered in a concentration camp has become one of the great mournful songs of Europe and the Middle East (Orfanos, 2014b). The music and poetry of "Song of Songs" make it not just a lament but also an act of peace.

Now in his early 90s, frail but as sharp and rebellious as ever, Theodorakis is a titan of Modern Greece. He may be her last hero. He is certainly a hero for me. In part, he is the father I never had. My own father was a harsh man who physically abused me. My mother did this too but I could often outrun her. My father was deeply wounded by his years in America and he often took it out on me. He didn't know what else to do (Orfanos, 2010). I suppose I escaped by reading about and imitating Greek heroes such as Odysseus. In choosing as my ethical guide Theodorakis, this old-school *grandezza* of a man, I was making a more mature choice. Unlike Odysseus, Theodorakis never left his people behind. He never acted superior to anyone while at the same time he understood his uniqueness and personal idiom. His community was the world.

Theodorakis has written over 1,000 songs, many of which Greeks know by heart. His signature genre was the popular art song. He has also composed symphonies, concertos, oratorios, and operas, which have been performed on the great concert stages of the world, though in Greece his work has had its most profound impact. Theodorakis set poems by Nobel Prize recipients like George Seferis, Odysseus Elytis, Pablo Neruda, and other well-known poets to music using popular instruments and singers, so beautifully that every taxi driver and intellectual in Greece was singing the same songs. He started a cultural revolution in his country in the 1960s. My mother, with only a first-grade education, and my father, with his sixth-grade education, sang Nobel Prize winning poetry because of Theodorakis.

I learned from Theodorakis that the world harbors dangers and that sometimes I had to be able to sit with the danger and the suffering and just be there and survive. I learned not to disengage from grief and mourning. Further, I learned that sometimes I have to oppose the tragic. I learned that the individual is always in relation to the other. I learned that there was great beauty in the world. I understand that life is not fair, it just is. His songs taught me much of this but so did our encounters. I've been to countless of his concerts both here and abroad and I have interviewed him almost every year for the last two decades in his home in Athens in a music room that overlooks the Parthenon.[4] Being in his presence, I feel that I love him and that I have known him all my life, this giant, this musical genius who transforms national and personal trauma into art. "Creative expression," he says, "is, above all, an act of freedom. I create means I am free—I become free. The message of art is the message of freedom." This sentiment, part romantic and part pragmatic, I believe, is also the message of psychoanalysis.

Ereikousa

I was born into a family that migrated to the island of Manhattan from the island of Ereikousa. Ereikousa had no electricity and no running water. There were only narrow, dirt roads. There were no medical services. My grandmothers mourned the death of fifteen young children and transmitted these losses to me (Orfanos, 2014a). My father "jumped ship" in 1948 in Baltimore and worked his way to New York City. He wanted to be in America for the simple reason of economic survival. He felt bitterness towards the Greek state for not providing jobs for its citizens. Greek unemployment back then was similar to the levels of today. That is, in the 30% range for adults and in the 60% range for those under 25 years of age. Today, Greece is in economic ruin due to predatory European loans, corrupt politicians, and gangster bankers. Back in the late 1940s, Greece was in economic ruins due to the Cold War between the United States and the Soviet Union. My father's experience in America was of being uprooted, dislocated, and dispossessed. He was "wounded by reality" as a friend on the Upper West Side might say. Coming to America did not feel like much of a choice for him and the others. It was not a land of new beginnings and self-reinvention. These were the feelings of all my Greek American relatives, every one of them. They appreciated the opportunities for work but immigration was a deep wound. Thus, all the members of my family seemed to suffer from a severe case of *nostalgia*.

The late Svetlana Boym, a brilliant Russian and Slavic scholar, wrote a remarkable history of "hypochondria of the heart" her poetic term for *nostalgia* (which seemed to me to possess enough poetry as a word itself). She traced the etymology of the word nostalgia to the Greek *nostos*-return home, an *algia*-longing. Boym (2001) defines nostalgia as a longing for a home that no longer exists or has never existed. Nostalgia is feeling of loss and displacement. It is also a romance with one's own fantasy, a yearning for the time of our childhood, the slower rhythms of our dreams. Boym believes that the mourning of displacement and temporal irreversibility, is at the very core of the modern condition. Nostalgia is about the relationship between individual biography and the biography of groups or nations, between personal and collective memory. I believe my mother was nostalgic but her feelings about being in America were ambivalent. In contrast, my father's feelings were profoundly nostalgic. He lamented coming from a land of fishermen and sailors to a country of waiters and bakers.[5] My father appreciated the opportunities America gave him but he belonged somewhere else and by extension so did I. My mother belonged on Ereikousa and also Manhattan and by extension so did I.

The reader will no doubt sense my own feelings of *nostalgia* in this chapter. There is no mystery why I taught, at an early stage of my academic life, immigrant history for 15 years at the Center for Byzantine and Modern Greek Studies at Queens College. No mystery why a significant portion of my practice is with immigrants and minorities of all types. No mystery why I married an immigrant—a child survivor of the Holocaust. No mystery why our daughter married an immigrant. I learned about nostalgia with my first milk. Even my younger brother Tatsi married an immigrant. The pull of home is eternal. I metabolize generations.

My mother's trauma prior to the trauma of immigration to America was the Wehrmacht occupation of Ereikousa during World War II. Prior to being occupied by the Germans Army the island was occupied by the Italians during the War. The Italian military understood the nature of the islanders, their innocence, their basic struggle to survive by cultivating the land and fishing. The fact that Ereikousa was so remote from mainland Greece (it took 6 hours by boat to travel there) meant that the people led their lives as if in the 19th century rather than the mid-20th century.

Most of the women who grewn up on Ereikousa before the 1960s received no schooling. My mother, however, did complete the first grade in the island's one-room schoolhouse. She learned early to toil in vineyards. And despite grieving the death of 12 siblings, her life was more or less fine. On occasion, our conversations would start with her saying she was "fine" to the question "How are you?" But then there would be a roundabout discussion of her early life's unbearable grief, shades of gray, and sheer terror.

Some of my first memories are as a 3-year old child huddled in the corner of the kitchen in the tenement apartment we lived in in Chelsea. My mother is holding my infant brother Tatsi. There was a huge bathtub in the kitchen covered by a heavy metal top. The WC was outside the apartment in the hallway. There were no books in the house. The memory is not murky. It is central to my self and my past. I am listening to my mother tell stories about how the Nazi army disrupted the idyllic island and how the islanders lost their innocence about the world. She would go on and on about these losses. I was her witness. I learned my empathy from her then and it developed into deep intersubjective moments. She knew that I knew that she knew she was suffering. I took her suffering in. I learned how she suffered and how the islanders suffered and how others suffered. I learned how to listen to those who suffer. We sat face to face: she in an old beat-up wooden chair and me on a cold linoleum floor. My rhythms were not completely my "own." I was in a coordinated dance with my mother and she with me (Beebe et al., 2016). An important aspect of my emotional life was sealed during those conversations in a way that I could never have imagined at the time. This was the process.

The content of the conversations was about an era of trauma. The Ereikousa islanders suffered. They may have been poor and uneducated but they understood the agony of famine and the deadly terrors of Axis occupation. For the ancient Greeks, philosophy alleviated emotional pain and suffering (Nussbaum, 2009; Orange, 2011). This moral philosophical practice, despite its values controversy, has become a fundamental position in my clinical work. I target suffering both formulated and unformulated. I learned this as a toddler from my mother.

Returning to the ceremony on the Tuesday summer day of 2015 on Ereikousa, here are some of my prepared words to those assembled:

> The events that took place on the small island of Ereikousa during the brutal Axis occupation of World War II bear witness to the power of the human spirit to overwhelm man's inhumanity to man.
>
> The German Third Reich repeatedly came to the island seeking the Savvas family. Everyone on the island knew where the Savvas family had been hidden and no one, absolutely no one, betrayed them. When the Nazis left Ereikousa disappointed, the Savvas family would join the islanders in daily activities, enjoy the lyrical landscape, and partake of bread and freedom. The Nazis would return like a bad dream and the hiding would begin again deep in the hilly forest of "Skotini" or the inaccessible "Bragini" coves. At night, women would bring them food and clothing to stay warm.

Ereikousa received two awards on that Tuesday: the "House of Life" Award from the International Raoul Wallenberg Foundation and the "Moral Courage" Award from the Association of the Friends of Greek Jewry. Later in the summer, the State of Israel issued a commemorative stamp marking the Ereikousa ceremony. The stamp displays an aerial photograph of tiny Ereikousa floating on a sea where the blue really begins. I can point to the forest where Israel Savvas, his three daughters Nini, Julia, and Spera, and niece little Roza Villeli were hidden by five brave young Ereikousa women one of whom was my mother Angelina.

In the mid-1960s after we had our first telephone installed in the Chelsea apartment there was a call from Idlewild Airport (later renamed JFK International Airport). I answered the phone, as was the custom in our family. It was a woman named Roza. She explained that she was travelling from

California to Israel. In broken English and with a thick accent she asked me, "Is this the home of Mitsis and Angelina Orfanos Bambinis?" Bambinis was the family nickname. I did not recognize her voice. But my parents certainly did when they picked up the phone. They did not know what had happened to Roza after the war. They were in indescribable joy as they talked to their old friend. It was memorable to me because my parents were often so depressed at home. Decades later on a Tuesday in the summer of 2015, I met Roza's children and grandchildren on Ereikousa. My heart weeps as I write this. I feel I know Roza and her children and her grandchildren. I know their faces. I embrace them. My tears flow.

Coda

Still later in the summer at the 90th birthday celebration of Mikis Theodorakis, thousands of Athenians attend a free concert at the Megaron Mousikis. Such concerts are often memorial acts culminating with the rousing and uplifting, spirited music of *Zorbás Dance*. But this time was different. In the context of Greece's economic depression, the worst human suffering in Greece since the days of World War II, the program ends with "Song of Songs." The song emotionally holds a community and a nation fractured by traumas past and present. The song is witness. There are three singers on stage. The first sings in Greek, the second sings in German, and the third sings in Hebrew. Lina enters the song last. She sings her Hebrew lines in a voice that is both plaintive and sublime. The intergenerational power of this is obvious to the audience. Their tears flow. She knows that they know that she knows they are suffering. While in command on stage she is suffering too. For me it is a full circle. I can only aspire to such intersubjectivity moments in my clinical efforts. That would be an aesthetic of almost unbearable beauty.

Notes

1 While the word retains some semantic indeterminacy (due to differences among Greek and European philosophers), current usage has it as a philosophy of beauty or the science of art. In this essay, I add the element of tone of voice.
2 *Beauforts* is a nautical measure of wind speed. When the Beauforts scale measures six red warning flags go up.
3 Giorgi's voice is part of my life's original poetry. I felt cherished by him. I sport a moustache like he did all his life. He taught me to fish, to read English, to cook, and to identify needs in myself and in others. He was a master *polymechanos*. On August 3, 2016, Giorgi passed away at age 85 on Ereikousa. He died the way he wished—prepared, alert, curious, surrounded by family, and knowing he had led the life he desired. I grieve deeply for him and I look forward to our conversations in dreams.
4 These days Lina, Sophia, and I pay social visits rather than conduct interviews. The pleasure in his company is Homeric.
5 The irony is that that is exactly what happened in Greece starting in the 1960s when tourism exploded.

References

Acocella, J. (2007). *Twenty-eight artists and two saints: Essays*. New York, NY: Pantheon Books.
Aron, L. (2016). Mutual vulnerability. In D. M. Goodman & E. R. Severson (Eds.), *Otherness and subjectivity in contemporary psychoanalysis* (pp. 19–41). New York, NY: Routledge.
Beebe, B., Messinger, D., Bahrick, L. E., Margolis, A., Buck, K. A., & Chen, H. (2016). A systems view of mother-infant face-to-face communication. *Developmental Psychology*, *52*(4), 556–571.
Bostridge, I. (2015). *Shubert's winter journey: An anatomy of an obsession*. New York, NY: Alfred A. Knoff.
Boym, S. (2001). *The future of nostalgia*. New York, NY: Basic Books.
Greenspun, W. (2011). Three dimensional treatment: The interplay of patient, analyst, and supervisors. *Contemporary Psychoanalysis*, *47*(3), 386–405.
Nussbaum, M. C. (2009). *The therapy of desire: Theory and practice in Hellenistic ethics*. Princeton, NJ: Princeton University Press.
Orange, D. M. (2011). *The suffering stranger: Hermeneutics for everyday clinical practice*. New York, NY: Routledge.
Orfanos, S. D. (2003). Imagining Ithaca: The impact of the analyst's worldview. In A. Roland, B. Ulanov, & C. Barbre (Eds.), *Creative dissent: Psychoanalysis and evolution* (pp. 113–125). London: Praeger.
Orfanos, S. D. (2006a). *Mythos* and *logos*. *Psychoanalytic Dialogues*, *16*, 481–499.
Orfanos, S. D. (2006b). Out of the dark: The psychoanalysis of an adolescent boy. *Journal of Infant, Child, and Adolescent Psychotherapy*, 5, 290–301.
Orfanos, S. D. (2010). On bread and wine. *Psychoanalytic Perspectives*, 7, 211–219.
Orfanos, S. D. (2011). Forward: Voyaging the relational sea change. In L. Aron & A. Harris (Eds.), *Relational psychoanalysis: Evolution of process* (Vol. 5, pp. xix–xxx). New York, NY: Routledge.
Orfanos, S. D. (2014a). An epiphany of the Acropolis: An open letter to Nikos Kazantzakis on the 50th anniversary of the publication of *Report to Greco*. *Contemporary Psychoanalysis*, *50*(4), 659–680.
Orfanos, S. D. (2014b). Music and the great wound. In S. Richman (Ed.), *Mended by the muse: Creative transformations of trauma* (pp. 156–173). New York, NY: Routledge.
Richman, S. (2002). *A wolf in the attic: The legacy of a hidden child of the Holocaust*. New York, NY: Routledge.
Richman, S. (2014). *Mended by the muse: Creative transformations of trauma*. New York, NY: Routledge.
Slochower, J. (2014). *Psychoanalytic collisions* (2nd ed.). New York, NY: Routledge.
Wachtel, P. (2001). A (inevitably) self-deceiving reflection on self-deception. In M. R. Goldfried (Ed.), *How therapists change: Personal and professional reflections* (pp. 83–101). Washington, DC: American Psychological Association.
Wilson, E. (1940). *To the Finland Station*. New York, NY: New York Review of Books.

Part II
Reflections

Chapter 14

Themes and variations

Linda Hillman and Therese Rosenblatt

> If you want to be a real psychoanalyst, you have to have a great love of the truth, scientific truth as well as personal truth, and you have to place this appreciation of the truth higher than any discomfort at meeting unpleasant facts, whether they belong to the world outside or to your own inner person.
>
> —Anna Freud[1]

What does it mean to be a psychoanalyst in today's world? Psychoanalysis has evolved significantly since Freud's first publications over a hundred years ago. Though much has changed and continues to be challenged, the fundamental tenets of the field have become embedded in our cultural and intellectual history. Current psychoanalysis incorporates several distinct schools of thought, as well as drawing on a rich cross-fertilization across a broadening array of disciplines, including neuropsychology, social psychology, and anthropology.

While we are inspired by these new developments in theory and practice, as a profession, we are also struggling to sort through what we have been taught and how we have been trained to determine how best to integrate the ongoing developments in the field. Even among those who agree on particular theories, there is wide room for differences in practice. Diverse theories filter through an individual analyst's mind. In turn, they bring to their work that which fits best with their own character and development. While psychoanalysis has acknowledged the subjective presence of the analyst in practice, making different styles theoretically more acceptable, open discussion about this subject has not yet found a place in the field.

What do we want to hold onto, adjust or transform? As we see in the narratives in this book, we are evolving constantly as analysts, and we want psychoanalytic education and training to catch up with the reality that these narratives reflect.

Our authors are deeply engaged in their work. We seek to be authentically who we are, while operating within a field that both espouses individual freedom and imposes stringent parameters. We resist rules and conditions we view as suffocating because they are outmoded, too broadly applied, or don't fit current realities. We strive to incorporate analytic love and warmth into our work. We want psychoanalysis to be relevant to the larger community and society. We want to figure out how to use our own selves to further our work. We want an evolved psychoanalysis that is not defined by yesterday's constraints, instead adapting to our evolving personal development within the contemporary context.

The chapters in this book testify to the elusiveness of the ongoing quest to find and refine our identity and voices as psychoanalysts. We search for what is only partially clear—as is often the case in analytic work—for something missing, beyond memory, beneath the conscious. We wish to be both true to ourselves and be relevant in today's world. The twelve narratives in this book are a testament to the ongoing work of finding one's identity and voice as a psychoanalyst. Even the act of putting our search for voice and identity into a traditional narrative format with a beginning, middle and end is necessarily imperfect. We use words, knowing that they cannot fully capture experience.

From the first sentence of each chapter we hear these analysts' unique combination of stylistic preference and personality traits in their particular voiceprint. We enter their world and atmosphere. As individual as each voice is, we find striking similarities in the themes of the narratives.

Our authors share an abiding interest in "the inner world of others and the relationships we create with them" as Jack Drescher puts it. That interest springs from a combination of intellectual curiosity and a drive to comfort and heal, although different authors stress one motive more than the other. Lissa Weinstein's initial instinct was intellectual, trying to understand another person's reality, but ultimately she is drawn to love in her repertoire as an analyst. Rachel Altstein was moved first by a desire to help people get out of their psychic prisons after first having helped people to get out of real prison in her life as a lawyer. Spyros Orfanos is also interested in "freeing people" and himself. In our case, Therese was always driven to "peer into the interiors of minds" and now aspires to offer patients "analytic rigor and analytic love."

Suffering and the wounded parent

Our authors all wrote movingly of having borne witness to the suffering of others (usually, but not always their parents). Certainly, the affectively laden memories described in every single narrative testify to how witnessing has become an ongoing part of their lives from very early on and continues in the form of bearing witness to their patients' conflicts. In addition to witnessing, these authors feel a great responsibility to "manage the anxiety of others" as Jack Drescher says, and certainly this inclination played a conscious or unconscious role in their choice of profession.

While some people remember very little of their childhoods, our authors remember a great deal, much of which is colored by pain or sadness. Lissa

Weinstein "feels her father's sadness, his terror and his dread," imagining that as he stares vacantly out the window, he is listening for the "distant hooves of the Cossacks in the Third Ave. El."

Most authors describe their impressions that one or both parents were psychically wounded and their sense of responsibility and preoccupation with their parents. This trend calls up the observation by Alice Miller in her book, *The Drama of the Gifted Child: The Search for the True Self* (1997), that people who become therapists start out as children who are gifted at understanding the needs of a psychically wounded parent and adapting themselves to that parent's needs. Linda writes that her role as a family therapist both fits her personal proclivities, and gives her a way to fit into her own family, supporting her parents who carried their own trauma and wounds. Many of us felt a sense of "urgent calling," as Therese puts it, to respond to our parents' pain and needs, something that had its genesis for Therese in her attempts to soothe her mother and understand her brother. It is not surprising that this calling lives on in our work as analysts, reinforcing a long held desire to heal psychic distress.

Others were affected by the suffering of their community. Dorothy Holmes who grew up in a "strictly enforced segregated city" is subjected to overt acts of racism. For example, in high school, she is encouraged to skip college in spite of being class Salutatorian and in graduate school, a mentor makes a racist interpretation of a case. She finds a sense of meaning in "becoming a psychoanalytic scholar whose focus has been to help herself and others to understand the multiple negative impacts of racism and sexism." Spyros Orfanos watches the Greek immigrant community in New York suffer from loss, poverty, uprooting and a fear of deportation, from his perch as a waiter in Greek diners.

Otherness, immigration, and the Holocaust

The analysts who were born to immigrant parents are deeply affected by their parents' stories of dislocation, loss, hardship and nostalgia. These analysts feel compassion for their parents even as they experience frustration with their parents' child-rearing judgments. Some have parents who flood them with age-inappropriate information about their traumatic past or expect their children to make up for their own pain and suffering through their success in this new world. For many, it is a matter of absorbing the weight of their parents' losses and grief.

These analysts feel both empathy as well as the contagion of the suffering of their immigrant parents. As Spyros Orfanos writes "we feel our parents' immigration wounds." Carolyn Ellman, while reading Joseph Berger's book *Displaced Persons* realizes that in all her years of treatment no one had picked up on her mother's Russian immigration story and her drive for her children to succeed in order to feel as if she belonged.

Psychoanalysis as a discipline is uniquely conceived to help patients grapple with two of the major difficulties that burden immigrants; experiences of disrupted identity and mourning for the losses incurred in leaving one's homeland—be they culture, family and friends, status or more. Having grown up with their parent's mourning and search for identity and belonging, the mission and spirit of psychoanalysis feels like a natural fit and a source of hope.

Being the child of immigrants presents an opportunity for new perspectives. We believe that in addition to the outside perspectives gained by having a foreign parent, these analysts have absorbed the sensibilities of their European, Israeli, and Latino parents, engendering a more philosophical approach, one that incorporates a sense of the soul. This tendency may have influenced their choice of psychoanalysis as a career, one that is perhaps less typically American as it is more philosophical and eschews quick solutions and the pursuit of the material world.

Among those authors with immigrant parents, several had parents who were survivors of, or were affected by the holocaust. The offspring analysts felt their parents' pain. We don't know that being exposed to victims and witnesses of victims of the holocaust moved people to become analysts. We do know that these analysts vicariously witnessed losses and suffering resulting from the holocaust. At the same time they also witnessed brave responses from family members and others who overcame a doomed fate by escaping and building a new, more hopeful life. Examples are the formative stories in Spyros Orfanos' account of hiding the Jewish family in Greece from the Gestapo and the countless stories Therese heard from her mother about the murder of two cousins while defending the new state of Israel and her holocaust-surviving neighbors. Jack Drescher describes his plucky mother who got her family to leave in time to save them from the gas chambers. These were stories of "Polymechanos" in Spyros Orfanos' words—the wiliness that aids in survival.

Themes and experiences of Otherness run prominently throughout the majority of the narratives. They spring from internal and external factors. Therese's immigrant mother clung to a "beloved and vulnerable homeland," and felt like a deserter. Mitchell Wilson's low socioeconomic status within his community, his mixed lineage and his father described as an "outlier of substantial proportions" fosters his "disquiet, insecurity, and doubt." Francisco González describes "growing up in an environment in which my sexuality was not socially recognized, and growing up as an immigrant in a bilingual family." Jack Drescher fights to be accepted in professional settings as a gay man. His parents were immigrants and holocaust survivors. Dorothy Holmes was one of a few black women in a profession dominated by white men. Psychoanalysts with their tendency to be introspective and sensitive, have a particular way of experiencing and dealing with Otherness that allows them to empathize with people's experiences of being different or excluded and finds satisfying expression in psychoanalysis.

Success below the radar

Our authors strive towards success and learning and prize high achievement. Some, like Ted Jacobs and Carolyn Ellman, feel the weight of the hopes of their parents. All aim to meet high internal standards of what success looks like in how they think, how they practice and the drive to heal. They enjoy their academic pursuits and accomplishments as well as other successes. Some have name recognition and stature within the profession while others are less known. But for all, much of the work—the work with patients—is private.

There is a tension in being achievement oriented and making the choice of a career in which the work is private, so private that it cannot be easily assessed by others. As analysts, we sit behind the couch both literally and figuratively, putting the needs of the patient and the work before our own. The work revolves around the patient's psychic life and we are sworn to keep it confidential. We listen, absorb, and analyze as the patient speaks. When they are silent, we watch and wait and wonder what is going on inside. The history of the analyst remaining anonymous contributes to this back seat position as does the technique of free association, which privileges the patient's voice.

As we try to understand what draws our authors to this field we are left with a complex mix of factors and speculation. Many authors note their own reluctance to yield to the pull of psychology and psychoanalysis as a profession. They take a path to another field but discover a deep identification with being a psychoanalyst. As Francisco González says, "it enlivened an inner current in me." We do not know what caused that initial resistance to choosing psychoanalysis as a profession. Certainly the history of feeling disenfranchised, "other," or poorly understood either by the community or family that characterizes many of these narratives, could lead to complex feelings about what it means to be on center stage, both the longing for it and the fears of exposing oneself or one's work. It could also lead to a desire to conquer the anxiety associated with exposure by helping patients to overcome similar fears.

The choice of psychoanalysis is also one that includes a high tolerance for ambiguity and no clear product by which to measure success. Analysts must accept long periods of not understanding, not knowing, and taking emotional risks (with patients and themselves). They often try but do not know if they will be able to offer a modicum of healing to their patient. For many, private recognition from the patient and the analyst's sense of having met his or her own internal standards, is sufficient. At times patients do not express their appreciation directly, if at all. The analyst must take satisfaction from the patient's improved functioning and mood. In addition, analysts know that the definition of cure can be ambiguous and have different meanings according to different theorists.

From intellect to a flourishing mind

These are authors who think about thinking—its content, form, and style. The narratives express how heavily the authors rely on their intellect from early in their lives to survive and make sense of their own suffering or that of their family members. Cultivating their minds and the activities that go along with that open up horizons for them and make possible a rich inner and outer life.

While never letting go of their love of learning and the mind, authors write about letting go of the less helpful aspects of an overreliance on intellect and theory. Carolyn Ellman describes withdrawing into a world of the intellect early on in her life, investing heavily in her wide-ranging intellectual curiosity. As her narrative unfolds, she blossoms into a fully humanistic professional. The journey of becoming a psychoanalyst involves becoming ever more self-aware and able to tolerate one's own painful, repressed, or dissociated feelings. The need for intellectualization as a defense lessens while the love of the life of the mind flourishes.

In addition, it is striking that early on several authors used theory to a great degree to ground themselves in psychoanalytic work but evolve to let in a form of analytic love. Therese relies on traditional Freudian theory early in her career until she finds a balance between a warm, more flexible authenticity and analytic rigor. Lissa Weinstein says that when she started her journey to become a psychoanalyst, "I was fascinated with how the mind worked ... and psychoanalysis seemed like the best, most humanistic way to explore the mind." Later she discovers a need and a way to integrate warmth and caring into the work.

Analytic love as an agent of change

Several authors speak of a conviction that warmth and analytic love need to be part of the work in order for therapy to be mutative. Their belief is founded in their perspectives as both patient and analyst. This idea is one that many patients (including ourselves) already know intuitively and find ways of bringing up in treatment—often to the discomfort of the analyst.

The idea of analytic love has the potential to bring up layers of conflict in analysts and patients alike. For the analyst it is often masked by theoretical prohibitions and admonitions: we do not cure through love; we do not offer corrective emotional experiences. We must distinguish between transference love and real love. We have expertise and practice a "real" scientific discipline. The latter sentiment echoes Freud's fear that psychoanalysis would be discredited if it were not considered a science. Ultimately, as relevant as these concerns are, we as analysts can experience personal conflict about giving our love, fears of boundary loss, fear of the exploitation of our "love" that we may have experienced earlier in life, or envy of our patients for receiving the love we wish for ourselves.

Ultimately, analysts are human with their own unconscious motivations. In analysis (as in life in general) the often unconscious wish to give and receive love with patients can be fraught with shame and uncertainty and defended against, leaving us feeling exposed, if only to ourselves.

It is as difficult to define and describe analytic love as it is to describe love in general. It may be even harder to describe how it is expressed. How does one give love to a patient without either crossing a boundary or simply behaving in a way that is neither thoughtful nor helpful to a patient? Our authors talk about it often from their perspective as patients. Therese says that in spite of considerable pain, she grew from a problematic analysis in which her analyst's warmth towards her partly offset his mismanagement of a painful set of enactments. Ted Jacobs credits the warmth of his first analyst with being able to reach the adolescent Jacobs when he became withdrawn and defensive. We use words like alive, engaged, and committed to describe fondly remembered and effective analysts. Some include as part of analytic love a description of how their aggression and frustration over being misunderstood was tolerated in the treatment. Linda describes how, "like a jujitsu master, he took my blows and redirected them where they belonged," and Therese describes her analyst "withstanding her anger, passionately wanting to understand" what at first he could not. Both analysts persevered, tolerated the aggression and made life-affirming meaning out of the pain, chaos and anger that was directed towards them as they worked.

Authors also speak about analytic love from their perspective as analysts. Some describe particular cases with disappointing outcomes in which a human element was missing in the work. Therese recalls an inhibited and withdrawn patient with whom, in retrospect, she believes that she came across as cold and uncaring. Analytic love often comes in the form of the analyst's sense of "being responsive to the patient rather than theory," as Therese puts it. Several analysts refer to an aliveness with the patient such as Linda's description of engaging with her patients in order to facilitate their own "vitality, life force, their quickening" (De Mille, 1991, p. 264). Some describe their drive to think originally and creatively about certain patients whose needs and vulnerabilities are not adequately addressed in the theoretical literature.

We show our love for our patients through our authenticity, vitality, emotional availability, deep engagement, commitment, and responsiveness to who they are. Revealing our caring provides a portal through which more of the analytic work can be taken in by the patient, thus facilitating the analytic process. Our inner selves are revealed through our humanness, caring, and sense of importance of the work.

We therefore risk feeling shamed. In working through the shame of wanting love from our own analysts, it becomes easier to give it to patients in a responsible and analytic way. In working through our own shame, we can understand and relate to these same feelings in our patients and as a result, enhance and deepen our work with them.

Nurturing independence and courage in the soil of orthodoxy

There is a pronounced independent-minded spirit running throughout these narratives. The analysts in this book have highly developed sensibilities about life and analytic practice and feel strongly about the integrity of their analytic personas. The authors take us on a tour through the development of their personal ideas about psychoanalysis. They often question analytic standard practices such as those Carolyn Ellman described as being "obsessed with neutrality, anonymity and parameters ... (with) so much rigidity in thinking." This questioning creates an opening and necessity for the analysts to find and use their own voice in their work. Of her early career training Ellman says, "I was already carving out my way of doing things and Shelly Bach was a tremendous help in supporting my search for ways to be with the patient."

Using the self is necessary to be an effective analyst, and it requires a certain measure of originality, independent mindedness, and questioning of established standards since there is nothing standard or routine about trying to coax out and befriend the unconscious of a patient. Being an effective analyst requires both adherence to rigorous analytic principals of restraint plus a mindful emotional spontaneity and attunement. We are all balancing constraint and freedom, structure and spontaneity. Each analyst must find his or her own resolution of this dialectic that by its nature is creative. There is an emotional risk involved in this process that could even be called courage.

It is not surprising that such independent mindedness often goes along with a strong inclination towards impatience with authoritarianism and orthodoxy. Several authors described how this impatience expressed itself vis-à-vis their training and particularly their institute. Most institutes are formally structured, hierarchical, and authoritarian. Many promote an orthodoxy of thought that was difficult for our authors to subscribe to, and in the cases of Dorothy Holmes and Jack Drescher, made the possibility of admission to an APsaA institute tenuous. The analysts in this book describe in different ways how they came to resolve and reconcile the tension between incorporating the rigor and discipline of the field together with finding their own voice and identity within these belief systems. Some, like Therese, found a less authoritarian institute in which she felt she could breathe, "become comfortable in her own analytic skin," and integrate her own beliefs with the theoretical orientations she chose to subscribe to.

In his description of the individuation process for the analyst who is an offspring of analysts, Jonathan Eger describes the special aspects of the struggle of those young analysts in training to separate and individuate from parents, teachers, and mentors, in the service of ultimately developing his own voice and identity. The endeavor to distinguish one's own identity from those of one's mentors, supervisors and teachers involves a destruction of the object followed by the internalization of the transformed relationship with those objects. This process ultimately results in taking responsibility for one's agency and autonomous functioning as an analyst and as a person. It seems safe to say that some form of the dynamics of separation-individuation described by Eger was experienced and described explicitly and implicitly by our authors.

As we saw in the narratives, courage in psychoanalysis can show up in many different forms—from small, quiet acts of courage unseen within the private confines of the consulting room, to more public settings in which long-held tenets of the profession are openly challenged. Therese discusses the anxiety of departing from the established psychoanalytic canon in her private work with patients, as a feeling of being "lost and alone in outer space, anxious that the road home is forever gone."

Dorothy Holmes and Jack Drescher challenged the establishment institutes they applied to and eventually joined. Holmes refused to sign the waiver form required by the APsaA institute she applied to, which insisted she not engage in clinical practice as a PhD graduate of that institute. Only MDs were allowed by those institutes, to practice psychoanalysis. She was admitted anyway. She also confronted her professor about his racist language and views on a clinical case. Jack Drescher applied to his psychoanalytic institute as an openly gay man and against the odds, was accepted. Drescher's applying was a risk and took courage, occurring at a time when being gay was seen as a pathological condition and could have been used as a reason to disqualify him from analytic training. In the 1980s, there was open discrimination towards homosexual analysts in many establishment institutes, but some adopted a "don't ask, don't tell" policy.

Finally, Ted Jacobs describes the way he publicly challenged psychoanalytic orthodoxy when he broke the silence around countertransference issues with his book, *The Use of Self: Transference and Communication in the Analytic Situation* (1991). His work was greeted with criticism and disdain, especially by his psychoanalytic institute. His work was discussed in pejorative terms and his qualifications for doing the work were maligned. Within just a few years, as the psychoanalytic field opened up to work by Klein, Winnicott, Racker, and others, Jacobs' formulations were recognized as ahead of his time.

The evolving role of social and cultural factors in the consulting room

The burgeoning literature on trauma theory has done a great deal to bring social and cultural realities into the treatment room and ironically has brought us closer to Freud's original idea that symptoms were caused by actual trauma, not fantasy (1917). The idea that cultural and social experiences not only affect us but are passed down out of awareness from generation to generation i.e. the unconscious transmission of trauma has had a great impact on psychoanalytic thinking. We see it in the links so many of our authors make between their legacy of trauma and their current sensibilities This particular understanding of development has opened a door for us to think in new ways about how violence, racism, war, immigration, displacement, and much more can be transmitted through the generations. Some analysts are more sensitive to social and historical events and issues and bring them more into play in the treatment room than they have in the past. Dorothy Holmes reminds us "whatever resides within us, in our personal psychologies, including our cultural experiences and histories, is the proper focus of psychoanalysis."

The way that psychoanalysts think of themselves and their role in society is also shifting. Francisco González was reluctant to acknowledge his emerging desire to become a psychoanalyst as it "smacked of elitism and clinical distance ... an ethical capitulation." However, he found theorists who helped him create a "synthesis between community mental health, sociopolitical critique, and conventional psychoanalysis."

Several authors spoke about their attraction to valuing and becoming involved in community. Spyros Orfanos frames his discussion about his growth and evolution as a person and psychoanalyst around embracing community. His hero in later life, Theodorakis, is a Greek musician whose "community was the world" and who created a cultural revolution for the Greek people through his music. Linda spoke of the ever-growing role that creating meaningful communities has played in her life through her work of advocacy and creating a support council for crises in her local community. She brings her psychoanalytic perspective to bear in all of these activities.

Some of our authors stress the importance of breaking out of the confines of the stereotyped model of the psychoanalyst who only attends to the inner world, only focuses on early family life and who has to remain anonymous in the world to effectively perform his or her work. In this reimagined role of psychoanalyst, we are no longer divorced from significant cultural and social factors. Rejecting the stereotype and instead seeing the origins and development of psychoanalysis as a progressive, even radical event, Dorothy Holmes makes a passionate plea to the field of psychoanalysis to include racism in our psychoanalytic understanding, teaching and work so that we are "worthy heirs" of a "truly radical discipline."

How art nourishes professional practice and life

Many of the authors write about the relationship they see between the creative arts and psychoanalysis. In addition, many point to the central role that art has played in influencing the development of their psychoanalytic voice. How do we understand the fact that Ted Jacobs has always viewed himself as a storyteller and says "literature was in my blood"? That both Francisco Gonzalez and Mitchell Wilson earned masters in literature while or before pursuing medical training, that Linda and Lissa Weinstein found their way to serious creative writing as adults and that Therese and Lissa Weinstein spent their early careers devoted to dance. Later in life, Spyros Orfanos became a music producer alongside his career as a psychoanalyst. What is the connection?

We know that artists and psychoanalysts are both highly connected to their inner life, to the imagination, dreams, and play. They use multiple modalities to formulate experience and express themselves. Artists and psychoanalysts have a heightened receptivity and strive to hone their ability to listen and observe. Artists, like psychoanalysts, tell stories through verbal and non-verbal mediums. Joan Didion makes the ultimate case for storytelling. "We tell ourselves stories in order to live" (1979). We tell stories through vision, sound, movement, or language.

Metaphors and symbols can take either verbal or non-verbal form in the treatment room or in artistic creation. In the treatment room, we pay attention to movement, mood, and tone as well as to language. Linda describes attending to "the flow, the rhythm, the stops, the gaps, the inconsistencies, the tone, the metaphors and the images." Formulating emotions and thoughts into symbols and stories gives us a sense of mastery over our feelings and experiences and is how we build meaning in our lives. Psychoanalysis like art opens up meaning even as it leads to deeper questions.

Writing is one particular mode of creativity, and it is one that a number of our authors consider to be an important marker in the development of their voice. We note that the authors in this book were chosen partly because of their interest in writing. The focus on narratives may have encouraged our authors to privilege their reflection on writing more than other forms of art. Jack Drescher describes the emergence of his "writing self" as a positive development of his first analysis. Carolyn Ellman became passionate about the topic of envy and "For the first time I had a burning desire to write a paper." In describing how an analyst comes into his or her own, she says "it also seems to come from writing and having people know you."

Transformative moments

Many of our authors described transformative moments, or what Rachel Altstein referred to as serendipitous moments. What are these? Are they moments of getting in touch with unconscious or dissociated parts of the self, a sudden insight? Are they moments of a complete reorganization of the self? Are they like dreams or poems where so much meaning and emotional resonance is contained in so few words or images? Are they moments of a hitherto long process of development, formerly semi-conscious, now coalescing in a conscious resolution? Or is it as Altstein says in paraphrasing Bion "when a preconception, which has yet to find shape through articulation, meets experience in the real world"?

Transformative moments may explain the past, the present and in some cases allude to our future. Even this book was conceived in a moment of serendipity, unexpected and sudden in a casual conversation between the authors. There is an accompanying sense of inevitability that follows these moments. Linda describes them as "both enlivening and unsettling, as if recognition and shifting are happening at the same time." Many of our authors highlight these experiences when describing the evolution of their identity. They range from traumatic moments to particular interactions with mentors, teachers, analysts, patients, friends, or readings to memories that suddenly come to mind and take on whole new meanings.

In a moment that led to a shake-up of the self, Altstein describes the subtleties of her actions to witnessing one of the planes fly into the World Trade Center on September 11. Using the metaphor of a dice popper, she says "all our parts were violently reshuffled, and we were other than we were before."

When he was young and visiting San Francisco with his family, Francisco González's father said that San Francisco reminded him of Havana. It was in the act of retelling this story to a friend later in life that he suddenly realized his father's nostalgic memory of Havana had "become planted in my aspirations, only to bloom when it came time to choose the place (San Francisco) where I would live the bulk of my life." González describes this as "the way meaning can move across places and times."

For several of our authors, encountering the writings of Freud for the first time is one of these transformative moments. Freud's ideas animated something unformulated and unarticulated when Linda discovered them in college, "The idea of the unconscious made the world fall into place." Ted Jacobs discovered in Freud someone who combined his interests in writing and psychology, a natural storyteller as well as a healer, and this was one of the factors in Jacobs' choosing to become a psychoanalyst.

The passion that Freud's work inspires in our authors speaks to the intellectual and human vibrancy that Freud transmits through his excitement about the workings of the human mind. For Therese, who was initially introduced to his ideas by her mother, it was reading Freud in a 12th-grade course that caused her to "fall in love with psychoanalysis," which then "became an abiding passion."

Reading texts and minds

The authors assigned varied roles and importance to reading in their life. Mitchell Wilson tells us "That the psychoanalyst is a practitioner of the symbolic order is why the analyst ought to read widely, be curious about many things and, most importantly, be curious about what he or she doesn't know." Carolyn Ellman refers often to her reading adventures, speaking of her favorite authors almost as dear friends, as does Spyros Orfanos. Francisco González says "Reading was an encounter and a transmission, a way of inhabiting the mind of another and of letting another inhabit you." Not just understanding another's perspective, but inhabiting another's mind through reading is similar to what Michael Moskowitz (2010) describes as "reading minds" in the social world or in relationships—understanding how a mind other than our own thinks and feels. Reading our patients as well as their reading us is what we aspire to do in the treatment room.

Therese writes about a different kind of reading experience. While many writers have been illuminating or entertaining and have added to her fund of knowledge and ideas, the ones who most affected her identity and voice as an analyst were able to "draw her into their worlds, minds, and ambience, affectively and vividly." In this way, they mirrored her feelings of becoming animated and absorbed by people and their communications.

Training as a foundation for lifelong development

Psychoanalytic training is a pivotal step in the journey towards forming our identity as psychologists. From a developmental perspective, the candidate has the job of taking in and incorporating a great deal of material and identifications. At the same time the candidate has to find his or her own differentiated voice as an analyst. Jonathan Eger describes the aggression required in order to loosen the libidinal ties to one's teachers and supervisors mirroring the separation process from one's parents. From an organizational perspective, our contributors raise the question of what kind of institution maximizes the potential for this kind of development. An institute that is too authoritarian will squash free thought and an institute that is too unstructured may leave the candidate with a lack of discipline and rigor.

Carolyn Ellman focuses on the conflict "between rigorous requirements and personal freedom." She observes how over-evaluation leads to inhibition and a lack of questioning and curiosity on the part of students. Ellman believes that the development of critical thinking—a quality that Freud exemplified— requires an atmosphere in which questioning and curiosity are valued.

Therese felt both enlivened and free in a way that promoted her growth as an analyst. The combination of rigor and freedom fostered an active engagement and ownership of the work. She says,

> Like a good enough parent, Postdoc provided a defined space in which I tested out the perspectives offered by the various theoretical orientations ... authoritarianism was minimal and autonomy was supported ... I felt like someone had opened a window and let air into a musty room.

Ted Jacobs writes "at the ... Institute I also learned important lessons about the interplay between warmth and restraint, spontaneity and discipline, lessons that I carry with me and use in practice every working day."

The authors in this book are at different stages in their lives and developments as psychoanalysts. Those who have been practicing longer are able to bring to their narratives a certain kind of perspective and hindsight about their earlier experiences. Though training recedes in centrality the further we are from it, it remains a foundation or keystone in analytic development.

Note

1 Extract from letter to 'John' by Anna Freud on display in the Anna Freud Room of the Freud Museum, London. The exact date this was written is not known, nor is the exact identity of John. Reprinted with kind permission of the Freud Museum.

References

De Mille, A. (1991). *Martha: The life and works of Martha Graham—A biography*. London: Hutchinson.

Didion, J. (1979). *The white album*. New York, NY: Simon & Schuster.

Freud, S. (1917). General theory of the neuroses—fixation to traumas—the unconscious. In J. Strachey (Ed. & Trans.), *The standard edition of the complete works of Sigmund Freud* (Vol. 16, pp. 273–286). London: Hogarth Press.

Jacobs, T. (1991). *The use of the self: Countertransference and communication in the analytic situation*. Madison, CT: International Universities Press.

Miller, A. (1997). *The drama of the gifted child: The search for the true self*. New York, NY: HarperCollins.

Moskowitz, M. (2010). *Reading minds*. London: Karnac Books.

Chapter 15

Rethinking psychoanalytic training and beyond

Linda Hillman and Therese Rosenblatt

> I think that a psychoanalyst should have interests beyond the limits of the medical field in facts that belong to sociology, religion, literature and history, otherwise his outlook on his patient will remain too narrow. This point contains the necessary preparations beyond the requirements made on candidates of psychoanalysis in the institutes. You ought to be a great reader and become acquainted with the literature of many countries and cultures. In the great literary figures you will find people who know at least as much of human nature as the psychiatrists and psychologists try to do.
>
> —Anna Freud[1]

Two key ideas about becoming a psychoanalyst rise to the surface in the stories in this book. The first is that becoming an analyst is a lifelong endeavor. We have seen how a diversity of analysts, from those in their training to those who have been in practice 40 or 50 years, continue to change and develop in both their understanding of theory and technique as well as their use of themselves in the treatment. While formal psychoanalytic training may be an important piece of this process, it is only one piece. Many of the analysts report continuing to grow in their analytic identity through a wide range of life experiences, including reading inside and outside the field, learning from their patients, peer supervision, study groups, and finally, their own reflective processes often facilitated by continued analysis. The second idea has to do with the central role of the analyst's personality, character, and ethics in the practice of psychoanalysis. As Jane Kite writes in her 2016 address to APsaA on Ethics "I know of no other profession where we bring so much of ourselves into what we do."

Michael Parsons (2000) agrees that it is hard to "separate out the analyst himself or herself from the thing that he or she is doing" (p. 14). He says, "Central to the identity of a psychoanalyst is the analyst's relationship to his or her own unconscious" (p. 3). He makes the case for the analyst to be prepared to trust the unconscious processes that transpire between him and his patient. No matter how well analyzed we are as analysts much remains unconscious so we need to be ready to mistrust ourselves. According to Parsons, the analyst needs to be both a repairman with the technical skills to help the patient, and a healer which involves "full respect for that person's spirit and commitment of his own" (p. 10). How does this impact our view of psychoanalytic training? Lacan (cited in Parsons 2000, p. 73) believes that in addition to technical training, institutes should set up conditions that foster the development of a certain kind of inwardness in the analyst.

In a 2015 paper, Ogden reimagines Bion's 1967 paper "Notes on Memory and Desire." He elaborates on the importance for both Bion and himself of intuitive thinking that is rooted in the unconscious mind. In this view, the analyst wants to do everything possible to be in the purview of the unconscious, viewing experience from multiple perspectives and dialectical modes of thinking. Thinking that interferes with the connection to the unconscious and that keeps the analyst centered in the conscious mind, including sensory experience, desire for cure or understanding or memory (memory of the past is a distraction for Bion, but not for Ogden who sees the past as essentially in the present) takes the analyst away from the ideal moment. The analyst's job is to "intuit that unconscious psychic reality by becoming at one with it" (Ogden, 2015, p. 294). Psychoanalysis happens only in the present. Once again, we are wondering about the implications of this for formal psychoanalytic training. How does one help an analyst develop intuitive thinking? According to Ogden, Bion is trying to say that

> we cannot be taught how to interpret what we sense concerning the patient's unconscious psychic truths. Nor can we be taught how to convey to the patient that we have intuited those truths, much less what it is that we have intuited.
>
> (2015, p. 286)

If this is a skill that cannot be taught, can we at least provide environments that will be conducive to the development of intuitive thinking? Here again knowledge of ourselves gained through our own self reflection and analyses, sharing with colleagues in a safe environment, life and clinical experience as well as any other form of self cultivation and development are all invaluable in this process.

Rycroft (2010) warns about factors in psychoanalytic training that can get in the way of the analyst developing an authentic analytic identity. According to Rycroft, candidates are prone to recover their sense of infantile omnipotence by idealizing and projecting omnipotence on their training, their analysts, supervisors, Freud, and psychoanalysis itself. In general then, through projective identification they reintroject the omnipotence. Additionally, he believes that when young analysts privilege transference in their work with patients, they further expand their own sense of omnipotence.

In addressing the developmental challenges facing the beginning analyst during the first years after training, Rosenbloom (1992) points out that in the midst of the loss of her analyst and training community, the graduate has the developmental task of building a professional identity or what Rosenbloom labels a "work ego" (p. 117). These emerging analysts must find ways to adjust stereotyped beliefs and practices learned in training so that their "psychoanalytic work superego" (p. 118) moves in the direction of greater flexibility and openness. He suggests that the training analysis has a significant impact on the success or failure of the new analyst's ability to build an optimal work superego. Although Rosenbloom focuses on the period post-training, we believe that it is possible to start to address some of these developmental issues directly during training through courses, seminars, informal mentoring, and group discussion. Institutes should encourage the faculty to support the developmental process that candidates are undergoing. In addition, institutes could offer support and a place to discuss this transition after graduation from formal training.

Several analysts have addressed the need to reimagine psychoanalytic training given what we know about its weaknesses and limitations. Eisold (2004) suggests democratizing psychoanalytic institutes in which candidates would have a voice in shaping and managing those institutes. Lacan (in Parsons, 2000) takes a more radical position, believing that the decision that one is ready to be an analyst is the individual's decision, not the institute's. Because of the inevitable infantilization that is inherent in any hierarchical training institute, Lacan believes that in order to become a fully formed psychoanalyst, it is necessary for the analyst to achieve independence and to proclaim his or her own authority. He compares becoming an analyst with becoming a poet. Eisold also addresses the idea of the ongoing nature of forming a psychoanalytic identity by suggesting that institutes "enlarge the concept of training to include lifelong professional development" (1994, p. 65).

Kernberg and Michels (2016) write about their ideas on the present state and future of psychoanalytic education. They consider how to make psychoanalysis more relevant in the academic world and influential in contemporary thought, particularly how to restore it to its former status as a an important contributor in the scientific and intellectual worlds. They identify serious shortcomings in the present state of psychoanalytic education including a "stultifying conservatism" (p. 479) in its methods and an "intellectual stagnation and a phobic attitude toward any questioning of basic theory and technique" (p. 482). The authors suggest opening up the system to make it less authoritarian and more connected to other academic and intellectual disciplines. At the same time they suggest instilling more rigor and substance in the academic aspect of psychoanalytic education.

After reading what the twelve psychoanalysts in this book had to say about their own training and development, we are left with some key questions.

What kind of training environment can best provide the requisite professional knowledge and experience and at the same time facilitate an openness to lifelong learning, character development, and a capacity for compassionate self-reflection in the analyst? How would an institute create a culture that allows for rich didactic instruction as well as the personal learning and the development of the analyst?

Institutes require candidates to be in a personal analysis that provides a unique and intensive opportunity for them to develop self-awareness and self-understanding. The problem with leaving this type of work to the analysis alone is that many institutes are structured such that the analysis is not independent of the training and hence, evaluation. Our narratives tell us that while a personal analysis is a critical professional and developmental experience, there are many other life experiences and interests that contribute to the formation of a personal psychoanalytic voice and identity. If the training institute is to lay the groundwork for the life-long, multidimensional learning and development that is the reality of professional growth, it would benefit by creating an open and receptive culture that facilitates the exploration and evolution of candidates' identities and voice.

The challenge for a psychoanalytic training institute is one that is inherent in any learning environment. When starting out, the learner has to tolerate feelings associated with being a novice, having limited knowledge and making mistakes. The tremendous value placed on knowledge, scholarship, and the intellect in institutes creates high expectations and a competitive atmosphere. The training experience is particularly fraught in these institutes because the learning is often intellectually and emotionally about the self. Does the Institute provide a relatively safe place for the young analyst to take risks, question or reveal his or her confusion? Is it safe to "not know"? Is the training institute a place where sharing and self-exploration can take place in an informal and constructive way as opposed to a place where competition, hiding and feelings of shame predominate?

Another challenge is how to take into account that students enter with their own voices already in the process of forming. As we have seen in these narratives, analysts bring their own interests, styles, and proclivities that have been evolving from early in their lives. While responding to their training experience, students are formulating (unconsciously or preconsciously) how they work with patients based on their personal style, interests, and proclivities. They are primed to be more interested in some schools of thought than others based on how those theories interact with their personal style. Do we tend to avoid confrontation? Do we always see the positive side? Are we comfortable being idealized or attacked? Do we need to be needed? Training at its best gives us the opportunity to find theory and practice that fit with our own developing voice. More importantly, the more we can learn about our own voices, the more we can understand what challenges us and how we can expand our professional breadth and freedom.

The non-evaluative encouragement of writing from early on in training could be something that might contribute to a deeper self-awareness and facilitate the development of analytic voice. One technique that seems promising as a way to bring our own proclivities to light and help us to enrich our own voices is the writing of personal narratives. Many of our authors shared with us how transformative and uplifting it has been for them to formulate and express their ideas, feelings, history, and experiences through the process of writing about themselves. There is something particular about writing that reflects and encourages the development of a voice and the nurturing of identity and self-awareness. Writing about ourselves forces us to actively recreate memories, renew and redefine how we think about ourselves. Often spontaneous and surprising, what emerges in our writing informs our thinking just as our thinking informs our writing. Writing becomes an act of discovery and rediscovery. Seeing our words on the page can act as a mirror in which we learn about ourselves by observing our reflection as it is seen outside of ourselves. In relinquishing our thoughts to the page we symbolize feelings and thoughts and gain a sense of mastery over these ideas. Hence, the feeling of wholeness and healing that writing offers to many people.

We suggest that institutes offer writing opportunities that encourage the development of self-expression and self-discovery through such mediums as narrative and memoir. Questions like "How did we arrive in psychoanalytic training," "Which theorists/schools of thought are we drawn to and why," and "Which theory do I react negatively to and why?" can serve as jumping off points for self-exploration. Small group discussions around these issues of self-style and interests are another option for this kind of growth. Institutes might encourage teaching and administrative staff to see part of their mission as encouraging self-discovery in their trainees. This in no way is meant to suggest any less rigor in the imparting of theory and experience. In fact, our belief is just the opposite. We believe the more one knows about oneself, the more effectively one learns. These analysts are not blank screens when they enter training, and the more they know about what is motivating them and who they are, the more they will be able to take in all there is to learn in the field, challenge themselves and allow their identity to solidify and their voices to flourish.

Post-graduation professional and clinical development

The narratives in this book reveal the tremendous amount of development that occurs in our authors after they complete their analytic training. Post-training is a fertile time in an analyst's life and career for personal and professional growth. Fogel and Glick's (1991) point that an independent psychoanalytic identity can only be achieved after the completion of training is supported in our author's narratives. We see the questioning and the growth that is fostered by greater distance from training. It is primarily after training that the newly independent analyst can more securely experiment with his or her own analytic persona including the more subtle music behind the words in developing his or her own voice.

Post training is a time of relative isolation, a loss of the community created during training with its classes, supervision, and other programmatic events. As Kernberg and Michels (2016) point out in their recent paper on psychoanalytic education, most analysts do not stay involved in the activities of psychoanalytic societies after they graduate from training. Michels says this "non academic majority" (p. 478) of graduated analysts "want to be left in peace" (p. 481) and are uninterested in further formal educational programs and the profession's continued concern with standards. Kernberg (2016) sees a different nuance in this disaffection. He proposes that analysts are concerned with standards precisely because they are so isolated, but they are discouraged and put off by the authoritarian atmosphere of the institutes.

To this end, we need to develop sources that can support and nurture the development of analysts at every stage of their career—a different kind of support and cultivation than for those in training. Some analysts create their own peer study and supervision groups and other forms of communities that are important to their functioning as analysts. They do this in part to combat the inherent isolation in the work especially after training. As we saw in the narratives, most analysts do develop stronger ideas about their own persona and voice as they mature into the profession. They may wonder what colleagues are doing and thinking about practice as they leave training farther behind. They may be wary about exposing themselves through questions or practices that differ from what they perceive to be established canons of practice, and they may come into conflict with certain of the standards of their own training.

This book is intended to serve as a companion to analysts in their ongoing development. The narratives in this book take us into the minds of twelve analysts as they trace the various influences on their thinking and attitudes starting in childhood and continuing throughout their professional development. As we mentioned in the first chapter, the presentation of new ideas and personas available for identification in the form of our author narratives can awaken a possibility for readers. Such a possibility may give form and expression to a nascent or hitherto unconscious impulse, feeling or belief, spark an insight or change of perspective, or simply give permission to a fledgling or disowned idea or thought.

Training institutes can expand their view of training to include the ongoing process of becoming a psychoanalyst. They can offer forums for graduates and more senior analysts to discuss their ideas about practice, separate from the formal lectures offered in conferences and panels. The object is to encourage informal dialogue about practice in an atmosphere that reduces fear of judgment and the need to impress or fit in with colleagues.

Note

1 Extract from letter to 'John' by Anna Freud on display in the Anna Freud Room of the Freud Museum, London. The exact date this letter was written is not known, nor is the exact identity of John. Reprinted here with kind permission of the Freud Museum.

References

Bion, W. R. (1967). Notes on memory and desire. *Psycho-Analytic Forum*, *2*(3), 271–280.

Eisold, K. (1994). The intolerance of diversity in psychoanalytic institutes. *International Journal of Psychoanalysis*, *75*, 785–800.

Eisold, K. (2004). Psychoanalytic training: The "faculty system." *Psychoanalytic Inquiry*, *24*, 51–70.

Fogel, G. I., & Glick, R. A. (1991). The analyst's postgraduate development: Rereading Freud and working theory through. *Psychoanalytic Quarterly*, *60*, 396–425.

Kernberg, O., & Michels, R. (2016). Thoughts on the present and future of psychoanalytic education. *Journal of American Psychoanalytic Association*, *64*(3), 477–493.

Kite, J. V. (2016). The problem of the analyst as person and the ethical unknown. Paper presented at APsaA, Panel on the Ethics of Psychoanalysis, New York City.

Parsons, M. (2000). *The dove that returns, the dove that vanishes*. London: Routledge.

Ogden, T. H. (2015). Intuiting the truth of what's happening: On Bion's "Notes on memory and desire." *Psychoanalytic Quarterly*, *84*, 285–306.

Rosenbloom, S. (1992). The development of ego in the beginning analyst: Thoughts on identity formation of the psychoanalyst. *International Journal of Psychoanalysis*, *73*, 117–126.

Rycroft, C. (2010). Why analysts need their patients' transferences. *American Journal of Psychoanalysis*, *70*, 112–118.

Chapter 16

Coda

Linda Hillman and Therese Rosenblatt

With this book, we set out to give voice to the reality of how we, as analysts, develop our identities and bring those to our professional practices. We wanted to unearth the hidden and unspoken, the reality of developmental experience that may not find expression within the confines of formal training paradigms and professional writings. These narratives provoked and expanded our thinking. We see how each developmental journey is unique, each voice distinctive. With courage, integrity, and humility each analyst has shared their personal thoughts, feelings, and struggles in finding their place in a field that is both professional and very personal.

In opening these windows onto others' experience, we found two overarching themes unified our authors' narratives. Our authors love psychoanalysis and they yearn to put the humanity back into their work. While these nascent ideas were brewing in us when we embarked on this book journey, we were reaching for something still in the process of formulating itself, of becoming. Our own personal lives informed our professional lives and vice versa. Our urge to express who we wanted to be as analysts, spoke to something that was missing, yet needed and relevant to our field of psychoanalysis.

Every essay here has the quality of a love letter to our field, speaking to that thirst for deeper understanding. There is gratitude and care for the people they have encountered, from teachers and mentors to patients. And they are devoted to the work, loving it in all of its flaws, committed to raising psychoanalysis to its highest potential. An aspiration that requires putting the person back in the analyst, to include their own ethics, to define what they believe in above and beyond what we are taught in our formal training, to find flexibility, independent thinking, humor, play, creativity, social awareness, a sense of mission, and above all, warmth and analytic love. In short, our authors have risen to the challenge of defining their own voices and identities and incorporating these into their work.

All the analysts in our book have struggled to find their own path to authenticity within a field that—like others—has developed its own rigid orthodoxies. In their own ways, they have each had the fortitude to challenge our thinking and expand our understanding of what is central to our personal and professional development. They took this risk out of their love for the field and their commitment to building a stronger, more inclusive and integrated psychoanalysis.

Index

abjection (Jacques Lacan) 57
adolescence 34
African-American children, research on learning 160
AIDS epidemic 90
Albert Einstein College of Medicine 30
Alexander, Franz 26, 74, 124
Alexandria, VA, Community Mental Health Center 163
Alstein, Rachel xiv, 188; brother 145; clinical writing 149; decision to become a psychoanalyst 148; first analysis 146, 149; grandmother 147; law career 149–152; psychoanalytic training 148; research on 9/11 with Beatrice Beebe 148; second analysis 149; trauma of 9/11 141–147
Altieri, Charles 51, 57
American Psychiatric Association 83, 85
American Psychoanalytic Association 86, 163, 194
analytic frame 43, 147
analytic person 6
anti-Semitism 80
Antonowsky, Anna 89
Appelfeld, Aharon 152
Aristotle, 168
Arlow, Jacob 59

Bach, Sheldon 69, 113
Bak, Robert 31–34
Baltimore Washington Psychoanalytic Institute 164–165
Barchelon, José 31
Barthes, Roland 57
Bass, Alan 147
Baumbacher, Gordon 58–59
Beckett, Samuel 107

Beebe, Beatrice 68–69, 148
behaviorism 158–159
Bergman, Martin 7, 69, 79, 114
Bernardi, Ricardo 6–7
Bion, Wilfred 38, 44, 153, 202
Bird, Brian 44
blank screen 3
body language 71
Boesky, Dale 75
Bollas, Christopher 8, 32, 126, 132, 133–134, 149
Borges, Jorge Luis 19, 21, 24, 37–38
Boym, Svetlana 180–181
Brandeis University 94
Brenner, Charles 33
Brooklyn College 80
Brooklyn Dodgers 28, 109
Browne, Thomas 19
Browning, Robert 56–57
Buechler, Sandra 128, 129–131, 136
Burke, Nancy 117

Cabinet magazine 37
candidate's difficulties in training 129–130
Carson, Anne 13
Case Western Reserve University 157
Casterline, Forrest 54
causality 78
Charles Evans Hughes High School, New York City 171–172
Chicago Institute for Psychoanalysis 30
child of therapist/psychoanalyst parents 124–128, 194–195
childhood pain and sadness, psychoanalysts' 188–189
Chodorow, Nancy 135–136, 138
Chrystal, Joyti 177

City University of New York Graduate Program in Clinical Psychology 97
clinical psychology graduate school 42
Close Encounters of the Third Kind 146
community mental health 15
Conrad, Joseph 94
Contemporary Freudian Society 116, 118
Contemporary Freudian Track, New York University Postdoctoral Program in Psychoanalysis and Psychotherapy 65, 69
Contemporary Psychoanalysis 89–90
corrective emotional experience (Franz Alexander) 74
Cossette, John 51–53, 60
countertransference 34, 46–47, 75, 89, 118, 119
creative arts, influence on psychoanalysts 196–197
creativity 73
Cuba 13–14, 20
cure through love 48

dance, study of 41, 67
Darwin, Charles 110
death of a patient 77
DeLeon, Charles 157, 159
desubicado 13–14
Didion, Joan 197
dreams of the authors 14, 56, 58, 59
Drescher, Jack xiv, 188; antipathy to orthodox Freudians 82; awareness of unconscious 81; being gay 86–89, 90–91; Brooklyn college 80; childhood 79–80; death of a patient 77; discriminated against in psychiatric and psychoanalytic training 86; medical school in Padova 80–81; parents' escape from Nazi-occupied Poland; parents' immigration to the United States 79; psychoanalytic training at William Alanson White Institute 88–89; residency at St. Vincent's Hospital and SUNY-Downstate 81–82; supervisors and teachers during psychoanalytic training 89; therapist to parents 80; therapy with Stuart Nichols 83; training analysis with Raul Ludmer, 88; University of Michigan medical school 81; writing self 89–90; writings on homosexuality 83

Du Bois, W. E. B. 23
Durocher, Leo 28
dyslexia 47–48

Eco, Umberto 178
Edwards, Henry (pseudonym of Henry Katz) 171
Eger, David 138
Eger, Jane 138
Eger, Jonathan xiv, 5, 194–195; childhood 123; defensive identification with teachers and supervisors 133; experience of having therapist parents 124–128; identity as a psychoanalyst 136; parents 123; walled-off inner world of 133
ego psychology 49, 97, 164
Ehrlich, Joshua 128–129
Eisold, Ken 5, 203
Eissler, Kurt 113
Ellman, Caroline xiv-xv, 69, 189, 191, 194; Brooklyn Dodgers fandom; childhood 109; comparison of institutes 117–119; envy, writing and teaching on 116, 117; experience of being in her own analyses 115, 119, 120; first therapy 111; husband, Steven J. Ellman 115; internship at Montefiore Hospital 113; mother 109, 120; New York University clinical psychology graduate school 111–112; New York University Postdoctoral Program in Psychoanalysis and Psychotherapy 114, 117–118; New York University undergraduate 110; seminar on Freud with Martin Bergmann 114; study group 116; subliminal perception research 112; supervision with Sheldon Bach; training analysis 115; University of California, Berkeley, graduate school 111
Ellman, Steven J. 42, 115
enactment 35, 69, 71–72, 169
Engel, George 161
envy 43, 116
Epstein, Lawrence 102
Ereikousa (Greek island) 167, 169, 180–183
Erikson, Erik H. 173
Esposito, Eleanor 100
examination for candidates at psychoanalytic institute 119
extractive introjection (Christopher Bollas) 133–134

father hunger 32, 163
female castration complex 112
Fenichel, Otto 16
Ferenczi, Sandor 113, 115
Fifty Miles of Elbow Room (African-American spiritual) 157
Fiscalini, John 89
Fitzgerald, Faith 81
Fogel, G. I. 6, 205
Fonagy, Peter 74, 148
Foucault, Michel 17–18, 57
French, Thomas 74
Freud, Anna 130, 187, 201; analysis with her father Sigmund Freud 128
Freud, Sigmund 2, 5, 7, 8, 16, 21, 23, 52 64, 70, 78, 94, 120, 136; 171, 195, 198; analysis of his daughter Anna Freud 128; view of homosexuality 84
Fromm, Erich 70
Fryer, John 85
Fuks, Betty 23

Gay and Lesbian Psychiatrists of New York, 83
gay applicants to psychoanalytic institutes 16
George Washington University 162
Gilligan, Carol 3
Glick, R. A. 6, 205
González, Francisco J. xv, 191 196; childhood, 22; choosing psychiatry 20–21; community mental health 15; ethnicity 22–23; *desubicado* 13–14; dream 14; first analysis 13, 14, 18; gay identity 17–18; motive for becoming a psychoanalyst 19; psychoanalytic institute 24; residency 15; San Francisco General Hospital 15–16; second analysis 23–24
Graham, Martha 94–95, 107
Gray, Paul 164
Grossman, Allan 98
Growing up observed: Tales from analysts' children (edited by H. S. Strean) 124–126
Grunes, Mark 114

Hammett, Dashiell 168
Heller, Doris 111
heterosexual imperative 18
Hillman, Linda i, 1–9, 193; 202–207, 208–209; Brandeis University as undergraduate 94, 98, 102; childhood 96, 100–101; choice to become an analyst 107; community involvement, 101; control case 101; doctoral study at City University of New York Graduate Program in Clinical Psychology 97; father, 101; first psychotherapy 103; first analysis 103; second analysis 103; initial interest in psychoanalysis 94; master's program at Teachers College, Columbia University 96; mother, 95, 101, 103; parenting 103–104; parents' separations and divorce 102; parents' traumatic experiences 99–100; plan to be an English teacher 95; poetry writing 98–100, 104–105; psychoanalytic training at New York University Postdoctoral Program in Psychoanalysis and Psychotherapy 96–98; radicalism in late 1960s; study group with Eleanor Esposito and Steve Solow; supervising young therapists 105–106; therapist to parents 101; voice as a psychoanalyst 99
Hirschfeld, Magnus 84
Holmes, Dorothy Evans xv; 189, 196; career as a clinical psychologist in Washington, DC 162–163; childhood 156–157; dissertation 160; divorce of parents 156; Doris (twin sister) 157; experience as an African-American 157, 159, 162, 163, 165; father 163; first analysis 163; first therapy 159; graduate school in psychology at Southern Illinois University 158; grandfather 157; grandmother 157; initial interest in psychoanalysis 158–160; internship at Department of Psychiatry, Case Western Reserve University 158–160; mother 157; post-doctoral fellowship at University of Rochester 161–162; practice in Bluffton, SC; supervision with Charles DeLeon 159; supervision with Irving Weiner 161; training analysis 163; training at Baltimore Washington Psychoanalytic Institute 164–165
Holocaust experience and impact 78–81
homosexuality 17–18, 21, 195; pathological view of homosexuality in 1980s psychoanalysis 86; history

of its treatment in psychiatry and psychoanalysis 83–84
Hooker, Evelyn 84
Horace Mann School 27–28
Hornick, Edward 31
Howard University 162
hugging the patient 73–74
Hultberg 133
Hunter, Robert 60
Hurvich, Marvin 102
hypochondria of the heart (Svetlana Boym) 180–181

identification 5, 6, 7
identity of psychoanalyst 5–7, 67, 132, 136, 201–202, 203
immigrant experience 22–23, 39, 63, 79, 100–101, 109, 120, 170, 180–183, 189–192
implicit theories 7
independence-mindedness among psychoanalysts 194
infant-mother research 68–69
Institute for Psychoanalytic Training and Research (IPTAR) 116, 119
Isaacharoff, Amnon 89
Isakower school of psychoanalysis 31–32

Jacobs, Ted xv, 75–76, 193, 195; childhood 26–27; choice to become a psychoanalyst, 29; countertransference 34–35; enactment, 35; father's depression 27; first psychotherapy 28–29; Horace Mann School 27–28; mother 27; novel *The Year of Durocher*; reading of Freud's case histories 29; residency 30; sports journalism 28; story-telling 27; study of adolescence 34; training at New York Psychoanalytic Institute 31–35; training analysis 31–34; University of Chicago Medical School 30; warmth of the analyst 33; writings 34–35
Jacobson, Edith 33
Jewishness 23, 39, 65, 80, 110
joke of old lady and the scientist 13
Journal of Gay and Lesbian Mental Health 90
Jucovy, M. 79
Jung, Carl G. 8, 115
Jungian analysis 14

Kalinkowitz, Bernard 111
Kaplan, Louise J. 147–148
Katz, Gil 69
Katz, Henry 171
Kennedy, John, assassination 111
Kernberg, Otto 133, 203, 206
Kerr, John 90
Kinsey, Alfred 84
Kite, Jane 6, 201
Klauber, John 7
Klein, George 112
Klein, Melanie 115, 116
Kohut, Heinz 82, 113, 126, 127, 132, 133, 137–138
Kuriloff, Emily A. 79, 120

Lacan, Jacques 22, 52, 57, 62, 202, 203
lack (Lacan) 21
LaFarge, Lucy 82
Levine, Susan 6
Levi-Strauss, Claude 57
Lewin, Bertram 26
Lipton, Samuel 2
Loewald, Hans 73, 135
love in psychoanalysis 59, 70, 72, 107, 192–194
Ludmer, Raul 88
Luria, A. R. 8

Mahler, Margaret 148
Makari, George 110, 114
Marx, Karl 40, 171
Mather, Cotton memory 142, 146, 152
Mental Health Consultation Center, New York City 114
mentalization 148
Metropolitan Opera, 178
Michaels, Robert 203, 206
Miller, Alice 189
Milner, Marion 24
Mitchell, Stephen A. 65, 89
Montefiore Hospital 113
moratorium (Erik Erikson) 173
Moskowitz, Michael 199
Moss, Donald 82

narcissism 14
narrative 7–8, 95
needing to destroy the object 135
neutrality 31, 35, 113
New York Psychoanalytic Institute 31–35, 38

New York University Postdoctoral Program in Psychoanalysis and Psychotherapy 64–69, 86–87, 90, 97–98, 114, 117–118
Nichols, Stuart 83

objectifying patients 97
Odysseus 169
Oedipus complex 22, 31, 33–34, 49, 70
Ogden, Thomas H. 4, 74, 106, 148, 202–203
omnipotence of analyst 202
Oneness and Separateness (Louise J. Kaplan) 147–148
Onorato, Richard 94
Opatow, Barry 82
Orfanos, Lina 167–169, 177–178, 183
Orfanos, Spyros D. xvi, 188, 189, 196; attending and being expelled from Polytechnic Institute of Brooklyn 172–173; caretaker of immigrant parents 170; Charles Evans Hughes High School, New York City 171–172; childhood 170, 175, 172, 181–182; clinical style 168–169; daughter Lina Orfanos 167–169, 177–178, 183; deportation of uncle, Plutarchos 176; father 175, 179, 180; introduction to psychoanalysis 174; first analysis 168; first hearing of Sigmund Freud 171; Giorgi (cousin) 172; 174–176, 183; identification with Odysseus 169; mother 175 179, 180–182; moratorium 173; musical production 178; "*polymechanos*" as personal idiom 169; relationship with Mikis Theodorakis 179–180; restaurant employment 173–176; running and practicing yoga 177; second analysis 168; talking with Jimmy the Mute 175; teaching at Queens College 181; wife Sophia Richman 169, 173–174
otherness experiences of psychoanalysts 190–191

parameters (Kurt Eissler) 113
parents who are therapists/analysts, suggestions for raising children 137
Parsons, Michael 201
Paul, I. H. 42
Paul, Irving 111
peer study group 206

Perlswig, Ellis 86
Perry, Helen Swick 89
phallic symbolism 39
Pine, Fred 4
play 96
play therapy 96
poetry writing 98–100, 104–105
Polytechnic Institute of Brooklyn 172
Possible Profession, The: On the Analytic Process of Change (Ted Jacobs) 34–35
post-graduation development 205
projective identification 202
Psychic Equivalent Stage (Peter Fonagy and Mary Target) 74
psychoanalyst's own psychoanalysis 203; Alstein, Rachel 146, 149; Drescher, Jack 88; Ellman, Caroline 115, 119, 120; González, Francisco 13–14, 23–24; Hillman, Linda 103; Holmes, Dorothy Evans 163; Jacobs, Ted 31–34; Orfanos, Spyros D. 168; Rosenblatt, Therese 64, 65, 69–76; Weinstein, Lissa 42–44; Wilson, Mitchell 58–59
psychoanalytic coyness (Jack Drescher) 87
psychoanalytic institutes 204
psychoanalytic training, its influence on psychoanalysts 199
PTSD 81

Queens College, Center for Byzantine and Modern Greek Studies 181

racism 162, 165, 166
Racker, Heinrich 35
Rader, Ralph 56
Rado, Sandor, view of homosexuality as phobic 84
Rapaport, David 38
regression in psychoanalysis 71–72
Reiser, Morton 31
relational psychoanalysis 106, 114
Research Center for Mental Health, New York University 111–112
resistance to becoming involved with psychoanalysis 191
reverie 148
Richman, Sophia 169, 173–174
Rilke, Rainer Maria 153
Robert Jay Fulton Projects, New York City 172

Robinson, Jackie 109
Romano, John 161–162, 165
Rorschach 160
Rosen, Marcia 89
Rosenbaum, Milton 30
Rosenblatt, Therese ii, 1–9, 189, 192, 194, 202–207, 208–209; acceptance at a traditional psychoanalytic institute 66–67; ballet 69, 71; brother's depression 63–64; clinical experiences 73–75; father 63, 66, 71–72, 73; first analysis 69–70; graduate school in clinical psychology 68; infant-mother research with Beatrice Beebe 68; initial interest in psychoanalysis 62; mother 62–64; motivation for becoming a psychoanalyst, 64; own psychoanalyses 64, 65; New York University Postdoctoral Program in Psychoanalysis and Psychotherapy 64–69; postscript 75–76; second analysis 71–72; teachers during psychoanalytic training 69; surgery for abdominal tumor 70; therapist to mother 64; third analysis 72–73; transference to training institute 67; True Self 65, 66;
Rosenbloom, S. 203
Ross, John Munder 82
Rousseau, Jean-Jacques 170
Ruefle, Mary 104
Rycroft, Charles 201

Sacks, Oliver 8
San Francisco 13
San Francisco General Hospital 15–16
savior complex 44
Schafer, Roy 7, 136
Schaffner, Bertram H. 83
Sendak, Maurice 143
serendipity 152–153
shame of candidate 130–131
shame of patient 71
signifier (Jacques Lacan) 52
silent analyst 69
Silverman, Lloyd 112
Slochower, Joyce 147, 172
Smith, Henry F. 5, 7
socialism 27, 39
Socrates 177
Solomon, Andrew 40
Solow, Steve 69, 100
Southern Illinois University 158

Spitzer, Robert 85
St. Vincent's Hospital, New York City 82
Steingart, Irving 114
Stepansky, Paul 90
Stern, Donnel B. 148
Stevenson, Bryan 150
Strean, H. S 124–126
subliminal perception research 112
Sullivan, Harry Stack 67–68, 88–89
SUNY-Downstate, Brooklyn 82, 89
Sutton-Smith, Brian 96

Target, Mary 74, 148
Teachers College, Columbia University 96
text, literary term 57
Thaler, Otto 161
Theodorakis, Mikis 179–180, 183
therapist to parent(s) 64, 80, 101, 188–189
tolerance of ambiguity, analysts' 191
transference 23, 32, 44, 49, 67, 71
transformative experiences of analysts 197–198
transitional objects and transitional phenomena 58, 96
trauma 107, 195–196
trauma recovery 145–146, 149, 151
True Self 64, 66, 72

Ulrichs, Karl Heinrich 83
unconscious transmission 35
University of California, Berkeley 56, 111
University of California, San Francisco, Medical School 56
University of Chicago Medical School 30
University of Maryland 162
University of Michigan medical school 81
University of Rochester 161–162
unthought known (Christopher Bollas) 149

voice 3–4, 51, 94, 98, 178
von Krafft-Ebing, Richard 83–84

Wachtel, Paul 170
waiver process of American Psychoanalytic Association 164
warmth of analyst 33
Warren, Marsha Levy 69

Weiner, Herbert 31
Weiner, Irving 161
Weinstein, Lissa xvi, 188–189, 192; choice of psychoanalysis 40; child therapy vignettes 45–47; childhood 39–40; clinical psychology graduate school 42; college 40; decision to apply to clinical psychology program 41; father 39–40; first analysis 42–43; motive for becoming an analyst, 44; mother 40–41; parents' leftist politics 39–40; repetition 46; research in Steven J. Ellman's laboratory 42; "savior complex," lack of 44; slowness in learning to speak 40; study of dance 41; training analysis 43–44; training at the New York Psychoanalytic Institute 38; writing about her child's dyslexia 47–48; writing for a Funeral of Psychoanalysis 37
William Alanson White Institute, New York City 88–91

Williams, Ted 53
Wilson, Mitchell xvi-xvii, 7, 8; baseball 52–54; baseball reunion, 60; childhood 53–54; divorce of parents, 53, 58; father 53, 58, 60–1; first psychoanalysis 58; first therapy 58; impossibility of writing truthfully about oneself 50; high school 54–56; high school reunion 52; Jewish, English, and Scottish ancestry 53; medical school 56; melancholy 58; mother 53; studying literature at Berkeley 56–57
Winnicott, Donald W. 58, 64, 66, 96, 115, 127, 135–136, 147
workplace environment 100
Wortman, Richard 160
writing of personal narratives 8, 205

Yeats, William Butler 168

Zwerling, Israel 31